Praise for *The Pivot*

"In *The Pivot*, Lori Michele Leavitt introduces a profoundly important new construct for getting everyone in your organization moving forward toward your strategic objectives. She calls it Aligned Momentum, and it's how the most successful leaders enable their organizations, at all levels, to initiate change and become more nimble, flexible, and adaptable, and speed miles ahead of their competition. *The Pivot* is full of compelling stories and examples of how successful organizations have used Aligned Momentum, as well as practical applications that you can put to immediate use. Mastering The Pivot is not optional. It is absolutely essential in a world where misalignment is costing businesses their talent, their competitive advantage, and their customer's trust."

> — **Jim Kouzes,** coauthor, *The Leadership Challenge* and the Dean's Executive Fellow of Leadership, Leavey School of Business, Santa Clara University

"Lori Michele Leavitt provides a fresh perspective on a well-worn term: pivot. She introduces the concept of Aligned Momentum and shows how to achieve it in order to execute the type of transformation that every business must undertake if it wants to survive today's challenging and ever-changing environment. Read *The Pivot* to learn from Leavitt's extensive experience helping companies thrive and grow through organizational momentum and culture change."

> — **Denise Lee Yohn,** author of *What Great Brands Do*

"I love this book! Understanding the art and the need to occasionally Pivot is essential to founders and their teams. Lori's approach offers both a good read as well as a hands-on resource. Go over sections with your team. Use it to spark discussion in meetings. I intend to use *The Pivot* as a valuable resource for the rapidly growing startups I advise."

> — **Frumi Rachel Barr,** author of *The CEO's Secret Weapon*

"Lori Michele Leavitt's book, *The Pivot*, presents an effective methodology for anyone aspiring to be a powerful leader in this unprecedented twenty first century global economic reality. As an MBA, management consultant, and executive coach, Lori (*"The Pivot Catalyst"*), is intimately aware of the rapid and unpredictable changes, growing complexities — as evidenced by multiple industry disruptors and accelerating, exponential growth.. not to mention major political disruptions, demographic dislocations and even major changes with Earth's climates. In this book you will find that Lori shares her wisdom and actionable methods with great clarity. She has captured the essence of pivoting and its practical applications.. highly recommended reading!"

> — **Jim Bergquist,** president and CEO of Creative Business Futures, Inc. consultant/coach for Seattle's World Famous Pike Place Fish Market

"Employees will do their best work when they're a part of an organizational culture that empowers them. In *The Pivot*, Lori Michele Leavitt shows us how to build and maintain an engaging culture, regardless of your current organizational dynamics."

> — **Sharlyn Lauby,** SHRM-SCP. president of ITM Group Inc. and author of the blog, *HR Bartender*

"Every leader should care about their employees' success and empower them to initiate change by identifying the best next step – which is not always the step that worked previously in a similar situation. In *The Pivot*, Lori Michele Leavitt reminds us that transformational change happens when many people make small shifts that are well orchestrated because employees understand how they contribute to the purpose of their organization. Lori has developed a very powerful set of key indicators to achieve the aligned momentum required to drive successful transformations."

> — **Andrea Sturm,** President & CEO of Samson Rope

The Pivot helps answer, "How do I attract the best and brightest and how do I keep them engaged?" Leaders influence, and leaders anticipate. In *The Pivot*, Lori clearly explains what should be done to develop a high performing culture that is prepared for change. As someone who coaches companies from $1M to $325M it's clear that what you tolerate, you encourage. If you are tolerating something you should not be, read this book and Pivot."

— **Ken Proctor,** CEO of The Grey Pointe Group, LLC.

"If you want to lead your organization from where you are to where you want it to be, you must identify and orchestrate *The Pivot*. Lori Michele Leavitt has provided a road map, rich with brilliant practical insight. I highly recommend *The Pivot* to every leader who wants to see their organization achieve much greater performance."

— **Glenn Hansen,** partner of One Accord Partners

"*The Pivot* shows how to be truly nimble — essential to any business today. A must-read if you want real advantage in today's rapidly changing world!"

— **Dan Barnett,** CEO of Make or Break Execution, CEO and owner of Primavera Group, former President of Van de Kamp's

"With *The Pivot*, Lori Michele Leavitt adds a new dimension to the world of enterprise and its contributions to society. We need this book. Leavitt makes a cogent argument for business leaders to fully engage every employee to attain vision, and even to accomplish a mission. She proves her understanding of business by being mindful of risks, real or perceived. Unlike many business publications aimed at coaches and others learning that craft, *The Pivot* speaks to all who themselves lead or aspire to that objective. Author Leavitt provides meaningful examples, stories and guidance within the book, and tops it off with an accessible assessment tool. This tool is a clear added value, so graciously shared with readers."

— **Steve Barchet,** MD, Rear Admiral, MC, USN Retired

"*The Pivot* provides important advice that every leader needs to build a great business. Author Lori Michele Leavitt describes a leadership culture in which all employees are aligned towards an organization's goals and help build the momentum needed to achieve business success. When alignment occurs, the company is ready to Pivot from the status quo to a level of performance that exceeds those of competitors. So, what does a leader need to do to initiate a Pivot and begin the journey towards great performance? Leavitt identifies the cultural norms needed for this process to take place. The Holy Grail of any business is to become the preferred provider of products and services in the markets it serves. Leavitt provides the roadmap to achieving preferred provider status, that is, the provider that customers and clients to go first."

— **Stan Silverman,** Founder and CEO of Silverman Leadership, speaker, advisor and nationally syndicated writer on leadership, entrepreneurship and corporate governance, former CEO of PQ Corporation.

"*The Pivot* clearly lays out how Aligned Momentum is a product of preparation, planning and orchestration. The author provides a blueprint that can serve all leaders and companies. The lessons from *The Pivot* will be valuable to our clients. I will make sure to give a copy to each of our coaches."

— **Stephane Panier,** Founder & CEO of BetterManager

"Whether you run a small neighborhood business or a Fortune 500 company, survival depends on continually adapting and innovating. In *The Pivot: Orchestrating Extraordinary Business Momentum*, Lori Michele Leavitt shows how enlightened leaders effect change through clear communication of goals. Clarity and repetition ensure that everyone in your organization is aligned with those shared goals."

— **Robert Spector,** co-author, *The Nordstrom Way to Customer Experience Excellence: Creating a Values-Driven Service Culture*

"Reading *The Pivot* will remind you what most of the business world has forgotten—long term success is almost never based on a big budget, headline-worthy strokes of strategic genius, but rather of small, seemingly infinitesimal, but ultimately highly significant, small steps. It's the turns we don't take, it turns out, that can take even long established businesses down. Lori Michele Leavitt offers up a new and insightful look at a multitude of ways in which the world's most progressive business leaders are changing their companies, their markets and their own mindsets. One page, one Pivot, one positive insight at a time, Lori's new work lays out a plethora of small, practical, meaningful tips that can take you and your organization to the next level! Take careful notes—the Pivot that might make or break your business is probably somewhere in its pages."

— **Ari Weinzweig,** co-founder of Zingerman's Community of Businesses and author of *A Lapsed Anarchist's Approach to the Power of Beliefs in Business.*

THE PIVOT

Orchestrating Extraordinary Business Momentum

Lori Michele Leavitt

LORI MICHELE LEAVITT

THE
PIVOT

Orchestrating Extraordinary
Business Momentum

Abrige
MEDIA

publisher@abrige.com

Ordering Information:
Quantity sales. Special discounts are available on quantity purchases by corporations, associations, and others. For details, contact the publisher at *publisher@abrige.com*.

Visit the author's website: www.thepivotbook.com

Publisher's Cataloging-in-Publication data
Leavitt, Lori Michele.
The Pivot : Orchestrating Extraordinary Business Momentum
p. 15.24 x 22.86 cm.

ISBN: 978-0-9990336-0-9 paperback
ISBN: 978-0-9990336-1-6 ebook
ISBN: 978-0-9990336-2-3 audiobook
ISBN: 978-0-9990336-3-0 hardcover
Library of Congress Control Number: 2017907789
1. Business/Leadership Guidance 2. Business/Management Practice 3. Business/Organizational Studies

First Edition

Published by Abrige Media
Bellingham, WA
Printed in the United States of America

DEDICATION

To my daughter, Emily, who inspired me and often stepped up as coach during our Pivot toward greater courage, choice, and joy.

CONTENTS

PREFACE 1

INTRODUCTION 3

PART 1: SET THE STAGE

1. ALIGNED MOMENTUM 17

2. MASTERING THE PIVOT 31

3. CHANGE THE CONTEXT 49

4. GAINING MOMENTUM 69

PART 2: SHARE THE VISION

5. CLARITY 97

6. FOCUSED AND NIMBLE 131

7. CHANGE THE SOCIAL CONTEXT 155

8. THE BOTTOM LINE 181

PART 3: TAKE ACTION

9. ALIGNED MOMENTUM PIVOTS 199

PIVOT TO CLARITY 207

PIVOT TO MASTERY MINDSET 213

PIVOT TO NIMBLE DECISION-MAKING 221

PIVOT TO STRATEGIC THINKING 228

PIVOT TO TALENT ADAPTABILITY 234

PIVOT TO COACHING 240

10. YOUR BEST NEXT STEP 245

APPENDIX 261

GLOSSARY 251

NOTES 263

ACKNOWLEDGMENTS 279

ABOUT THE AUTHOR 281

FIGURES

Figure 1: The Pivot, page 9.

Figure 2: Aligned Momentum, page 10.

Figure 3: Aligned Momentum Key Indicators, page 25.

Figure 4: Van de Kamp's breakthrough performance, page 32.

Figure 5: The Pivot, page 38.

Figure 6: Hierarchical structure, page 52.

Figure 7: Matrix structure, page 55.

Figure 8: Flat or horizontal structure, page 57.

Figure 9: Open structure, page 59.

Figure 10: Personal Brand Alignment, page 75.

Figure 11: Gap Assessment Process: Five iterative phases, page 102.

Figure 12: Define and Discover phases, page 103.

Figure 13: Assess and Prioritize phases, page 104.

Figure 14: Track phase, page 105.

Figure 15: Leadership and Personal Alignment, page 166.

Figure 16: The Growth "S" Curve, page 186.

Figure 17: Sample Talent Assessment Matrix for Talent Adaptability/Right Fit, page 189.

Figure 18: Global market share held by smartphone vendors since 2009 143, page 193.

Figure 19: Worldwide smartphone operating system market share 144, page 194.

Figure 20: Sample Aligned Momentum Readiness Assessment chart, page 201.

Figure 21: Large business: typical assessment results, page 202.

Figure 22: Medium-sized business: typical assessment results, page 203.

Figure 23: Small business: typical assessment results, page 204.

Figure 24: Startups: typical assessment results, page 205.

Figure 25: Fixed vs Growth Mindset, adapted from Carol Dweck's book, Mindset (2006), page 213.)

Figure 26: Strategic Thinking: Leads to and Avoids, page 229.

PREFACE

After stepping out of the corporate world in late 2000 to consult with Fortune 500 companies, senior executives often asked me, "How did you do it?" They didn't have a compelling desire to be an entrepreneur; they simply didn't feel fulfilled in the corporate world. These executives felt they had more to offer than what they could do from their corner office. Specifically, they wanted to initiate change and they wanted the people they managed to be better able to speak out and step up.

This was a catalyst for me, to step up and speak out for business vibrancy, which in my terms includes leading a great business and a fulfilling place to work. Being the employer people choose to work for is available to every business. I believe that if the businesses we served had been vibrant, not rigid, and interested in change, we may have stayed.

Leaders I now work with aim to lead a great business. They are open to discover where the business has grown rigid and why, where, and how to Pivot to become more nimble in a way that doesn't place ongoing operations at risk. Cultural health is very important to them. This book is for them, and for you.

You have what it takes to positively influence people. You are open to trusting the people who work in the business to initiate change. I offer this book to help you orchestrate change, gain momentum and, while doing so, create the type of workplace that is more fulfilling for you, and attracts and retains capable leaders.

Lori Michele Leavitt
lori@lorimicheleleavitt.com
March 2017

INTRODUCTION

"A journey of a thousand miles must begin with the first step."

— *Lao Tzu*

Too often, a push toward a specific target brings only short-term success to you and your business. You tell people what is needed, you seek buy-in, and you feel you are making a smart, nimble decision. Yet any success realized during the push doesn't stick.

You are in authority; your employees want to comply so that they get noticed by you or keep their jobs. Perhaps you are seen as the hero; your employees want to please you. But, whether employees are acting out of compliance to direction from above or in hopes that your heroism is the magic they need right now, their exertion is not sustainable. After the push, everyone falls back to "work-as-usual," and business growth stalls.

There's a push and an acceleration, but, subsequently, there is a stall. Momentum is lost because there was never alignment of employees' visions of what they want with what is required of them to execute your business strategy (i.e., all that is in your strategic plan). Commitment to a new way of working or a higher level of performance is not gained. In this book I will refer to such heroic or authoritative turn-on-a-dime attempts at change as a pivot. If you see this phrase in lower case, read "quick turn."

A pivot has become a commonly used term to describe *a quick turn,* usually in response to changing external variables: turning away from one customer segment and focusing on a new one, for example. Or, changing a government policy; an unplanned career change; going for the big, quick win (being the hero); and so on.

In this book I describe a method to gain and sustain momentum, to be nimble, without the frenetic rush and without the top-down push of a turn-on-a-dime change. This method is The Pivot. If you see this phrase in upper case, read "orchestrated change."

Whereas, a pivot refers to a quick change of direction, The Pivot represents a specific and long-term change. As this book sets out to show you, The Pivot is a method (not a quick action) for gaining and sustaining extraordinary business momentum.

The Pivot requires employees to be empowered to initiate change aimed toward the strategic objectives set by the leadership team. The Pivot requires the leader to orchestrate these many changes initiated by many people, to ensure brilliant execution.

> **The Pivot** *describes a method for readying many people to initiate changes that are in alignment with the organization's strategy, and that, over time, and when well-orchestrated, generate extraordinary business momentum—even performance breakthroughs.*

When you see Pivot (capitalized) in the following pages you will know that it refers to a method to carefully plan strategic change. When you see pivot (lower case) you will know that this refers to an attempted turn-on-a-dime change. A pivot may be heroic, egotistic and/or desperate. It is always reactive.

A HERO'S TURN-ON-A-DIME PIVOT

I begin with a cautionary tale of what The Pivot is *not*: it is *not* a turn-on-a-dime pivot, which may be perceived as heroic, but is rarely successful.

The hero of this turn-on-a-dime pivot story is Antarctic explorer, Ernest Shackleton, best known for his Imperial Trans-Antarctic ex-pedition on the ship, *Endurance*. Shackleton has been mythologized as a hero for being the architect of the survival of the ship's 27 crew members. The goal of the expedition was to be the first to traverse Antarctica. Shackleton's charisma helped attract investors, scientific explorers, and a ship's crew, but in the end he didn't come close to fulfilling the promises he made on behalf of the expedition. Of all its goals, the expedition achieved only the survival of its men.

Endurance set sail on December 5 1914 from South Georgia Island. Despite having been warned by a number of experienced Norwegians who manned the nearby whaling stations about the dangers of pack ice (comprised of large pieces of ice floating together in one mass), Shackleton overconfidently sailed south in search of his intended Antarctic landfall site.

The journey was abruptly stalled by the daunting pack ice. On January 19 1915, *Endurance* became frozen fast. Unprepared and un-versed in the properties of pack ice, captain and crew thought that with springtime's warming water *Endurance* would be released, but the ice never relented its frozen grip. Shackleton then rallied the crew to focus on survival.

In late October 1915 the crew, abandoning their sinking ship, set up camp on a floe of pack ice. To merely survive it was now critical to find and make land. A small crew was selected to take a lifeboat and set forth in the treacherous waters. During subsequent enormous trials lasting over a year, luck and persistence kept everyone alive until their rescue in late August 1916.

That they all survived such an arduous journey makes this one of the greatest survival stories of all time. Yet, it is not a great story of success: the terrible events could have been avoided. Shackleton's hubris worked against the expedition's principal objective. Not only had he not researched the environment before setting off, he also ignored subsequently received critical facts and advice from the Norwegians living in the area. Instead, he relied on a discussion he had had with a colleague *before* the trip—a colleague who was a fellow explorer who had not traveled this route. Shackleton was unwilling to change his plans even when potentially fatal conditions forced a situation of immobility on his ship.

Luckily for this crew, Shackleton's heroic instinct to pivot saved their lives, even though his pride was responsible for putting their lives in peril in the first place. The expedition failed—hugely! Investors realized no return. Shackleton, applauded by some as an entrepreneurial leader, launched many subsequent opportunistic ventures that similarly failed to prosper. He died a hero, but heavily in debt. His reputation was ruined for many years. A heroic turn-on-a-dime pivot may mitigate loss, but rarely will it achieve anything else.

A hero may be a good leader. He or she may earn the respect and confidence of others. A *great* leader, though, inspires by building up others' confidence in themselves. Others gain confidence that their leader cares about them and wants them to be successful.

> *Are you the hero who allows risk to become unbearable so that you can save the day? Or are you ready to take up the gauntlet of true leadership, and the orchestration of extraordinary business momentum?*

What might have been possible if Shackleton had prepared the crew by sharing information on the potential hazards ahead? What might have been different if he had focused all members of the crew on the strategic objective, rather than on blindly following his command? With preparation and empowerment of his crew, a Pivot could have led them to success in achieving their strategic objective—to be the first to traverse Antarctica.

When there's more than just you involved, The Pivot, well-orchestrated, gets everyone aimed toward achieving strategic objectives.

You may know someone like Shackleton: an adventurer, exciting to know and to be around. These personality types make people feel good about themselves. Yet, you find that they also readily take funds, effort, property, etc., for their ventures and rarely return the investment, offering no accountability all the while. A leader may bring employees along on a journey. A great leader engages employees in a shared commitment to achieve strategy objectives.

Your business may have many more employees. As the number of people grows, the chance that a heroic, turn-on-a-dime pivot will succeed dwindles.

A GREAT LEADER'S ORCHESTRATED PIVOT

A great leader feels no need to be the hero. A great leader builds a team and supports them being a hero in their role.

The better way to succeed with change is to Pivot, with the leader orchestrating many small shifts made by well-prepared people who have been empowered by knowledge and resources.

A Pivot is possible when the organization does not require that only the leader or leadership team be empowered with initiating change. Business success today cannot be dictated by a single person (the leader), or a limited few (the leadership team).

As most great leaders discover, the very thing that drives business success—people—is often the main roadblock to being nimble and quick in the marketplace. The process of aligning every person in your organization to take advantage of opportunities and steer clear of mishaps doesn't follow a straight line, nor does it require a major change in direction.

Alignment is realized through small shifts that keep bringing business performance back on track with strategy.

ABOUT THIS BOOK

I've written this book for leaders.

You are most likely leading a proven, mature company and still want and need to grow—revenues, profitability or both. You know you must become more nimble to keep up with industry changes. You have several employees to move forward with you. You've done many things "right" and certainly no longer consider your company a startup. You see your company as stable, and positioned to be successful, in part due to your ability to strategize and innovate.

Alternatively, you may be leading a young, fast-growth company and you don't want it to lose its edge, or worse, grow into the type of corporate culture that you find "ugly." You've grown beyond the small core team and lean start-up stage, but because you are still growing fast, you don't see yourself as a small or medium-sized (SMB) business.

Momentum can become alive in your culture, as can engagement, alignment, productivity, achievement, and growth. To enable such a healthy culture requires leaders who care about bringing others across the finish line with them. I call this a culture with *Aligned Momentum*. Aligned Momentum allows you to build leadership at all levels of the organization: It re-engages people who are not performing at their best; it opens lines of communication; it allows strategy to inspire change organization-wide; and, it results in the company being committed, collaborative, innovative, and quick. When Aligned Momentum thrives in your organization, you will experience *extraordinary* momentum.

> *Ordinary momentum is incremental.*
> *Extraordinary momentum reaches new heights.*

Your strategic plan likely contains objectives that, if executed well, will position your business for an even better future and closer to your vision. Brilliant execution requires alignment, with everyone being aimed toward a shared vision, and momentum that leads to achieving objectives at the optimal time.

THE CONCEPTS: THE PIVOT AND ALIGNED MOMENTUM

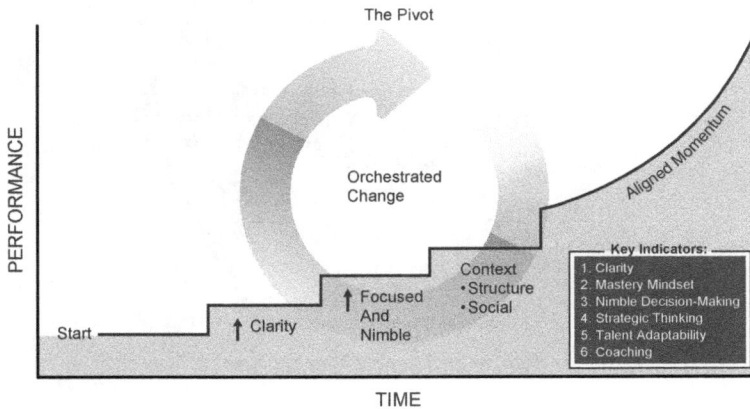

The Pivot

PERFORMANCE

Orchestrated Change

Aligned Momentum

Key Indicators:
1. Clarity
2. Mastery Mindset
3. Nimble Decision-Making
4. Strategic Thinking
5. Talent Adaptability
6. Coaching

Context
• Structure
• Social

↑ Focused And Nimble

↑ Clarity

Start

TIME

Figure 1: The Pivot

The Pivot illustration shows what success looks like: a progressively increasing level of performance. What does progress look like? How will you know if you are moving toward these objectives? How will employees know if their actions are driving progress? What key metrics will indicate progress?

> *As a leader you want to gain and sustain momentum in your business. You know that you need alignment so that the momentum leads toward a shared vision. To execute brilliantly and make breakthroughs possible as you move forward together, you will orchestrate The Pivot.*

In my work and training, with hundreds of leaders over the years, I have encountered various theories that attempt to identify the key indicators of business leadership success. A key indicator answers the question, "What does progress look like?" When combined, the six "Aligned Momentum Key Indicators," shown below indicate that your business is positioned to gain or sustain momentum:

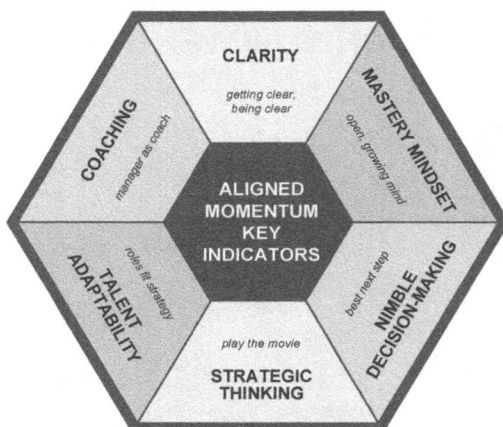

Figure 2: Aligned Momentum

Indicating brilliant execution of strategy:

1) **Clarity**—*getting clear, being clear (about strategy, including vision, purpose, values and direction).*

2) **Mastery Mindset**—*open, growing mind.*

3) **Nimble Decision-making**—*best next step.*

Indicating readiness for a better future:

4) **Strategic Thinking**—*play the movie[1] (think through to the likely end before a judgment call).*

5) **Talent Adaptability**—*roles fit strategy.*

6) **Coaching**—*manager as coach.*

In the following chapters, I elaborate on the Aligned Momentum Key Indicators, using them in examples and recommending Pivots and best next steps toward strengthening each one. I share stories and case studies to illustrate what The Pivot and Aligned Momentum look like in organizations both large and small, even if these terms were not used within those companies at the time.

The stories and examples incorporate what I've learned from leaders and their teams, worldwide, as well as from thought leaders who share my purpose of improving leadership and business vibrancy. I have found that while a leader may have the will and capability to Pivot, sustainable business growth becomes available only when they fully grasp Aligned Momentum.

WHY THIS BOOK?

It is possible for any business to be vibrant and nimble; highly valued, ahead of the competition, and a great place to work. Being vibrant and nimble is also possible for any person including you, the leader. Most of us need a few concrete steps to get us moving forward. This book provides guidance and best next steps for you and your business to take from whatever position you are in today. This book is your catalyst for gaining momentum.

There are many books about successful businesses, good strategy, strong execution, and great leaders. I am grateful to their authors, some of whom are chief executives of Fortune 500 companies and well-known thought leaders. I've grown from their teachings and I've had the pleasure of meeting several of them. I admit that as I write this book I have wondered, "Who do I think I am to join these authors?" Yet, when I do the work I do, and synthesize concepts and models into *best next steps* for my clients, coach them to *orchestrate change* toward their vision, and guide them toward a workplace culture with *Aligned Momentum,* I see their businesses grow bigger or stronger, or both. Often my clients become more fulfilled at work and in life. This ripples through to employees, families, customers, vendors, communities, and others. How, then, could I not write this book? These benefits are what I wish for you. I intend to, in my work and with this book, increase business vibrancy and to do so in a way that is fulfilling for leaders and all employees. I especially hope that leaders who read this book will expand their positive influence.

The ideas advanced in this book will have a significant impact on your employees' alignment with business strategy, execution excellence, and momentum. *Your business will be more nimble.*

The recommended Pivots and best next steps in this book are based on the common growth paths of many of the businesses I've worked with or observed, with proven results. However, I cannot guarantee that if you pick up one idea and move forward with its recommendations that you'll realize your desired results. Your organization, the culture, your leadership, the market dynamics, and your strategy are unique, and are very likely changing over time. Consider this book as my offering to you of insights for greater awareness, more nimble decisions, and gaining momentum—even extraordinary business momentum.

HOW THIS BOOK IS ORGANIZED

This book is organized into three parts plus an appendix:

Part I: Set the Stage helps you prepare for Aligned Momentum and The Pivot in your organization.

Part II: Share the Vision addresses the critical aspects of organizational readiness required to share a single vision, including: communication; thinking; intentions; and habits.

Part III: Take Action presents Aligned Momentum and The Pivot in practice, and is designed for both reading now and for your future reference.

An **appendix** containing a code to access a Pivot / Aligned Momentum Assessment and other resources is provided at the end of the book. You'll be directed to www.thepivotbook.com.

I hope this book will prove useful to you now, and be nearby as you grow. The Pivot and Aligned Momentum online resources will be kept relevant and current to serve you over time.

PART 1

Set The Stage

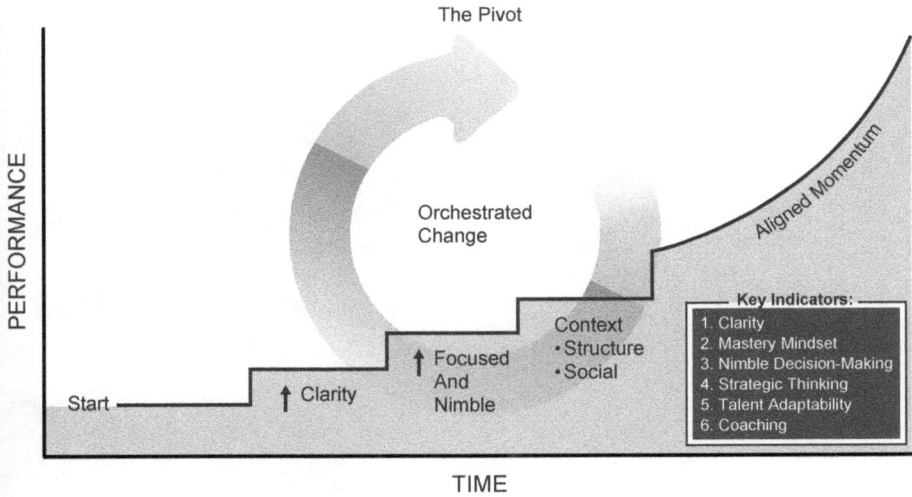

The Pivot

Orchestrated
Change

Aligned Momentum

PERFORMANCE

Context
• Structure
• Social

↑ Focused
And
Nimble

↑ Clarity

Start

Key Indicators:
1. Clarity
2. Mastery Mindset
3. Nimble Decision-Making
4. Strategic Thinking
5. Talent Adaptability
6. Coaching

TIME

CHAPTER 1

Aligned Momentum

"So much of what we call management consists of making it difficult for people to work."

— *Peter Drucker*

When every employee is clear about how their individual performance *can* make a positive difference in your organization's performance, you have alignment. If you are able to maintain alignment, but lack significant improvement in business performance results, you need to gain momentum. Change is often required. What does the combination of alignment and momentum look like?

In *Open Book Management*,[2] John Case tells a story about a hotel manager who was mentored by Jack Stack, CEO of SRC Holdings Company and co-author of *The Great Game of Business*.[3] The performance breakthrough described in this story is a natural result of a well-orchestrated Pivot.

The hotel was underperforming at a 67% occupancy rate—and worse, it was losing money. Following Stack's advice, the hotel manager shared the occupancy rate with all the employees— maids, bellhops, everyone—every day, explaining what it is and helping them understand how they can affect it. The occupancy rate became what Stack calls the "Critical Number." Then, as advised, the manager offered a bonus to every worker when the occupancy rate rose above a target of 72%. Now, the employees understood what the Critical Number was, what achieving the Critical Number meant to the business, what part they played in achieving the Critical Number, and what was in it for them when the combined efforts of all the employees brought about the desired results.

Getting clear and being clear about the objective and how each person could make a difference created alignment. The manager got clear on what was needed from people in order to execute the strategic objective of significantly improving the Critical Number, which was the occupancy rate. The manager was clear with employees so they understood the Critical Number and knew how they could impact it. There was *alignment* between what the manager needed people to execute brilliantly and what people actually did. In response to the manager's clear communication, employees changed how they worked and collaborated in order to achieve the occupancy-rate objective.

In addition to alignment, when the path and the destination are clear, you will experience momentum. This was the situation at the hotel; as Stack continues in his story to Case,

> They were no longer just clocking in and out. Now, they were pulling together to improve their Critical Number, which would result in meeting the hotel's strategic objective—and so that they'd all make more money. And the daily number felt like a scoreboard.[4]

He then pointed out,

> At the end of eighteen months, they were up to 85%. The funny thing was, they now had people running out, carrying bags, greeting customers, being personable. For all that time before, what kept the manager from thinking that all the employees could understand that Critical Number—and could respond to it?[5]

Stack ends on a rhetorical question. He understands that too often managers are not comfortable sharing with employees more than the minimum information necessary to perform their jobs. What the hotel manager discovered was that the information necessary to execute brilliantly included their Critical Number.

Stack's story describes a Pivot and all that was required to move *from* low employee accountability for the occupancy rate *to* high accountability. There were many changes initiated by the employees, which were orchestrated by the leader (the hotel manager) to create a better overall result. And the result was a breakthrough: profitability with an 85% occupancy rate.

Although it is not in the story, we can presume that the targeted 72% occupancy rate was a standard level of profitability and that the increase from 67% to 85% was a breakthrough. Over 18 months there was momentum building, with quarter-over- quarter increases, until the 85% occupancy rate was reached.

The momentum expressed by this story is not ordinary—it is extraordinary. But not impossible. Considering Stack's observation that the sharing of the Critical Number led to noticeably improved customer service as well as higher occupancy rates, it is reasonable to say that both alignment and momentum came alive in the culture during this time. I call this "Aligned Momentum."

TRUE LEADERSHIP AND ALIGNED MOMENTUM

A culture with Aligned Momentum indicates the business is nimble, and able to Pivot. Later in this chapter, and throughout this book, I describe how to Pivot toward Aligned Momentum and how to track progress. With a well-orchestrated Pivot, extraordinary momentum and performance breakthroughs become possible; otherwise your business faces incremental improvement only, and is at risk for a stall.

You can begin your Pivot toward a culture with Aligned Momentum with just one decision: to practice true leadership. You agree to prioritize building up others so that everyone grows and succeeds. To do so, you commit to creating the tone for an organization where every person knows that their manager (or similar) wants them to be successful. You will take steps toward getting clearer and being more clear in your communication. You will dispense with any desire to be a hero in your leadership role. You will take steps to ensure that positive influence trumps authority-based power and you will be a model of this in action. Finally, you agree to participate fully in any Pivots that involve you and to orchestrate the changes that employees will initiate naturally as you build Aligned Momentum into your culture.

> *Aligned Momentum is not about fixing those who are not meeting your expectations. Aligned Momentum is possible only with* **your** *true leadership, full commitment and participation.*

If you've been a business owner or top executive for a long time, you may have lost sight of what it's like to be an employee. For instance, while you have your finger on the pulse of the company, at the highest level to often the minutest detail, most of your employees don't have this luxury. They weren't in the room when you and your leadership team forged your strategic plan. And even if your employees were in the room and had that plan in-hand, they may not be able to translate the strategic objectives into digestible and measurable goals related to how they do their work or what to do next. Too often only the leadership team sees the entire plan. Others see only a small portion that is translated into quantitative budgets. To get everyone aligned, your vision must be shared. Your strategy—vision, purpose or mission, values, direction and game plan—must be translated into clear objectives. Then these objectives can be translated into priorities and then priorities can be defined in a measurable way by those closest to the work to be done.

Great leaders crystallize their game plan and priorities into memorable, overarching themes. Alan Mulally, while CEO of Ford Motor Company between 2006 and 2014, created a bold theme for a 10-year Plan: "One Ford." With One Ford,[6] the employees of Ford were to unite around the communal shared goal of returning to the basics of automobile manufacturing. One Ford was clear and inspiring. And it was executed. You will find a bit more detail about One Ford in Chapter 5. To give you a sense of the impact an inspired theme, following is a quick before and after:

In 2006, Bill Ford Jr. hired Mulally, then president of Boeing Co.'s commercial aircraft division, to save the struggling car company from the brink of bankruptcy. As Mulally puts it, "We had been going out of business for 40 years."[7]

By 2014, Mulally was handing over the CEO position to Mark Fields, having achieved his goal.[8] The company, with Mulally orchestrating its Pivot *from* disparate business units and cultures to One Ford, saved itself from bankruptcy and did so in less than 10 years.

PREPARING TO IMPLEMENT ALIGNED MOMENTUM

As was the case in Ford prior to its Pivot, your business may be experiencing a lack of shared goals. Employees in many departments may not be clear about the vision or strategic direction of your business. It may be that only your sales team has clear and measurable goals and priorities that all tie directly to the strategic plan. What about employees in accounting, marketing, technology, human resources, operations or even your own executive assistant? Can they tie their daily work into the strategic direction of the company? Can they articulate what the company is trying to accomplish in a sentence or two? Do they understand what you're trying to do and how? Do they know how their role fits and what they can do to catalyze momentum?

Defining roles

Before a company starts on the road toward Aligned Momentum, most employees are usually focused on just meeting the job-related goals that are outlined in their performance plan—that is, if they have one. In some cases, employees are trying to do their best at guessing what constitutes optimum performance *per* their job description, or they are working around that description to get their job done. Employees are likely to move toward incremental improvement in the area that the manager emphasizes during any performance conversation. Too often what one's role describes and what one's manager reviews are not aligned with what matters to the company *now*.

Lack of alignment can occur quickly with a new hire. Hiring into a role that isn't clearly defined can lead to quick turnover, especially in entry-level positions. Holding a performance review that relies on a comparison of an employee's work to an obsolete job description is painful for both the manager and the employee. The disjunction between what one is doing in a role compared to what is needed from the role to meet strategic objectives is compounded by an employee's focus on meeting their own annual review goals, rather than seeking out how they can best support the company's strategic objectives. This common shortsightedness creates an illusion of alignment—the employee is doing what the manager seems to want from them—but what they are doing is actually *not* strengthening strategic alignment. It is also not contributing to the business's momentum. Misaligned busywork is not momentum.

To avoid that scenario, adjust the description of roles to match the performance of your best employees in those roles. No matter what role they are in, the employees who are "best fits" for a culture with Aligned Momentum want to perform at their peak level of performance. They want to perform so that their work not only advances their own careers, but advances the company as well. Your best employees want to initiate change that supports the organization's objectives.

Communicating strategy

As the business leader, there's a good chance you have a clear idea of what you need to accomplish this quarter, this month or even this week in order to move your company forward. If every employee in your company has that same Clarity— congratulations, you have achieved alignment.

But that doesn't mean Aligned Momentum is woven into your culture. For Aligned Momentum to live and breathe in your organization, your entire team needs to understand clearly the strategic direction that is based on what is possible *in the future*, where they are *now* and where they must reach together, and they must be *able and willing to take the best next steps*. That is, getting clear, being clear and doing so with people whose minds are wired for mastery must be the norm in your culture. In Aligned Momentum terms, we call this "Clarity" and "Mastery Mindsets."

Asking someone in your company to take the next logical step based on what has been done in the past typically yields incremental work improvement and ordinary business momentum at most. They've done Step 1, which they followed with Step 2, so Step 3 is logically next. *Looking to the past rarely creates the desired future.* What is needed is the readiness and willingness to take action and Pivot toward the desired future. In fact, Aligned Momentum requires minds wired for Mastery. Take note: this will necessarily result in some failures as you grow.

Failure is feedback

Taking best next steps, and change, toward a desired future will involve taking some steps that don't work out. If failure is never an option, you'll miss out on opportunities and innovations. If complacency is tolerated, your best performers are going to leave. If your business is continuously churning through people, especially if such people are your rising stars—i.e., those with a Mastery Mindset—then Aligned Momentum will not be possible.

Have you equipped employees with a procedure for communicating their feedback? Do they have access to information and training? Is there a process in place for them to initiate their ideas? Do they know it is safe—and without repercussion—to speak up, step up, ask questions or request support? Do your organizational structure and social norms support initiative, collaboration and innovation? If you cannot answer, "yes" to those questions, you have not yet created the environment where any employee can initiate change. You have drastically limited the potential for individual Pivots that lead to breakthroughs and greater momentum for the company. As a result, change comes at a predictable pace and likely behind the pace of competitors, economic factors or what the market expects—if it comes at all. Momentum is lost because the company becomes more rigid and less nimble over time.

As the market inevitably shifts, your business may fall so far behind that catching up requires turning on a dime, which is rarely successful. *Aligned Momentum is the antidote to rigidity.* It creates a company that is more flexible and more nimble.

MEASURING ALIGNED MOMENTUM PROGRESS

Planning for the outcomes you want is a best next step toward realizing these outcomes, but it is not the only step. Stop at planning and you are unlikely to realize the objectives written in your strategic plan. Strategy must be brilliantly executed.

How will you know if you are making progress? As the saying goes, you get what you measure. Affirmatively nodding heads don't always translate into excellent execution. To help you measure progress use these six Aligned Momentum Key Indicators:

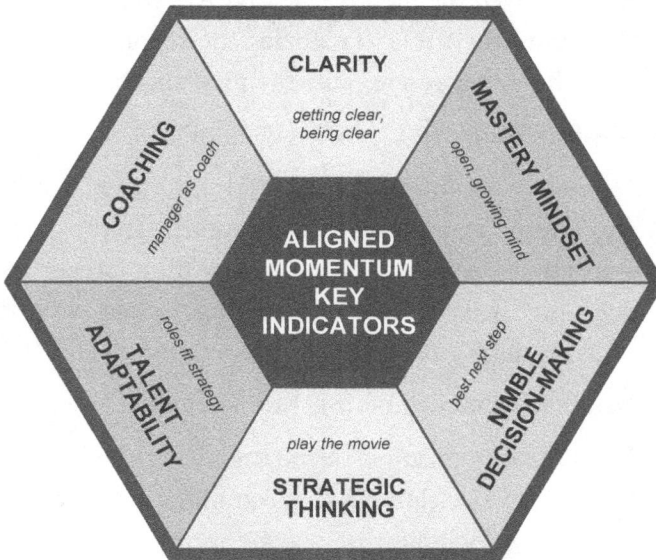

Figure 3: Aligned Momentum Key Indicators

Aligned Momentum Key Indicators help you track progress in your Pivot *from* an incremental, traditional and/or rigid business culture *to* a culture with Aligned Momentum. Aligned Momentum leads to brilliant execution of strategy.

Aligned Momentum Key Indicators

To support brilliant execution of strategy

1) **Clarity**: Getting clear, being clear.

Are you and every member of the leadership team clear about your vision and the strategy to realize that vision? Can you describe what success looks like? Are you ready to be 100% clear in communicating vision and strategic objectives throughout your organization?

Do you receive feedback that confirms that employees have received the message clearly? Are you certain that they know their role in realizing the vision and understand how they can execute their part brilliantly?

2) **Mastery Mindset**: Open, growing mind.

Do employees approach their work, interact with others and engage in training to continuously improve their strengths? Do they step up to apply their strengths, in ways that will require new learning, to best serve the organization's goals, purpose and values?

3) **Nimble Decision-making**: Best next step.

Does the organization's structure, delegation and culture afford decision-making, or initiation of change, at the level or area that will be most impacted? Are employees sufficiently clear about how their role aligns with the organization's vision and strategy, and current priorities and initiatives, to enable them to make effective daily choices, judgment calls and decisions?

To prepare you for a better future

4) **Strategic Thinking**: Play the movie.

Is every individual trained on how to look ahead and from a strategic viewpoint before taking their best next step?

5) **Talent Adaptability**: Roles fit strategy.

Are leaders and hiring managers skilled at predicting future talent requirements? Are individuals and teams across the organization able to collaborate, and share talent, effectively?

6) **Coaching**: Manager as coach.

Does every employee know that their manager (or lead) has their back and wants them to be successful? Are people in positions of authority given the training (and coaching) needed to assess and grow their strength as a coach?

Executing a plan requires alignment. Executing on time requires momentum. Executing brilliantly, including shifting quickly when the facts change while staying on track with strategic objectives, requires Aligned Momentum.

Aligned Momentum exists **when**:
- people know they are valued and trusted in their role;
- the strategic plan is bold and purposeful;
- people are clear about strategy and their part in it;
- excelling in one's role also meets personal goals;
- the Aligned Momentum Key Indicators are strong and consistent across the company.

To realize your strategy, and even before attempting a Pivot, you must ensure that each person you are relying on to execute brilliantly knows they are valued and trusted in their role. They know that a person who can influence their success (typically their manager) cares that they are successful. They also are empowered to initiate change.

Then, create a bold strategy that fits the purpose, that "why do we exist," for your company, and get very clear about how you will communicate it, what success looks like, and what progress looks like. For many leaders, clearly communicating how everybody's role fits the business strategy is the best next step toward strengthening alignment and opening up for the possibility of business performance breakthroughs. Few, if any, business strategies include execution plans for the training, coaching, communication, delegation and structural or social context changes that a bold new strategy requires. Bold new strategies are then executed poorly, resulting in certain failures. What can then happen is that people opt for a less bold strategy to avoid further failures. Future phases of the strategy may be diluted as a compensatory measure, and your business starts falling behind or stalls.

Strengthen alignment even more, as well as employee engagement, by paying attention to personal goals. Align the intrinsic satisfaction a person seeks with what they can realize when they perform well in their role and with your company. I call this "Aligning you with your Role" and I describe the concept in Chapter 4: Gaining Momentum. When people move *from* complying with what they've been told is expected, *to* committing to generate a win-win situation for themselves and the company, alignment grows stronger and business momentum can be extraordinary.

Finally, address what might be getting in the way of brilliant execution that you, the leader, can affect, such as communication of Critical Numbers, putting in place an organizational structure that now fits execution of your bold new strategy, and assessing and closing gaps in how work is done now compared to what is needed for the future. This latter step includes addressing social norms and training managers to be coaches. When Aligned Momentum Key Indicators are strong and consistent across the company, execution of strategy will naturally strengthen. For many, continued focus on a culture of Aligned Momentum creates a natural Pivot *from* "ordinary" *to* "extraordinary" business momentum.

Now, orchestrate this momentum, generated by changes initiated by many and in alignment with strategy, toward business performance breakthroughs. To do so, master The Pivot.

CHAPTER 1: KEY POINTS

1) In order to maintain alignment, change is often required.

2) You have alignment when every employee is clear about how their performance impacts the organization's performance.

3) You have momentum when every employee is taking their best next step toward fulfilling strategic objectives.

4) Aligned Momentum describes a workplace where people and the company are aligned, and gaining momentum in meeting strategic objectives.

5) These Key Indicators will help you track progress toward Aligned Momentum: Clarity, Mastery Mindset, Nimble Decision-making, Strategic Thinking, Talent Adaptability and Coaching.

6) Aligned Momentum *exists* when:
   - people know they are valued and trusted;
   - the strategic plan (strategy) is bold and purposeful;
   - people are clear about strategy and their part in it;
   - excelling in one's role also meets personal goals;
   - the Aligned Momentum Key Indicators are strong and consistent across the company.

7) In a culture with Aligned Momentum, changes initiated by many, aligned with strategy and well-orchestrated in a Pivot can lead to breakthrough performance.

CHAPTER 2

Ͻ

Mastering The Pivot

———————————

*"We value our people and encourage them
to be adaptable and innovative."*

— *Sir Richard Branson*

*"If the rate of change on the outside exceeds the
rate of change on the inside, the end is near."*

— *Jack Welch*

The Pivot is a well-orchestrated change over time, comprised of smaller changes or shifts initiated by many people. Mastering The Pivot is critical to extraordinary business momentum and makes performance breakthroughs possible.

The Van de Kamp's brand, currently owned by the Pinnacle Foods Group, offers a great example of The Pivot leading to breakthrough performance.

Van de Kamp's wanted to be #1 in the frozen fish market. When Dan Barnett stepped in as President, they were a distant third.[9] Within three years, the Pivots Barnett's team took resulted in significant progress toward moving from #3 in their market to #1. Van de Kamp's share of the frozen fish market started at an 11% share of the space compared to Mrs. Paul's, which had 28% in the #1 spot, and Gorton's in the #2 spot with 21%. After five years, Van de Kamp's held a 22% share and claimed the #1 spot, while the other two brands fell respectively to #2 and #3.

If you were to chart Van de Kamp's success in executing their strategic objective, you'd see a "hockey stick" on the graph—an inflection point between an earlier flat line and a new fast-climbing line depicting the performance breakthrough from this well-orchestrated Pivot. Here's an even simpler visual from Dan that presents Van de Kamp's market share takeover from competitor, Mrs. Paul's (see Fig. 4).

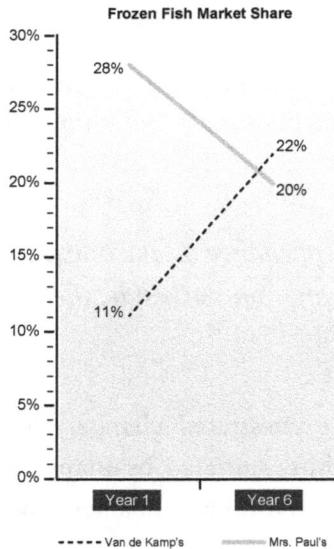

Figure 4: Van de Kamp's breakthrough performance

To begin this Pivot, Barnett identified and communicated *one simple idea* that Van de Kamp's needed to increase their market share in the frozen fish category. The strategic objective was to grow revenues, which required an increase in market share. Market research identified that the market cared about freshness of fish, even in frozen fish. So the idea that Barnett communicated was that the company had to become synonymous with the word, fresh, which became a theme: "Fresh!"[10]

From the highest-ranking executive to the fisherman at sea, everyone knew that "Fresh!" was the critical thing they had to get right and do right.

Note that in his communication Barnett wasn't telling everyone what to do; instead, he empowered others to Pivot from what they had been doing to what they had to do to ensure this one thing—"Fresh!"—was done exceptionally well and better than anyone else.

This Clarity, accompanied by empowerment, fueled further Nimble Decision-making and Strategic Thinking. For example, the company adopted a relatively new way to flash-freeze fish while the catch was still out at sea. Also, their advertising drove the "Fresh!" point home, depicting fish flipping out of a shopping cart where a box of their frozen fish had been placed.

A SPORTS ANALOGY FOR THE PIVOT

I've been in the business world long enough to have learned that a sports analogy helps most leaders visualize a concept. Perhaps this one will work for you. If you've ever played golf, you're probably already familiar with the concept of a pivot. The proper pivot can greatly improve your swing, especially if you learn to turn early, keep your eye on the target, maintain flexibility, and follow through.[11] It is not too fast. A smooth tempo is critical. It is not heroic. Smashing the ball typically leads to the opposite result of what you were wanting.

In many respects, a Pivot in business is the same as a pivot in golf. Except that you are orchestrating a smooth transition and powerful performance result, consisting of small shifts made over time by many people. The Pivot is orchestrated. And, it is an intentional and purposeful shift that keeps you and everyone in your business aligned with the target, to achieve the desired outcome. On the golf course, a proper pivot sends the ball on its correct flight path. In business, the same principle can be applied in terms of achieving strategic objectives. Both require intentional preparation, clear direction, orchestrating many parts or movements, and brilliant execution.

> *For the purposes of achieving Aligned Momentum, you want to think of a Pivot as small shifts made by many people that only appear to be a single shift because they are so well orchestrated.*

WHAT TO AVOID: LACK OF PREPARATION AND ORCHESTRATION

Turning on a dime, so to speak, may work for an individual or a small startup where the people deciding the new strategy are the same people who will execute that strategy.

But too often an urgent turn-on-a-dime, "heroic" pivot comes too late. Maybe the company survives, like the *Endurance* team. Usually, the result is unmet objectives. The very term "pivot" can send chills down the spines of investors in a startup company that isn't gaining traction in the market and is now burning its way through cash. In these cases a pivot may not be seen as a smart business strategy, but, rather, an act of desperation. FlightCar gives us an unfortunate case study of an attempted turn-on-a-dime pivot.

FlightCar was an airport car-sharing startup that paid outbound travelers to share their vehicle with incoming travelers who wanted a vehicle during their stay. The company was successful in attracting car owners who traveled extensively and liked receiving a monthly payment rather than paying for long-term parking. In fact, FlightCar wooed those customers with advertisements covered in dollar signs. They were also successful in attracting $40 million from several investors.

At its peak in 2015, FlightCar had expanded to 17 airport locations and around 150 employees—but quality hadn't scaled with growth. While FlightCar quickly gained traction from those early customers, the company missed important telltale signals that these customers were not, in fact, the ones the company needed to target for long-term business growth and profitability.

Interim CMO, Julie Supan, who was brought in to help FlightCar pivot, told it this way:

> We built the entire model—the business model, the operations model, the marketing model—around a target who didn't embody the sharing economy. Those users didn't value their role or see themselves as part of a car sharing community helping people become more self-reliant.[12,13]

FlightCar had attracted customers that stunted its growth. These early customers wanted excellence and they would post a negative review before reaching out directly to FlightCar for help toward a solution. Supan comments: "Because there was very little goodwill, the company was not given the benefit of the doubt as it expanded from one airport in the U.S. to 17 locations."[14] The company lost or let go half of its workforce including two of the three founders. In May 2016, FlightCar announced that it had learned from its mistakes, implemented reforms to "rethink the customer journey," launched an Android app so the service was more widely accessible, improved employee training, enhanced the look and feel of its stations, and much more.

This attempted pivot to a shared focus on quality was rushed, pushing for a significant change to be achieved without taking time for proper planning or orchestration. It failed. By July 14, 2016 FlightCar had closed all of its locations and was no longer taking reservations. Its technology assets were sold to Mercedes-Benz.

Preparation and orchestration are very important parts of The Pivot, and were missing from the turn-on-a-dime pivot described above. If there was a business hall of shame it would be filled with examples of pivots that did *not* come from empowered shifts made by many people who were clear and aligned with strategy. These attempts at pivoting are not examples of The Pivot within a culture with Aligned Momentum. These pivots were too late, too jumbled or ineffective. They were acts of desperation rather than plans of action designed to implement and continually drive change.

> *Once your company grows beyond the small startup phase, turning on a dime is truly an act of desperation and rarely works.*

Former Microsoft CEO Steve Ballmer's attempted pivot is another example of a dictated change—rather than a planned and well-orchestrated Pivot.[15,16] His publically announced restructuring of operations toward becoming more innovative fell on the deaf ears of his board, who believed the change could not be accomplished. Others in the industry chimed in, saying Ballmer's personality ran counter to the innovative culture he was envisioning. Aligned Momentum was not possible because line staff didn't believe he was the right person to orchestrate a Pivot. Their experience of him made him, at least in their eyes, part of Microsoft's problem, not its solution.

Achieving the "One Microsoft" vision is now in the hands of Satya Nadella, whose leadership style and dynamic presence inspires, engages and empowers employees in a new way.[17] Having employees embrace a Pivot toward a more innovative culture is now not only possible, but is the step forward that the company needs to make. Tim O'Brian, General Manager of Microsoft Global Communications, shared his optimism about Nadella's leadership in a May 2016 interview with Kunal Dua for *Gadgets360.com*:

> [At Microsoft, under Satya Nadella there has been a] change from a very fixed mindset, know-it-all culture to a more of a growth mindset, learn-it-all culture. Where there's an openness to learning, the pursuit of acquiring knowledge, rather than imparting your knowledge on others.[18]

Orchestrating a Pivot involves building up small shifts made by many people. A Pivot will not work and Aligned Momentum will not thrive if your workplace culture does not expect change. For most organizations it takes time to prepare, and become nimble. People must be able to initiate small shifts in their work and in how they work with others for this to occur. If there is internal competition, mistrust or resistance, perhaps as a result of a recent merger or acquisition, a Pivot will be difficult, if not impossible, to achieve. Preparation of people is required, which usually takes the form of communication, modeling, training and coaching.

When two workplace cultures combine in an acquisition, and there is no preparation, the most common result is not at all nimble. According to a recent report by the *Harvard Business Review*, the failure rate of mergers and acquisitions is somewhere between 70–90%.[19,20] These aren't always headline-making failures. Many are small failures, ones where the newly combined company underperforms or experiences write-offs. Sometimes the strategy is off. In nearly every case, there is some level of culture clash between the two companies.

In 2008, Microsoft purchased aQuantive for $6.3 billion.[21,22,23] Five years later, Microsoft took a $6.2 billion write-off, in large part due to this acquisition. According to former aQuantive staffers, it was simply a culture clash. It became increasingly difficult to combine the engineering-centric culture of Microsoft with the advertising-centric mindset of aQuantive.

Aligned Momentum is about aligning people to do the right things in support of strategy. The least painful and most effective way to achieve this is to enable The Pivot in your company. This takes preparation. I use the term "weaving" to create a visual of effective Pivot preparation and the ongoing attention to sustain it.

WEAVING THE PIVOT INTO YOUR CULTURE

A Pivot doesn't have to be an earthshaking change in your business. It may be comprised of many small shifts. The Pivot is prepared well in advance of any major shift. Let's take a look at an illustration of The Pivot:

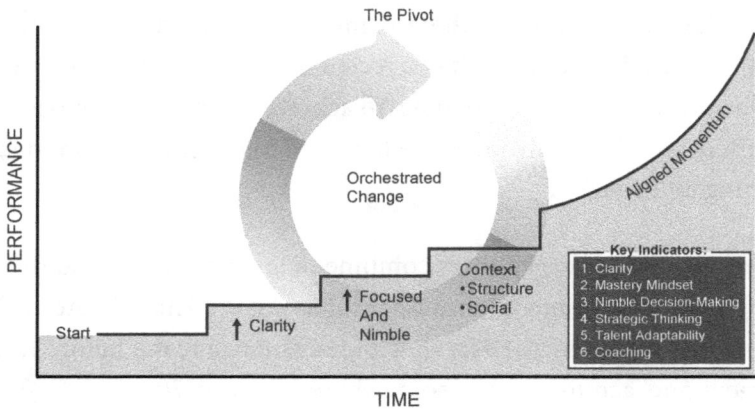

Figure 5: The Pivot

- Before beginning a Pivot, you know what it takes to gain **Clarity**, and you practice this.

- As you move into a Pivot, employees are trained to be both **Focused and Nimble**. They are empowered to initiate the changes to best meet priorities and remain aligned with strategy.

- As you orchestrate **The Pivot**, small shifts are made continually by many people to keep individual roles aligned with strategy.

- A continuous state of **Aligned Momentum** within the culture ensures that bold strategies are brilliantly executed, building extraordinary business momentum and creating opportunities for breakthrough performance.

> *If you want to master The Pivot, you must pay attention to the foundation before you start. Masters do the work. They are prepared and they practice. Being culturally ready is critical to mastering The Pivot.*

As you **Start**, these three cultural truths must be in place:

1) it is safe to step up and speak out;
2) employees are empowered to initiate change;
3) strategy is clearly communicated.

Preparation and practice of these foundational cultural truths are critical to mastering The Pivot. They are described in more detail below.

The following three cultural truths must be in place to effectively Pivot.

Cultural Truth #1: A culture where it is safe to step up and speak out

A safe culture does not mean that people can knowingly underperform. Rather, a safe culture is one where people feel safe to speak out as they step to do their best work: work that is aligned with the company's strategic objectives, values and purpose. Respect, trust, transparency and accountability are a few of the key characteristics of a safe culture.

A culture becomes unsafe when unhealthy characteristics are openly or unwittingly rewarded or tolerated, including unwanted bureaucracy, positioning, gossip, manipulation and short-term focus. If you find these unhealthy traits in your organization, start preparing your culture for The Pivot by looking at you and your leadership team. You must model the way forward. Ask:

- Are you spending time in the workplace, meeting with people, at eye level?

- Do you seek input about company performance and your performance? *This is not only about feedback. Input includes such information as discoveries and ideas that are not prompted (say, for example, by a specific question that you ask directly, via survey, etc.).*

- Do you listen to first understand and then take action?

- Does power of leadership through positive influence trump power of authority in your organization?

- Do you ask what people need to perform at their best?

- Do you fairly and consistently hold others accountable?

- Do you hold yourself accountable?

- Do company policies apply as strictly to you as to others?

Be a leader, not a boss. British journalist Russell H. Ewing describes the difference well:

> A boss creates fear, a leader confidence. A boss fixes blame, a leader corrects mistakes. A boss knows all, a leader asks questions. A boss makes work drudgery, a leader makes it interesting. A boss is interested in himself or herself, a leader is interested in the group.[24]

You are a model for your entire workplace culture. What you say and do, and how you are being every day, sets the tone.

> *A safe culture is one where **every person** knows their manager has their back and wants them to be successful.*

You can positively influence employees' feeling of safety (to step up and speak out) with three best next steps:

1) Get to "yes" on all the questions you've just asked, above.

2) Lead all communication, regardless of what levels, units, divisions, functions or teams are involved, with a collaborative "we."

3) Engage a coach who will challenge and guide you toward success with the first two steps, and beyond. Leverage your experience with your coach to help managers gain coaching habits. Consider also fast-tracking their growth, with a coach.

> *Every employee, even an executive, needs a manager and/or a coach discovering what they want and holding them accountable in a way that shows they **care** about that employee's success.*

Cultural Truth #2: Those closest to the work are empowered to initiate change

If you've identified roles and placed people in those roles who have talent and who fit into your culture, you're ready to empower them. If roles haven't kept pace with the work to be done to execute your strategy, or if you don't have the right person in the right role, you may still need to mentor, train or reassign. In particular, make sure each of your managers is in the right role, so they can succeed.

> *Empowerment requires letting people be, and giving them the tools, direction and support to do their best.*

Train every person in leadership and Strategic Thinking. In particular, give people a voice to identify their strengths and weaknesses, and give them the tools to be aware of threats, opportunities and trends. Help them practice "play(ing) the movie" for each situation; to forecast scenarios that might result from the changes they initiate or the choices they make.[25] The "play the movie" concept fits Strategic Thinking to any skill level, role, age, gender and nationality.

> *Any person can be trained to think strategically.*

Some employees will choose not to think strategically, even though they now know how to do so. They do not fit in a culture with Aligned Momentum.

Whether setting priorities for the year or day, modeling scenarios, making a sales call, dealing with a misunderstanding, or making a decision, by first "play(ing) the movie" forward, the best next step will be more clear. In business, the best next step is not always the step that worked previously in a similar situation. Often what was done before is not what is best done now. In a culture where employees are empowered to initiate change, the employee is trained to identify the best next step.

> *Mastering The Pivot includes creating an organization-wide process by which employees can initiate change.*

One of the best processes that empower employees to initiate change was designed by Ari Weinzweig, Co-owner and Founding Partner of Zingerman's. As the Zingerman's Community of Businesses continues to grow Weinzweig nurtures nimbleness using empowerment and an organizational change process he calls Bottom Line Change®.[26,27] He shared his Bottom Line Change® formula with me, as follows:

$$d \times v \times f > r$$

dissatisfaction x vision x first steps *overcomes* resistance.

True to Zingerman's form, he also provides a recipe:

> Combine a pinch of an organization's time, with a tasty dose of data, the right people, trust in the process and a willingness to ask for help ... Create a clear and compelling purpose for change, create a positive vision of the future and develop leadership agreement on that vision, engage a microcosm to determine who needs to know and how to get the information out, officially present the vision and create an action plan, and finally implement the change.[28]

What I learned from Ari is that when people know how to get involved, and they have a clear path set out to pursue the difference they can make, then their engagement at work is guaranteed to go up. He and I are both saddened that many in authority believe that those at lower levels aren't geared for decision-making and don't matter much. Of course, this does not describe you!

Placing the initiation of change in the hands of the people closest to the work—especially with those deemed "non-decision-makers"—can feel very risky at first. The benefit is greater than the risk. Great leaders do this, and their businesses grow stronger. Also, the risk (of an unhappy surprise by a change you didn't command) is mitigated when the act of empowering others to initiate change is part of a culture with Aligned Momentum. Employee empowerment will play a major role as you strengthen the six Aligned Momentum Key Indicators. Like Zingerman's, you too can implement training and processes to empower all employees to initiate change.

Cultural Truth #3: Strategy is clearly communicated

Communicate your strategy, including direction, values and objectives, as frequently as you can and in different ways. When people start asking questions to clarify their own understanding and best next steps, you are making progress with Clarity. When employees start repeating your words as they go about their day, you'll know you've communicated effectively.

In the beginning, communicating more information more frequently may feel risky, a bit awkward and unproductive to you, especially if you are used to telling and doing. Training all employees in The Pivot may seem counterintuitive. It may even seem like busywork. Initially, a lot of bad ideas may be surfaced by your team as they begin to align their roles and understand that they have input into reaching the company's goals and aligning with the strategic plan. Don't give up.

Identify milestones based on what you expect realistic progress to look like, and stick with it if those signs of progress are positive. If not, perhaps adjust the messages. If that doesn't work, then you need to back track above to Cultural Truth #1 "A culture where it is safe to step up and speak out" and look to see if the structure and norms in your organization are inhibiting progress in the change process.

ORCHESTRATING EXTRAORDINARY BUSINESS MOMENTUM

Envision the change you want to experience for you and for your business. Now, consider what it would be like for you if you were a conductor (as a leader, you are) and orchestrating many small changes into a significant Pivot with the potential to be leading to breakthrough performance and extraordinary business momentum.

The best picture I've found of the "orchestration" that only a leader can do comes from conductor Roger Nierenberg. Nierenberg offers

The Music Paradigm leadership training experience and describes the benefits of orchestration in his book, *Maestro* (2009).[29,30,31] I've had the good fortune to experience both, and I hope to do this work justice as I paint the picture for you now.

Consider the view from your position, at the top. Although you aren't involved in the details of each employee's role, you observe and receive direct reports about overall performance. At any time you could find out more about the performance of an individual, function, process, or system.

It may be tempting at times when performance isn't meeting expectations to tell others what to do (you see it so clearly!) Although others may comply, the performance rarely rises to where you think it should be, "if they truly were embracing what you've just told them to do."

When conducting an orchestra, feedback that your communication is not leading to a better outcome comes quickly. Even when each musician is doing his or her best to comply with what a good (but not great) conductor instructs, what's missing is the vibrancy, energy, and passion of a shared vision. To gain the vibrant performance desired, a *great* conductor knows to acknowledge the capability of each musician; that instead of telling them what to do, he or she will point out something for them to focus on to help them find their own way. In the orchestra, this focal point might be another section of instruments, or it could be playing to the tempo written in their sheet music. In your business, this focal point could be your strategic theme, such as Barnett's theme of "Fresh!" at Van de Kamp's, Mulally 's "One Ford" or the hotel manager's Critical Number related to occupancy rates, as shared by Stack.

A great conductor also understands that what might be clear from the podium might not be clear at all from one of the chairs. With this understanding, the conductor can improve Clarity for each musician, without growing frustrated.

> *Communicate for understanding. Observe. Listen.*
> *Communicate again, a different way. And again...*

You are orchestrating the good work and initiated changes of many who are inspired by the vision and the entire strategy. Roger Nierenberg comments that "With the right leadership, there is a special feeling that blossoms in an orchestra when it is really absorbed and fascinated by its own sound." When your leadership is effective, everybody in the company will feel more engaged with their work.

For you to Master The Pivot, consider your own leadership. If you are not nimble, Pivot *from* fixing your mind on the comfort of what you know and what is *to* rewiring your mind for nimbleness and mastery. You have accomplished much to get to where you are. Don't stop growing.

CHAPTER 2: KEY POINTS

---

1) A successful Pivot is planned and well-orchestrated. The leader orchestrates the many changes that empowered and strategically clear employees initiate.

2) The Pivot does *not* involve:
   - turning on a dime;
   - a show of heroism or of desperation;
   - top-down commanding, or even telling or selling.

3) Aligned Momentum involves weaving The Pivot into your business culture.

4) The Aligned Momentum Key Indicators keep you on track. Before you start, you will enable three cultural truths:
   i. It is safe to step up and speak out.
   ii. Employees are empowered to initiate change.
   iii. Strategy is clearly communicated.

5) As a leader, you orchestrate performance. Orchestrating involves:
   - creating a focal point rather than telling people what to do;
   - ensuring clarity for each individual, and
   - inspiring through vision rather than work intervention.

6) Pivot as a leader *from* complacency *to* mastery. Master leadership and The Pivot.

CHAPTER 3

○

Change The Context

_____

ORGANIZATIONAL STRUCTURE

*"In times of rapid change, experience
could be your worst enemy."*

— *J. Paul Getty*

*"I cannot say whether things will get better if we change;
what I can say is they must change if they are to get better."*

— *Georg C. Lichtenberg*

You can't change a person, but you can change their context. In an organization, each employee's context is often defined by that organization's structure, their role in it and the social norms of that workplace. How an organization is structured influences those who work there. This can either align or conflict with how home and school environments influenced their development. Organizational structure (along with social context, addressed in Chapter 7) affects the ways in which communication and information flow. Structure also influences retention, learning, innovation and many other aspects of your organization's culture.

A common impediment to Aligned Momentum is ineffective organizational structure. If your business has existed for decades, its structure may have served the business well at one time, but it may not be serving your strategy now. Have you considered the design of your organization's structure and the influence it has on the flow of communication and information?

Any one structure is not necessarily "better" than another; there will be different structures to suit an organization's strategy, including its purpose, objectives and its current game plan. Consider if structural adjustments in tandem with changes in strategy will lead to a better execution of that strategy. Alan Mulally adjusted the organizational structure of Ford to improve collaboration for his "One Ford" strategy aimed at turning Ford around.

Your organization's formal structure should be considered in the strategic planning phase. At minimum, you will want to answer: "How can our structure help ensure that we brilliantly execute this strategic plan?" Before you determine The Pivot(s) that will strengthen Aligned Momentum in your business, first consider how its organizational structure will support or impede progress.

The examples given in this chapter are intended to help you envision the structure that best fits your culture and strategy. My words are not intended to be your sole source for learning about different organizational structures. Two highly recommended reads include: *Reinventing Organizations* (2014) by Frederic Laloux and *Accelerate* (XLR8) (2014) by John P. Kotter. [32,33]

My words are also not suggesting you plan out every detail of work and the workplace. Once you envision a workplace in which your employees are brilliantly executing strategy, you can compare your vision to the current state of the workplace and begin orchestrating your best next steps, including any steps to a better-fitting structure. Think of this as a solid framework; the amount of detail you can provide from your viewpoint at the top. And *then* be ready for employees to initiate change in their roles, in how information flows, how to effectively communicate and how to truly execute strategy brilliantly.

Resist the desire to prescribe and manage every aspect of work. I love how Ari Weinzweig recently expressed a better way of thinking about decisions to a gathering of business leaders, *"You (the leader) know some things that they don't know. But they (your employees) know some things that you don't know."*[34] Ralph Stayer, former CEO of Johnsonville Sausage, a company with about 1,400 employees at the end of 2016, realized this over half way into his 47 years at the helm. He wrote about his discovery for Harvard Business Review in 1990.[35] Empowerment of employees didn't come instantly though. He talks openly about some of the stumbles as the Johnsonville leadership team improved their thinking. Writes Stayer, "We tried to plan organizational structure two to three years before it would be needed—who would be responsible for what and who would report to whom, all carefully diagramed in boxes and lines on charts. Later I realized that these structural changes had to grow from day-to-day working realities; no one could dictate them from above, and certainly not in advance."

To be nimble in your business be prepared to Pivot and adapt structure to best fit people, work, and strategy.

MODELS OF ORGANIZATIONAL STRUCTURE

Four organizational structures that are representative of today's workplaces are as follows:

1) Hierarchical

2) Matrix

3) Flat

4) Open/Networked

Your company may adhere to one of the structures listed above, or you may be structured differently. The structure you choose is based on what best fits executing your strategy, which includes living the company core values, adapting to market and location dynamics and sustaining business momentum. Your structure should not be based merely on what's is in place today, what other businesses have in place, or what worked decades ago for a company you hold as a model of success.

1) Hierarchical Structure

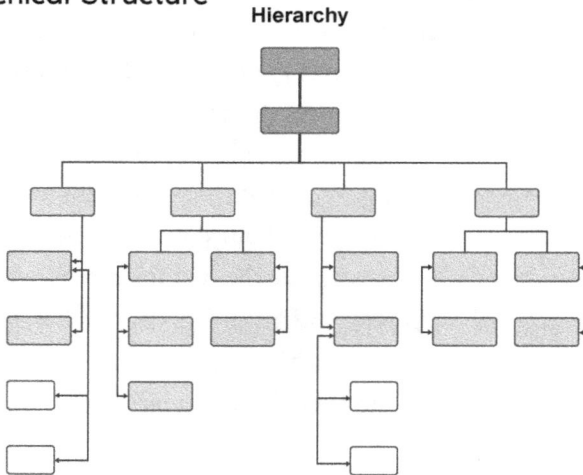

Hierarchy

Figure 6: Hierarchical structure

A hierarchical organizational structure has been in use in business for decades. This structure lends itself well to efficient one-way top-down communication and supports predictability and repeatability of daily work. Bottom-up communication is possible but typically very slow. Communication between functional groups tends to become weak or even absent, which has lent itself to the term "silo." Organizations where mentoring and review are important, such as a public accounting and law firms, often maintain this structure. Communication in a hierarchical structure most often cascades downward through organizational "levels" where employees at lower levels often have less authority over their work and less of a voice upward than employees working at superior levels, although it doesn't have to be that way. (A hierarchical structure is so common still today that phrases such as "at all levels" may be stated by a person who has no idea of the structure associated with their audience's business(es). Be careful not to take phrases that imply hierarchy literally; the person communicating may mean "throughout.")

That said, remember that organizational structure is selected for the best "fit" with strategy; no structure is "good" or "bad." There are hierarchically-structured organizations with highly effective communication, including bottom-up. SRC Holdings, for example, is a hierarchically structured organization that values and nurtures bottom-up communication. Jack Stack, CEO of SRC Holdings ("SRC"), best known for remanufacturing industrial engines, and also the source of the hotel's Pivot story in Chapter 1, gives us an SRC story about how a janitor helped save the company during a downturn. If bottom-up communication was not encouraged at SRC, the helpful voice would not have been heard, and likely the janitor would not have felt safe to speak out. The story follows:

In an interview with BBC Radio 4 (2009), Stack discussed what prompted the beginnings of his open book management principles, which naturally encourage employees to understand and speak out about the financial health of the company.[36] One night when leaving the office late, Stack was disappointed by the fact that all lights and air conditioning had been left on, although everybody had gone home. He realized that employees did not understand the impact that seemingly simple procedures like turning off lights could have on the company's profitability. He decided to create an intelligent organization where everybody would understand the financial situation and have the confidence to use their initiative to act and communicate independently, rather than feeling the need to await instruction.

Then, Stack had a chance meeting with the janitor, who asked him: "So Jack, getting ready for the downturn? As I am sure you know, [in] the U.S. agriculture follows the biblical cycle of seven years of fat cows followed by seven years of hunger."[37] Stack had no idea, so he went in his office, looked at the numbers and realized that the man was right. Sales of engines for farming equipment would be impacted. Immediately, his team and he acted upon the hint and traveled safely through the downturn. If the janitor had not felt safe to communicate his thoughts to Stack, the company could have been hurt during the downturn. Stack had created a safe place for bottom-up communication where voices can be heard, by implementing employee-empowering principles into the culture. His company, SRC, is an excellent example of what John Case meant when he penned the term Open Book Management, defined as "letting information permeate a company," and based on his finding that business bottom-lines were improved when people see themselves as partners in the business rather than as hired hands.[38]

The hierarchical structure is meant to yield consistency, predictability and minimize risk. Decisions are made at the top and communicated downward through levels of management to all employees. Some benefits of hierarchical structure are that reporting lines are clear and career ladders are clear. Even nimble start-up companies, such as PlanGrid, adopt this structure.

PlanGrid, a Silicon Valley fast-growth startup currently disrupting the construction industry, recently Pivoted to a hierarchical structure from an open one. Speaking with *Entrepreneur Magazine*, CEO Tracy Young commented that:

> [When we launched, we] decided to run PlanGrid with no titles and a flat management structure. We were just going to build this

business together. When we hit around 50 employees, someone came up to me and asked what her career path was. I looked at her and wanted to say, "Don't you see we're all drowning in work? Why are you asking me about career paths? No one even likes career paths!" But these things matter. Basic business structures work and career paths are there for a reason. Our biggest mistake was trying to be creative about how we ran the business instead of focusing all that creativity on our product.[39]

Aligned Momentum can live in a hierarchically structured organization if managers cultivate a safe workplace culture.

Care must be taken to combat the inherent negatives that can seep into the culture when structured this way—such as controlling management styles, lack of collaboration (both horizontally and vertically), and a focus on upward advancement to the detriment of deep expertise. A hierarchical structure does not have to take on negative workplace norms such as positioning, politics and slow decision-making, most often associated with a bureaucracy. A bureaucratic organization will likely be structured as a hierarchy. However, hierarchy and bureaucracy are not synonymous.

2) Matrix Structure

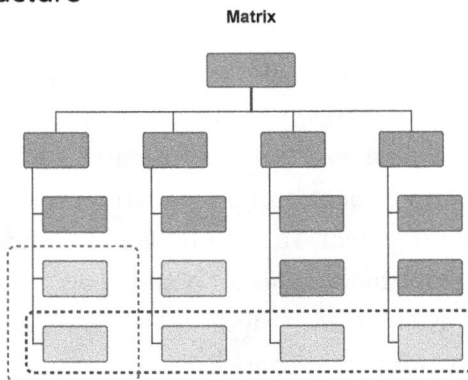

Figure 7: Matrix structure

A matrix organizational structure weaves project or product teams into the hierarchy. Employees still have their respective functional divisions and a manager of that division to report to and turn to for career advice. But for many employees, their day involves significant time on one or more project or product teams, along with employees from different functional divisions. There is a reporting hierarchy and also cross-functional teams.

Collaboration happens more naturally in a matrix structure, compared to one that is only hierarchical, due to the necessary communication across divisions for product or project work. While communication is still primarily top-down in a matrix, there is lateral communication within each team and often across teams as well.

However, setting and communicating priorities to employees can be more complex in a matrix than in a hierarchical structure. While performance expectations for any project may be clear, the goals of the staff under the functional division "manager" and the goals of the project team assigned to a team "lead" (who is often also a division manager) are not always aligned. Sharing an employee can be confusing to all parties. Aligned Momentum can exist when both the functional manager and team lead are aligned, and share a commitment to strategic business objectives.

To become *more nimble*, 3M combined their hierarchical management structure with cross-functional teams, to form a matrix structure.[40,41] Known for maintaining a culture where innovation thrives, 3M's cross-functional teams improve coordination. Team members also work with customers so that customer needs are a shared focus. Alignment and engagement around a shared customer focus helps speed product development. To *stay* nimble, 3M forms multiple small divisions throughout the organization and gives them the same authority as a business unit; each divisional manager has full autonomy and accountability for performance.

3) Flat Structure

Flat Organization

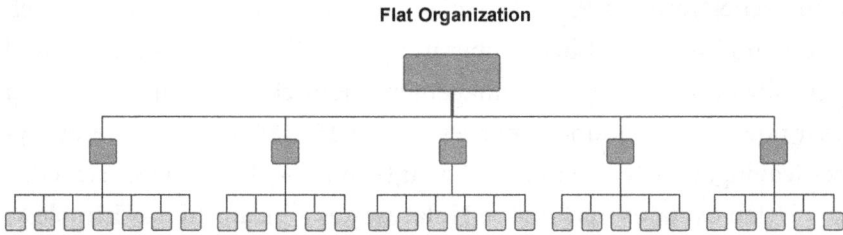

Figure 8: Flat or horizontal structure

A flat or horizontal organizational structure has fewer managers compared to a hierarchical or a matrix structure, and a higher degree of autonomy for all. In the purest translations of a flat structure, all employees are empowered to make important decisions for the company—that is, they follow the model of individual self-management.

Critics claim that flat organizations can conceal power structures and shield individuals from accountability; that power cliques can readily form and cause harm to the organization, a problem which is usually exacerbated by a lack of diversity or collaboration. However, if the culture is nurtured in such a way to prevent such power cliques from developing, a flat structure could lead to breakthrough innovation.

Indeed, advocates claim that a lack of bureaucracy lets employees collaborate more freely, which leads to Nimble Decision-making and innovation. A good example of a flat organization is Zappos. As of March 2017 all Zappos' 1,500 employees belong to some 500 self-governing teams called circles.[42]

Tony Hsieh, CEO of Zappos, hoped the move to self-management would help the company maintain a start-up feel even as it grew. Zappos is known for its unique policies, such as paying new employees to leave if they feel they are not the right fit for the company.

In 2013 Tony Hsieh began experimenting with Holacracy, a new model of flat organizational structure relying on self-management and self-organization.[43,44] No managers. By March 2015, Zappos was well into orchestrating a Pivot to Holacracy and, per a letter from Hsieh to all employees, had been "operating partially under Holacracy and partially under the legacy management hierarchy in parallel for over a year now." The announcement resulted in 15–18% of Zappos' employees leaving, which also means that at least 82% of employees stayed.

Hsieh explains his Pivot to Holacracy as a means to stay nimble as the company grows. In a 2016 article in *Zappos' Insights* he explained why he decided to Pivot to Holacracy:

> Research shows that every time the size of a city doubles, innovation or productivity per resident increases by 15%. But when companies get bigger, innovation or productivity per employee generally goes down. So we're trying to figure out how to structure Zappos more like a city, and less like a bureaucratic corporation. In a city, people and businesses are self-organizing. We're trying to do the same thing by switching from a normal hierarchical structure to a system called Holacracy, which enables employees to act more like entrepreneurs and self-direct their work instead of reporting to a manager who tells them what to do.[45]

Amazon purchased Zappos in 2009, before Zappos' Pivot to Holacracy. The cultures at each company have remained separate and it is not expected that Amazon will also Pivot to a self-managed structure. Jeff Bezos, CEO of Amazon, has, however, selected some aspects of the Zappos culture that he feels will work well at Amazon; for example, the policy to pay customer service hires to quit after a four-week training session if they feel they are not the right fit. Amazon now offers its warehouse employees $2,000 to quit after their first year and $1,000 per year more up to $5,000. "The goal is to encourage folks to take a moment and think about what they really want," Bezos writes to shareholders. The letter to the employee who has made it to a year in service is entitled "Please Don't Take This Offer."[46]

4) Open (or Network) Structure

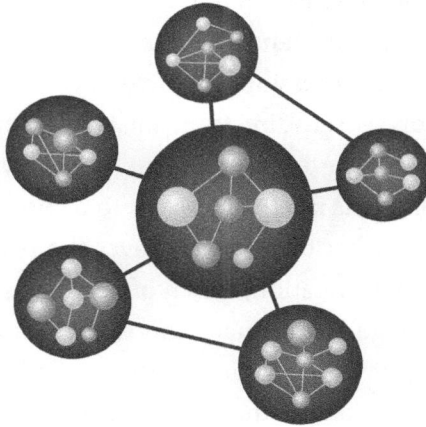

Figure 9: Open structure

An open structure pulls the informal networks that form even in a traditional hierarchy, infuses organizational authority into those networks, and drops the hierarchical structure. Most often there are a few managers or team leads in an open or network structure. A role of manager also may be temporarily designated and given to the person accountable for the team's performance, rather than in a permanent, traditional managerial role.

The aims of adopting this organizational structure include:
- the strengthening of shared values;
- free-flowing information and feedback;
- Nimble Decision-making; and
- rewarding people based on their merits and use of a Mastery Mindset, rather than on position.

James Whitehurst of Redhat and General Stanley McChrystal, former U.S. commander in Afghanistan, describe this nimble structure in *The Open Organization* (2015) and *Team of Teams* (2015), respectively. [47,48]

An open structure is comprised of teams grouped into multiple and often overlapping circles. An employee may be on several teams, and teams can form and disband based on the work to be done. Often a key component of a successful open structure, one that best avoids employee confusion, is self-direction. That is, an employee may be invited to join a particular team, or an employee may request to join a team, but the employee is never instructed to be on a particular team. Telling an employee what to do often leaves the reason for their assignment open to interpretation, which often creates anxiety. When a person is told to change, human nature most often concludes that they have done something wrong or that something bad has happened.

As listed above, one aim of the open structure is for the business to maintain its nimble, entrepreneurial spirit without becoming bureaucratic as it grows. While there is still an executive team, risk-taking and decision-making are driven by all levels of the organization.

Properly executed, an openly networked team structure can draw out tremendous innovation and creativity, as employees don't encounter roadblocks from management or top-down decision-making in the organization. Communication occurs organically and is shared "throughout and to the edges" of the organization.

In some open-structured companies, such as Valve, a gaming company best known for its video game series *Half-Life*, individuals who have an idea for a project recruit their own teams. Often, it is a mutual choice whether an employee joins a team or not, rather than an instruction directed from the top. This can work well as long as cliques are held at bay. Desks, even the CEO's, are on wheels so team members can move into clusters to work on a particular project. Employees simply roll their desk and chair over to the team they are working with at any one time.[49] Valve also leverages an open office space format, which can be energizing, but may require meeting rooms and headphones for productivity.

Alignment in open-structured organizations is typically achieved by communicating through many mediums, such as meetings, team huddles, online chat facilities and project management applications. The work, by nature, must be aligned with the organization's strategy or it dies on the vine. Aligned Momentum is likely to occur organically in an open organization.

Which structure fits your organization best?

The descriptions above are not meant to convince you to abandon an existing structure and adopt a new one without proper assessment and planning. What structure best fits your strategic plan? If your strategy is to be bolder, will the existing structure enable brilliant execution? The descriptions above intend to provide awareness and to help you envision what structure will best support your vision. I *do not* recommend attempting a turn-on-a-dime pivot to a new structure. The structure or hybrid structures best fitting your strategy should be woven in as you Pivot toward Aligned Momentum.

PIVOTS TOWARD ALIGNED MOMENTUM

Aligned Momentum exists when:
- the strategic plan is bold and purposeful;
- people are clear about the direction and their part in it;
- people know they are valued and trusted in their role;
- excelling in one's business role results in fulfilling one's intrinsic, personal needs and goals.

Your organizational structure needs to support these outcomes. How might Aligned Momentum exist in your organization, in your preferred structure? The following are recommendations based on what's worked for other organizations, grouped by type of structure. Your Pivots and best next steps may vary.

Pivots when structured as a hierarchy

If your organization is structured hierarchically and has become too reliant on command-and-control management when you seek to be more nimble, you must Pivot to a less rigid structure. Rigidity will block you from reaping the benefits of Aligned Momentum. The following Pivots preserve efficiency and accountability, while bringing in nimble practices:

> Pivot **from** *top-down communication* **to** *a more lateral communication style.*

You've likely put together cross-functional teams for special projects in the past. How can you incorporate cross-functional teams into the course of your normal daily work? Can you give these teams the authority to initiate change within their own areas of responsibility?

> Pivot **from** *commander* **to** *coach.*

Train managers how to coach. As coaches they still are in touch with what's going on and they remain accountable for outcomes; operational efficiency and accountability are not lost. What shifts, however, is the tone, context and frequency of communication. Your managers are doing this correctly when employees trust that their manager has their back and knows that their manager wants them to be successful. Make sure managers get this same coaching, including performance conversations, so that they too can increase their trust and sense of value. They will then flourish and help model the way for others.

> Pivot **from** *traditional performance management with only infrequent reviews* **to** *frequent performance conversations.*

This shift creates a more natural and timely way to assess and improve performance than the more formal quarterly or annual performance reviews. These regular conversations focus on priorities and become an excellent way to ensure alignment between what people want and do and what the organization needs them to do to achieve the business's strategic goals.

Here's a way to weave performance conversations into your organization:

1) Each employee shares with their manager (via email, private messaging, software app, etc.) their top one to five accomplishments of the previous month and their top one to five priorities for the current month.
2) The manager receives the email and promptly responds with one of the following:
   - Yes, continue;
   - Please consider ___ and send it again; or
   - Let's meet.

When using coaching skills to provide feedback in this way, this simple process will start aligning what is being done with the business's strategic direction, objectives and initiatives. In other words, the right things will be done right. Having this performance conversation be initiated by the employee deepens their commitment. For both the employee and manager, this process can more quickly identify any awareness, training, coaching or Pivot needed than a periodic performance review can.

In Gallup's Q12 employee engagement survey (12 questions, each given a rating from one to five), the first question asks, "Do you know what is expected of you at work?" The sixth question asks, "Is there someone at work who encourages your development?"[50,51] Frequent performance conversations with a manager who cares will increase employee engagement as well as their willingness to be part of your organization's change to becoming more nimble and experiencing extraordinary momentum.

Pivots when structured as a matrix

If your organization is structured as a matrix and you want to reap the benefits of Aligned Momentum, first identify and remove conflicts created by managers "sharing" an employee and assess the overall effectiveness of each project team. To move toward Aligned Momentum, start with one of the following Pivots.

> *Pivot* **from** *conflicting management styles and direction* **to** *team leads who are expert resources yet will leave management of people to each employee's functional manager.*

The team lead will best serve the individuals on the team, and the company as a whole, if they become a go-to person to provide advice, guidance and additional resources related to the project.

> *Pivot* **from** *know-it-all fixed mindsets* **to** *Mastery Mindsets.*

Experience will lead to greater knowledge, but wisdom requires both professional and personal growth. For your company to be nimble you need Mastery Mindsets. If you have experienced people who are not open to growing, are controlling and commanding, and base everything on experiences from their past, your company's growth will suffer. In some cases, the know-it-all can begin to shift toward growth if you award achievement rather than only hierarchical advancement (i.e., into management). For example, create a mentor program so that your achievement-oriented experts can grow the knowledge in your company without being expected to manage others.

> *Pivot **from** managing work and roles **to** managing people with managers who are trained to coach.*

Train managers how to coach. In their coaching capacity, managers can really get to know what each direct report's strengths are as well as that person's personal and professional goals. In fact, the fifth question in Gallup's Q12 survey asks, "Does your supervisor, or someone at work, seem to care about you as a person?"[52,53] Alignment and engagement grow stronger when people feel that what they do is fulfilling their needs.

Creating a more aligned and engaged workforce will lead to more successful Pivots, and extraordinary business momentum.

Pivots for both flat and open organizations

If your organizational structure is flat or open, you are already well-positioned to reap the innovation and Nimble Decision-making benefits of Aligned Momentum. Another benefit is that these structures create greater opportunity for an individual to continue to grow through further *achievement* without also needing to *advance* into higher levels of management. Reward for achievement without a requirement to advance into management is something your experts may desire.

The Pivots listed below can help a flat or open organization strengthen Aligned Momentum. An organization wanting to flatten or become more open may also find guidance in these Pivots.

> *Pivot **from** no traditional management roles **to** managers-as-coaches.*

It doesn't matter what you name the managerial role. You want managers who aren't merely managing work and processes, but managers who can coach their employees to excel in their positions and, at the same time, understand their role in and contributions to the team and the organization. Make sure that everyone in the company has someone with more experience or resources than they do to mentor and coach them to be successful personally and professionally.

> Pivot **from** *disparate team goals* **to** *teams aligned toward shared strategic objectives.*

A flatter or more open culture is predisposed to becoming chaotic. Creating greater Clarity around the company's strategic objectives can help teams prioritize their work to closely align with those objectives and, in the process, create the conditions for brilliant execution.

> Pivot **from** *lack of Clarity in direction when self-managed* **to** *some structure of peers-as-partners or managers-as-coaches that supports Clarity and accountability.*

Within teams or between the sparse number of leaders and the many others, it is not uncommon for there to be a gap between those who have up-to-date skills, but not years of experience, and those who have years of experience and wisdom, yet not the latest training. It becomes difficult for the wiser person to resist checking in, which the others may see as micromanaging. A simple solution is to create accountability through a reporting process.

You (or the team leader) are accountable for clearly communicating the strategic direction and explaining not only what changes are being made, but why they are, as well. Instill the means and sense of expectation for each individual or team to feed-forward (i.e., report) the current status at any point in time. This creates a different tone than the traditional top-down structure, because they are following through on a clear expectation; you are not telling them exactly how to report or checking over their shoulders. A discipline, or call it a rhythm, of reporting will keep everyone engaged and you informed of progress, without the need for traditional command and control management.

Once you have a clear vision of the organizational structure that will best suit your business to execute its strategy, you are ready to gain momentum.

CHAPTER 3: KEY POINTS

---

1) You can't change a person, but you can change their context.

2) A common impediment to Aligned Momentum is having an organizational structure that no longer serves you or your people.

3) Envision the structure that will best fit your strategy.

4) These organizational structures are common and may help you envision the structure that will be your best fit:
   - Hierarchy
   - Matrix
   - Flat
   - Open.

5) There are Pivots you can orchestrate to bring more nimble practices into your organization, without any change in its current structure.

6) With the right structure you can move your business toward Aligned Momentum and extraordinary business momentum.

CHAPTER 4

Ö

Gaining Momentum

———————

"Those who build great companies understand that the ultimate throttle on growth for any great company is not markets, or technology, or competition, or products. It is one thing above all others: the ability to get and keep enough of the right people."

— *Jim Collins*

Earlier chapters covered alignment via The Pivot and Aligned Momentum. Now, let's get clear about momentum: continuous forward movement toward your objectives and, ultimately, your vision.

Why might you want extraordinary business momentum? If your people and your business have been moving at a slow pace or even stalled for some time, how might you Pivot toward extraordinary momentum, gain momentum and avoid further stalls as you Pivot? What will success look like? What will progress look like? How might you track progress and generate performance breakthroughs? When momentum builds, a breakthrough can happen.

A breakthrough is a dramatic achievement. It may seem like magic—an instantaneous success—yet, in fact, a breakthrough usually comes after intentional focus and consistent effort have been applied over several years. Van de Kamp's idea to focus on freshness in order to move from third to first in the frozen fish market is an example of a business breakthrough after a well-orchestrated Pivot.

Another example is 3M's Post-It® notes product, invented in an environment that allowed mistakes, which in this instance led to a big win. We previously looked at 3M in Chapter 3 as an example of a matrix structure organization. That structure played a part in the company's success.

3M is the owner of some of the best-known consumer brands, including Scotch®, Post-it®, Scotch-Brite®, and Scotchgard™. If you started your career prior to the availability of smart phones, you will remember how sticky notes aided personal productivity. They remain a popular choice for group brainstorming. Although sticky notes were created during a failed attempt at inventing a highly sticky glue, the breakthrough result hints of magic (as if some secret to success had been revealed spontaneously).

3M leadership had successfully prepared and orchestrated The Pivot. The engineer was clear about the strategic direction and his role in it. He felt safe to initiate change, in this case through experimentation, and decide his best next steps.[54,55]

What if 3M had relied only on past experience to guide their next steps and hadn't allowed room for trying and failing? We might not have had sticky notes.

Business breakthroughs most often happen through people. Only when the right people are committed to achieving the best results possible in line with a shared vision can business breakthroughs happen.

Commitment strengthens when the work to be done and the vision to be reached align with the employees' own purpose. When you follow a clear purpose you are aligned with who you really are, how you intend others to experience you, and where you want to go or what you intend to do. Knowing your purpose—*why* you do what you do—is a uniquely human quality and one that is extremely powerful. When work aligns with purpose, employees often describe "feeling alive and engaged" at work. When you are fully engaged and in alignment with your purpose, the results you've wished for can seem to come almost effortlessly. It is under these conditions that personal breakthroughs can occur, which in turn may lead to team and business breakthroughs.

BREAKTHROUGHS AREN'T MAGIC, YET THEY OFTEN DEFY LOGIC

Breakthroughs are not magic or simply good luck. Luck in timing a situation can support a breakthrough, but the sure path to business breakthroughs is with Aligned Momentum and well-orchestrated Pivots. Both breakthroughs and extraordinary momentum require a Pivot *from* a focus on the past *to* a focus on the future. Stop limiting future momentum by what was or wasn't achieved in the past. Focusing on the future may run counter to traditional workplace dynamics, yet this is required for Aligned Momentum.

Traditional management thinking calls for projections into the future based on statistically significant data drawn from past performance. This is logical, but may not prove most successful. A rigid historical analysis too often omits important factors such as considerations of future possibilities. Traditional management also focuses on removing risk, and may lean so far that way that the trial and error process that is required to innovate cannot happen. Yet, innovation is needed to fuel momentum.

Peter Drucker explained this unfortunate misinterpretation of management in *Management Challenges for the 21st Century* (1999):

> All traditional assumptions led to one conclusion: The inside of the organization is the domain of management. This assumption explains the otherwise totally incomprehensible distinction between management and entrepreneurship. In actual practice this distinction makes no sense whatever. An enterprise, whether a business or any other institution, that does not innovate and does not engage in entrepreneurship will not survive long.[56]

Drucker wrote those words in 1999. Are you holding onto traditional business assumptions that are not serving you today? Pivot *from* traditions that cannot support a bold new strategy *to* Aligned Momentum.

A few large organizations have been nimble and successful in innovation for decades, such as 3M.

Relying solely on what one might predict with logical methods suppresses innovation and defies breakthroughs. Don't throw out your models, but do question if the past alone will support Nimble Decision-making. Do position your company for breakthroughs. Create a space where breakthroughs are granted a chance; aim toward the future, communicate the direction and objectives clearly, and let those closest to the work determine what is best done next. This is how you can be the conductor of well-orchestrated Pivots.

Ask yourself and your employees, "What will this (situation, problem, opportunity, roadblock, etc.) look like in the future, based on where we (or I) expect to *be* over the next few years?" To plot a path toward your vision of the future, you need to answer that question and then plot your path in reverse: step back and back and back from this future possibility until the best next steps in the present become clear. Looking forward creates Clarity. Then looking back to the present with that future in mind helps you communicate more clearly.

LEADERS, IT STARTS WITH YOU

Knowing that you can generate extraordinary momentum and create performance breakthroughs in your business should be more than compelling to orchestrate Pivots. It seems a no-brainer to align your employees and their roles with your strategic objectives. And yet, you'll likely be a first-mover in your industry and region to do so; and you'll benefit from the competitive advantage this creates.

Aligning what people want for themselves with their role in your organization doesn't even require an overly complicated long-term plan. It can be started in the next quarter. Or how about now? I hope that as you read these pages you'll gain Clarity around what your culture with Aligned Momentum might look like; what performance breakthroughs you may experience together; what will be hard; what your best next steps will be; and how you'll know if you're on the right track.

To be clear, this starts with you, the leader. Aligned Momentum demands active leadership that fosters human connectedness and authenticity. It does not thrive in a culture that relies on the power of (coercive) authority to get the best work done. "Corporate doesn't care" is not a good excuse for a lack of human connectedness in business, and it does not fit in a culture with Aligned Momentum. When a leader is clear about wanting breakthroughs, the business' culture will respond. Collaboration will become more common. The workplace will become more connected. More human.

INDIVIDUALS AND ALIGNED MOMENTUM

How will you help current employees adapt to this changing culture? To support individuals in their Pivot to a culture with Aligned Momentum, you want to ensure they understand, assimilate and experience the following:

1) clarity and accountability related to their performance;
2) trust in those who can influence their success;
3) access to resources, including training, that strengthen their ability to adapt.

When these points are in place and observable, you can be reasonably sure that your shift in culture is not holding anyone back. Yet, still, not all employees will be sufficiently ready to Pivot *from* what they are used to. Here's what you can do: make certain to respect and address the fact that not only do people desire to be part of something bigger than they are, but also that every person desires to have their unique voice heard.

Here's another compelling reason to consider individual alignment: when it comes to empowering others to initiate change in your business, you want individuals who are aligned with business objectives *because* executing those brilliantly will also align with what they want for themselves.

And finally, let's talk about you. Read through the following pages of this chapter once with yourself in mind. You may gain more Clarity around why you do what you do, if a few tweaks or even challenges might bring you more fulfillment in business and life, and how to be your best self.

Personal Brand Alignment: Overview

There is an aspect to extraordinary momentum that brings out each unique voice. When it exists, individuals grow even faster. I call this Personal Brand Alignment.

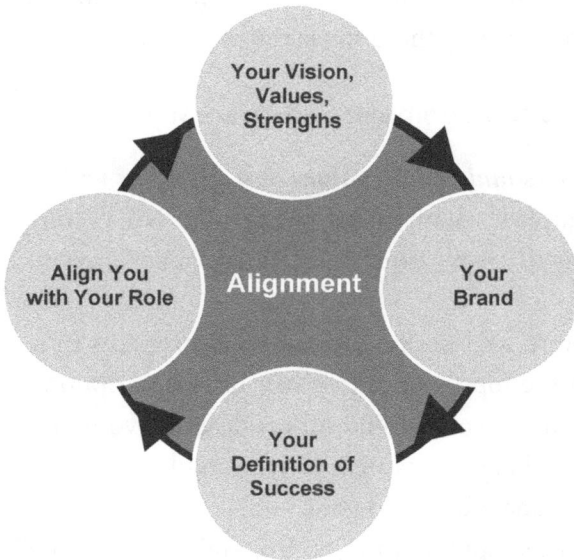

Figure 10: Personal Brand Alignment

Personal Brand Alignment entails:

- awareness of your personal vision, values and strengths (your brand);
- alignment of your brand with a definition of success;
- alignment of your brand and definition of success with your role.

Personal Brand Alignment is too often overlooked in business strategy and organizational structure. However, to get every individual aligned and part of your business momentum, they must be personally involved and invested. As a leader and a coach, it is an invaluable consideration. When people feel fulfillment in their lives through their work and they are being authentic to themselves, your business benefits. They proactively seek alignment. They step up and speak out in productive ways. They are engaged; they look forward to each day, stretch to meet or exceed goals, support their peers, subordinates (if any) and manager, and they remain focused on priorities even when it is hard to do so. Whether you are working on yourself or coaching others when following these steps, the process is the same.

Personal Brand Alignment: Self-assessment

Align your personal vision, values and strengths with your brand
If you accomplish what you set out to do (your vision), what might you be doing 10 years from now? What values are you living every day?

If you were to describe each of your strengths in a single word, what would the top five be? Create a brief description of each word and how each fits you. Would others describe your strengths in this way? How would others express your strengths if they were describing them to someone other than you?

Every day, simply in how you live and work, you define and further your personal brand. This is driven by your purpose—the "why" behind what you are doing now and intend for the future. How are you seen by others (and is this how you intend to be)? What commitments are you making? What promises are you keeping (or not keeping)?

Consider how you behave, what you say and what you do. Are you showing up in ways that are consistent with your personal brand? What is going right? What needs to stop? Do you need to Pivot?

Align your brand with a definition of success
A vision provides a snapshot of the future, but success is not a snapshot or destination: *success is a journey that is in alignment with your brand.* You may have successfully completed a goal. That is one achievement. You may *hope* it will lead to your success, but you only *know* it is part of your success path if that goal aligns with your brand. Here's a helpful exercise:

1) Describe a time when you knew you were moving ahead on your success path.

2) What percentage of the time do you define yourself as being successful? (Remember that success is a journey on a path you've defined for yourself.)

3) Describe an instance where it was clear you were checking items off of a list and it made you feel productive or met a job requirement, but it was not on your success path.

4) What percentage of the time are you checking off to-dos that are not leading you along your chosen path?

5) How often are you aware that what you are doing, being or saying is moving you forward (on your chosen path) or not? How often are you aware of when you are merely reacting to what is in front of you rather than acting purposively?

6) What elements of your business might you track to understand more fully when you are on your path, when you are off your path temporarily and need to Pivot, or if you are on the wrong path?

7) How will you stay accountable when tracking your journey and shifting, if you move off track? Who might you ask for support or candid feedback?

Aligning you with your role

Most of us aim for growth in five areas over our lifetime: financial, relationships, learning, health and achievement. When considering alignment between what you want as an individual and what the company needs from you in your role, ask the following:

1) How does this company align with your personal brand? What roles do you see here that best fit your success path?

2) How do you align with this company? What values and strengths do you bring that best fit both your success path and the strategic objectives of this business? (If the translation from company to individual is not clear or not yet shared, you can point to mission, purpose, values and functional goals that can be shared.)

3) How and how well does your role (or the role you are seeking) align with you? In what ways does your role not align with you? What might you do to create better alignment? What have you done or are you doing to create better alignment that is not yet reflected in the job description for your role?

4) In what ways do you align with the manager or team leaders you work with? In what ways is alignment lacking? What might you do to create better alignment? What might your manager do to foster better alignment?

5) Mutually agree and commit to a role scorecard, which describes the performance and values expected of you. Identify expectations that are aligned with you, performance expectations that are not aligned with you and that can be delegated or shifted to another role, and what roles others are performing that might propel you along your chosen path of success.

6) Once roles are identified, aligned, shifted or reassigned, update job descriptions to match the new/changed job responsibilities.

Personal Brand Alignment: in your workplace

Following are a few questions to ask employees. Of course, you may start with yourself. These questions are related to aligning a person with their role, to help them get clear about how their role aligns with the business' strategic objectives. After the questions I'll recount a story that I hope will give you a better idea of the level of readiness you are looking for.

> *When the questions below can be answered with ease, your workplace culture is primed for success with Aligned Momentum and The Pivot.*

Accountability questions

1) Are you clear about the business's current strategic direction and objectives? How do you know you are?

2) What *functions* are you accountable for? What functions must you answer for if performance is not meeting expectations or not leading to expected objectives?

3) What *processes* are you accountable for? What processes must you answer for if the process is taking performance off track or could be improved?

4) How do you know if others you're relying on to do the right things right are clear about the required direction and objectives and the fit with strategy?

5) How might you create the space for you and others to meet performance expectations?

6) Who is accountable for a function or process that you affect, but do not hold the ultimate accountability for? How might you better contribute to their success? How might they contribute to your success?

7) How do you know you are on track? How do you know that a function or process you are part of or accountable for is on track?

Commitment questions

1) Do you stay true to your values and brand, even in the toughest of times?

2) When you commit to a goal and you are on the right path toward achieving it, and things get tough, do you stay the course?

3) When you are moving toward a goal and the facts change so the path you are currently on is not going to get you there, do you make the needed needed changes or Pivot that these new facts require?

Trust questions

1) How aligned are you with your team? Do you inherently support the success of others at work? Is this clear to them?

2) Do others at work inherently support your success? How do you know?

3) Describe a recent experience when you stepped up or spoke out for the greater good of the organization. How were you treated? How was your idea or step treated?

4) Describe a recent experience when someone who relies on you or whom you manage stepped up or spoke out to support the greater good of the organization. How did you feel about them? How did you feel about the response to their action or words?

It may take time—months or years—for the alignment between a person and their role, and between each role and strategy, to be complete and entirely natural.

> *What is required to "Set the Stage" for The Pivot and*
> *Aligned Momentum is* **commitment to** *Clarity around*
> *what professional and personal success looks like.*

I promised you a story that would help you understand the level of readiness you are looking for, and to give you hope that the time it takes to be complete is worth waiting for. Here's that story:

Dr. Atul Gawande[57,58] shared a story with *The New Yorker* about a man named "Bill" who had experienced severe migraines starting at age 19. They were so severe that he often became very ill with each episode. By the age of 57, the migraines happened every few days; as one was improving another one would hit. They were taking a toll on his body. He'd had to quit his job because he couldn't function.

He tried a new specialist, Elizabeth Loder, and together they orchestrated a Pivot. Both had to be patient, keep momentum, and adapt to each new finding. It was an incremental approach using a variety of treatments that finally did the trick. "I am actually quite optimistic about his long-term outlook for improvement," Loder wrote in her notes that spring.

> I detect slow but steady progress. In particular, the extremes of headache at the upper end have come down nicely and vomiting is much less of a problem. That, in my experience, is a clear sign of regression.[59]

Dr. Gawande noted that Bill wasn't so sure. But after another year or so of adjustments he, too, began to notice a difference.

The interval between bad attacks had lengthened to a week. Later, it stretched to a month. Then even longer. When Dr. Gawande met with Bill in 2015, Bill had gone more than a year without a severe migraine, "I haven't had a dreadful attack since March 13, 2014," Bill said, triumphantly.[60] It had taken four years of effort. But Loder's systematic incrementalism (Dr. Gawande's term for this) or Pivot (my term for this) had done what nothing else had.

After four decades of agony Bill had achieved a breakthrough. He finally had his life back.

Mastering The Pivot benefits individuals, teams or the entire organization at any point where changes need to be made—whether a change in a function, a process, an overarching strategy or even a state of mind. But, as you have likely experienced as a leader, even when something is good for an individual, they often don't commit to it until *they* choose it.

> **Committing** *to a change requires* **choosing** *to change.*

The personal brand alignment process will help reinforce a choice of change when that change leads to alignment with what one wants for oneself. Choosing the change will lead to committing to that change. The best result is that these choices create an instinctual and ongoing alignment; as strategy changes, a person naturally changes how the work they do gets done, and at times even initiates a change in the work itself. Reinforce alignment in performance conversations and when communicating bold new strategies. Over time change becomes natural, and (Talent) Adaptability (to change in work and roles) is what employees expect; it is simply part of working there.

> *When people have a Mastery Mindset, are Adaptable, and have the skills to make Nimble Decisions, they'll commit to your bold new strategy more readily, and change will come more naturally.*

THE ROLE OF THE LEADERSHIP TEAM
IN GAINING MOMENTUM

For many organizations, it's easy to stick with what is working now, based on what seems to have worked in the past. But does this gain momentum? No. Today, sales may be brisk, your warehouse may be at optimized turns and your balance sheet may shine. Setting your sights on achieving momentum does not mean you must change everything right now, but I do not recommend getting to the point where you must desperately attempt to turn-on-a-dime. You need to look ahead to see how to gain momentum toward the future. The market has a way of moving and changing faster than you can change with it. The risk you face when becoming complacent is being blindsided by an impact you didn't see or didn't take seriously.

Decades ago, the workforce was focused primarily on internal operations. External forces were relatively stable or at least were known and could be contained. Change came at a comfortable, even predictable pace. Leaders in a top-down structure had time to respond to external changes with incremental internal changes.

> *Today, that same top-down structure can become a stranglehold if not adapted to the realities of the global marketplace.*

Your competitor is no longer just down the road or across town. A competitor can be on the other side of the world, totally out of your view. Vast local and global networks generate a connected power. Networks are comprised of a multitude of moving parts. How might you strengthen the power of networks within your business? In traditional business, the old model, knowledge was power and was held solely at the top. Today, to maintain business momentum, you must reach out to and hear from all employees.

> *To strengthen the internal and external networks powering*
> *your business, knowledge must be shared and the individuals*
> *stepping up to lead throughout the company need to be*
> *able to communicate change quickly and clearly.*

LEADING BY EXAMPLE

This new paradigm of vast networks can be unsettling to traditional-ly-minded leadership teams. It can even feel threatening to a leader accustomed to seeing power as a function of one's authority or to a leader basking in celebrity as a business hero.

> *To experience Aligned Momentum the leader and leadership*
> *team must Pivot **from** wielding power based on authority*
> ***to** having influence based on positive modeling.*

Leaders best serve by guiding the business toward the smartest strategic direction, as expert resources, and as the cultural tone-setters. In a culture with Aligned Momentum, the leader also orchestrates a Pivot. Managers ensure that what is planned to be done gets done, in keeping with this tone.

What is the tone? The phrase "tone at the top" has often been used in the realm of corporate governance and ethics. The leader is the model of transparency and ethical behavior: they create a safe place for employees to speak up, provide training and not only hold others accountable, but also hold themselves accountable. Tone is so much more. You have an opportunity to gain and maintain momentum by being a true leader, a positive influence and a person that others *want* to follow rather than one they must follow to survive in your company. The tone you set can create a better place to work, which is critical if you want to get the right people into the right positions and keep them engaged.

When people feel engaged in their work they are more likely to stay aligned, accountable and adaptable without needing to be rigidly managed. Gallup, referenced in an earlier discussion about employee engagement, also found a positive correlation between employee engagement and business results.[61]

Employee engagement scores have barely budged over the past 20 years. If we continue to lead businesses in the way they've been led in the past, we can't be surprised to also struggle to achieve and maintain business performance momentum.[62] Internal stats won't change unless you change. By applying traditional top-down leadership to a world comprised of vast networks, we will just make personal and business life even more complex. Simplifying work can lead to gained momentum. Simplicity doesn't have to mean there's a straight line from point A to point B. That's rarely engaging. Simplicity in business can be translated into shared expectations and commitments, clear strategy and ensuring that our own network of people are primed to take their best next step.

Even when traditional leadership was still effective, Einstein warned us with these words, "Any intelligent fool can make things bigger and more complex ... It takes a touch of genius—and a lot of courage to move in the opposite direction."

> *Simplify what it takes to orchestrate change by stepping back and letting your aligned and engaged employees reach performance breakthroughs naturally.*

The culture in your business doesn't have to be perfect before starting The Pivot or a move toward Aligned Momentum. It simply needs to be less rigid.

BE YOUR BEST RESULTS

We've talked about your role. Now let's talk about *you* in your role—your personal brand. Without even being aware of it, *you* could be playing a part in the *company's* rigidity. Warren Buffet, known for his financial prowess, but also one of my go-to voices on leadership reminds us, "It takes 20 years to build a reputation and only five minutes to ruin it. If you think about that, you will do things differently."

As a leader, there are steps you can take to be your best self and lead in a way that will reignite momentum. It can be difficult to be authentic at work. You may feel an expectation to always be in control, to have all the answers. You may feel you need to embody authoritative attributes based on what others expect (or you think they expect) of your role and "place" in the organization. As such, you create a work "persona" that becomes the "you" that everyone sees and gets used to. But this persona is not the real "you." Applying The Pivot to how you *are* at work can require more courage than orchestrating a significant Pivot for the company.

> *If your company is not keeping up with the market or the times, the first Pivot may have to come from you.*

A culture based on *fitting into* a role (as opposed to *aligning* a person with a role) is a culture that has become rigid. If you and your leadership team are not consistently re-evaluating how you *are* in your respective role, then perhaps you have become rigid. Remember, as a leader you set the tone for the company's culture.

THE RISK OF BEING RIGID

Rigidity is the opposite of being nimble. Giving the floor to only one style of communication is not nimble. Valuing only one style or noticing only a certain skill, trait, gender etc. in employees is not nimble. Creating obstacles to innovation and collaboration is not nimble.

A successful, mature "grown-up" business has taken the time necessary to become operationally efficient and there is value in doing so. However, when the initial way becomes the only way, rigidity becomes the norm rather than the exception. Even though protocols, policies, processes and systems were smartly implemented to reduce risk and increase efficiency in the business, this rigidity may now put you at risk of stalling. Unless you were particularly mindful of what was engaging people as you "managed" how the work was being carried out, you may have fueled disengagement.

> *Rigidity can lead to a lack of employee engagement or even to disengagement; it drains energy and leaves no room for individuality. Not feeling committed to one's work drains a company of its momentum.*

One sign that your employees are not engaged is compliance: when people in your organization only do what they are told they should do. This will not lead to momentum. Sure, some employees may do what you tell them to do in the short term. But eventually, when there is no positive change and they have no voice, they will disengage. They will start going through the motions and do nothing more while they look for a better place to work or figure out a way to get back at the company, such as calling in sick more often, becoming contrary, or stealing from petty cash or supplies. A seeming initial victory—total compliance—becomes a failure over the long term.

In *Radical Honesty* (2005), Brad Blanton provides a view into the failings of a culture where those at the top tell and those beneath comply:

> We know that being a wage slave, for most people, is not all good. We have all seen how people who stay stuck there, tolerating it while their life recedes to the background, are not all happy or

> even secure. We know that the people at the top … have often
> developed the capacity to not give a damn about people unless
> it affects the bottom line. Everyone who is not rich and doesn't
> stay ignorant is coming to know this, and everyone who is rich
> already knows that "security" provided by money is not the
> answer.[63]

Another view comes from the *Harvard Business Review* article
"Discovering Your Authentic Leadership."[64] Authentic leaders make
time to examine their experiences and to reflect on them, and in doing so they grow as individuals and as leaders. Authentic leaders also
work hard at developing self-awareness through persistent and often
courageous self-exploration.

You know that rigidity is not what you want. By now you also get
that compliance, or "wage slaves" as Brad Blanton so bluntly puts it, is
not what you seek. You may even be shying away from emphasizing
buy-in, which is a form of selling. Compliance (people doing what
you tell them to do) and buy-in (people doing what you compel them
to do) both have their place. Take care to use these methods when
they are the best way, and not as the norm and the only way. Shifting
to empowering others and delegating authority to them takes courage,
in addition to learning.

Knowing your style, your "as is" in gap assessment terms, and its
impact on others, requires self-awareness. We'll start there. David
Pottruck, former CEO of Charles Schwab, tells a story of his journey
to self-awareness, which I shall now share with you:

After completing his MBA at Wharton and a stint with Citigroup,
he joined Charles Schwab as head of marketing. He worked hard and
could not understand why his colleagues resented the hours he put in
and his aggressive push for results:

> I thought my accomplishments would speak for themselves … It
> never occurred to me that my level of energy would intimidate
> and offend other people, because in my mind I was trying to help
> the company.[65]

Pottruck was shocked when his boss told him, "Dave, your colleagues do not trust you." As he recalled,

> That feedback was like a dagger to my heart. I was in denial, as I didn't see myself as others saw me. I had no idea how self serving I looked to other people. Still, somewhere in my inner core the feedback resonated as true.[66]

Pottruck realized that he could not succeed unless he identified and overcame his blind spots. It was only after his second divorce that Pottruck was finally able to acknowledge that he still had blind spots: "After my second marriage fell apart, I thought I had a wife-selection problem." Then he worked with a counselor who delivered some hard truths: "The good news is you do not have a wife-selection problem; the bad news is you have a husband-behavior problem." Pottruck then made a determined effort to change. As he described it, "I was like a guy who has had three heart attacks and finally realizes he has to quit smoking and lose some weight." These days Pottruck is happily remarried and listens closely to feedback. He acknowledges that he falls back to his old habits at times, particularly in highly stressful situations, but now he has developed better ways of coping with stress.

If there's a chance that the tone you've set for your organization is too rigid, what will it take for you to set a new tone? What will it take for your employees to feel that they are *choosing* to come to work and that there is a mutual *choice* of the right role for them at your company? Spend some time on your own personal brand alignment, and then seek feedback from others to determine if they see you in the way you see yourself. This takes courage. Being vulnerable to ask for feedback and being open to it and any change it requires takes courage. You are a leader; BE courageous in your personal growth.

Lead your employees by example and weave self-awareness into your culture. Once someone who is in the position of being a hiring manager understands the importance and value of personal alignment, it can become part of every new hire and promotion process. A self-aware person has the courage to seek feedback. When a person can be authentic at work, they are more likely to be engaged and aligned with their role. Pivot toward a culture where every employee knows how they fit in their role and within their team, how their role fits the strategy, and that their manager cares about their success.

WEAVING PERSONAL BRAND ALIGNMENT INTO YOUR CULTURE

In this chapter I've introduced a few concepts that will help you gain momentum. I recommend some of the most common best next steps below. For some, a Pivot will be required:

Keep job descriptions current: including yours

For Aligned Momentum and The Pivot to be successfully woven into the culture, it is important to revisit roles as you update the organization's strategy. This can be a huge undertaking if job descriptions are rarely updated. Alignment with outdated rules will not help you gain momentum. Once the business is practicing Aligned Momentum, job descriptions will align with the current strategy in a more organic way.

Confirm that all roles, when combined, properly cover what is needed to execute the company's strategic objectives, and also remove functions, tasks or reporting that have become obsolete. Be sure you update the review mechanism as well, so that performance conversations are based on the work that matters today and in the future.

For example, the perfect time to solicit employee feedback is during a performance conversation: view the conversation as an opportunity to revisit the employee's job description.

Stay calm during change

It's important to keep everything in perspective as you Pivot. At the very minimum, remember that a Pivot is planned; it is not a leap of faith into the unknown. This is why we look toward the future rather than the past for the right path.

In a Pivot, one foot is always kept on the ground while everything else shifts toward a clear and measurable destination. While it may feel uncomfortable, it should feel possible. As each person masters The Pivot, it will become natural, and simply part of your culture. When change feels natural, stress is lowered and performance improves. Momentum is gained.

Another reason to maintain calm is that once a particular Pivot is woven into the culture, everyone knows that someone else has their back, from the bottom to the top *and* from the top to the bottom (or out to the edges for those of you not organized hierarchically). No one performs at peak efficiency when they think they are out there all alone. Everyone deserves to know that their manager cares about their success. The business will benefit from the momentum this fuels.

Aim personal ambition toward mastery, not perfection

Change is less risky for the organization if each person changes for their own personal reasons, including staying true to a personal brand. If one learns to change often without needing to be perfect, they are far more likely to grow. It also creates a culture of continual learning, where mistakes are used as lessons, not as opportunities to call someone out.

Understand belief systems

Commitment to perform and Clarity about what is expected are more likely to be present when you pay attention to personal alignment. Even so, your employees may not have the courage that you do to be open to constructive feedback about their own blind spots or to respond to the feedback with questions to become more self-aware. Blind spots usually stem from ingrained and unchallenged beliefs. Beliefs can keep people stuck, and stuck people hold business momentum at bay. You can let them go or you can coach them. If the issue is with their beliefs about change—not about their performance in the role they were hired to do—you may have an opportunity to help them grow. You may gain champions for future business momentum.

You may have been taught that, as a leader initiating change, you can expect 20% of people to be champions, 60% of people to go along, and 20% to resist. If you coach people, create a safe context in which they can become more aware, and communicate for complete Clarity throughout the organization, you'll engage more champions and gain momentum.

CHAPTER 4: KEY POINTS

---

1) When momentum builds, breakthroughs can happen.

2) A breakthrough is a dramatic achievement, which usually comes after consistent intention and effort.

3) Business breakthroughs most often happen through people when they are committed to a shared vision.

4) Commitment to a shared vision is strongest when the work to be done is aligned with an individual's purpose (personal and professional).

5) Feeling engaged and alive shows up as commitment.

6) Breakthroughs aren't magic, yet they defy logic. They:
   - happen when the focus is on the future with a clear vision, without knowing exactly how to get there, and without telling everyone how you (the leader) expect them to get there.
   - don't happen when applying a traditional, logical, history-based approach to moving forward.

7) The leader must model the way. You (the leader) create "the tone at the top."

PART 2

Share The Vision

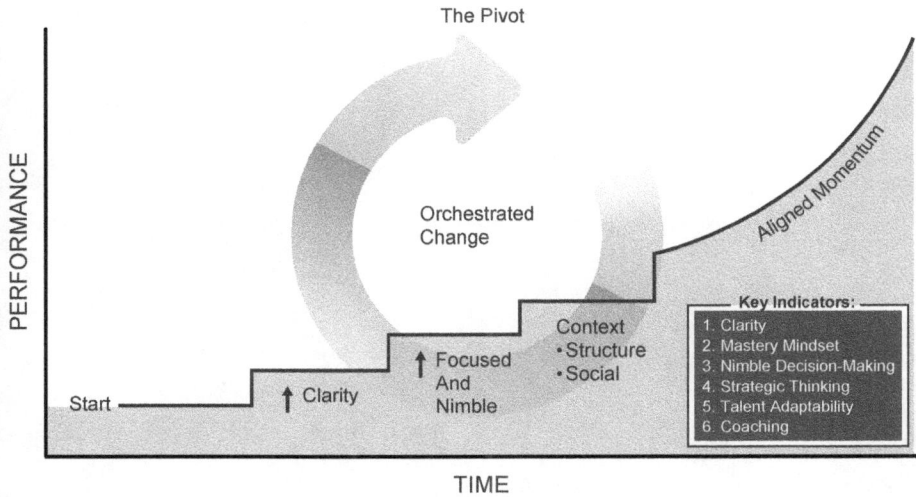

The Pivot

Orchestrated Change

Aligned Momentum

PERFORMANCE

Context
• Structure
• Social

↑ Focused
And
Nimble

↑ Clarity

Start

Key Indicators:
1. Clarity
2. Mastery Mindset
3. Nimble Decision-Making
4. Strategic Thinking
5. Talent Adaptability
6. Coaching

TIME

CHAPTER 5

Clarity

GETTING CLEAR AND BEING CLEAR

*"People are working harder than ever, but because they
lack clarity and vision, they aren't getting very far. They,
in essence, are pushing a rope .. with all of their might."*

— *Stephen Covey*

Clarity is the quality of being clear, as in the quality of being coherent
and intelligible, of being easy to see, and of being certain. In business,
you must *get* clear about where the company is headed, and the strategy, and then you must *be* clear when communicating this to others so
that they might execute brilliantly.

It's easy to get lost when you're mired in the day-to-day operations
of the business, or if you are too detached from operations; Clarity
can suffer. When you have a clear sense of direction and strategy, it's

far easier to take the next steps and to articulate those steps to others. And when you empower others by bringing them to Clarity about their role in the execution of strategy, you free yourself to be working more *on* the business than *in* it.

Clarity is required even before you begin to orchestrate a Pivot, which is why this Aligned Momentum Key Indicator has a full chapter dedicated to it. A successful Pivot requires Clarity. Aligned Momentum cannot live without Clarity. The following pages take you through what it means to get clear and be clear, so that Clarity is achieved.

PEOPLE WILL DO THEIR BEST; IT MAY NOT BE WHAT YOU WANT

By not being clear, you may be unwittingly causing your employees to "push a rope." The result is that strategy is not brilliantly executed, you don't gain extraordinary business momentum and you may find the business soon stalls.

Perhaps you recall the poem about the six blind men who all "see" an elephant in a different way, based on where they are touching the mammal.[67] The man touching the side of the elephant was sure it was a wall. The man touching the trunk of the elephant was sure it was a snake. And so on. Of course, they were all right in what they ex-claimed about what the part they were touching felt like, but they were all wrong in guessing what they were actually touching. The poem reminds us of how misaligned even well-meaning people can be when Clarity is lacking. Misinterpretation can result even when the facts are presented plainly and right in front of people. It can be even more dif-ficult to gain Clarity about what one cannot see—such as the future.

As a leader, it's imperative that you clearly communicate your vision of what the company will look like in the future: what it will have accomplished, who it will be serving, what its purpose will be, its values, and the guiding principles that everyone in the organization will be living by. And, you need to clearly communicate how that vision translates to current strategic direction and objectives, and even to this quarter's priorities. Then, managers and their teams need to become clear about how they will execute the current strategy.

LACK OF DIRECTION LEADS IN THE WRONG DIRECTION

Lack of Clarity can lead to moving in the wrong direction, missteps, and more. When well-meaning people are not clear, they will do their best to accomplish what they think they are *supposed* to be doing. The result may not be at all what was expected by managers or leaders.

To this point, Koen Smets, an expert in organizational development and founder of Care IQ U.K., shared with me, and an intimate gathering of business leaders, a televised human behavior experiment directed by the magician, Derren Brown.[68] The experiment went something like this:

Several people were placed into a room which had a timer on the wall with 000 displayed, a door that was closed and locked, and many colorful, large, plush cushion-like objects strewn throughout the room. The only information Derren gave them was that, to open the door, they needed to get the timer up to 500. Then Derren left the room.

At first, some of the people in the room asked each other what they thought should be done and gave the impression that they didn't really know what to do. A few people were more hands-on and started stacking the cushions. After a few cushions had been stacked, people noticed that the timer had increased from 000 to 017. They got excited and started stacking more cushions. As they did this, the timer went up to 047 and then to 072, but then suddenly started falling back toward 000.

At this point, it was concluded that one or more of them must have done something wrong. They then huddled together to discuss and figure out what that might have been. Frustration crept in. Some people got heated. A few people started doing things on their own, while others gave up entirely and did nothing.

In walked Derren Brown. The people in the room asked him what they were supposed to do and shared their frustrations with him. Derren Brown then revealed that there was actually no purpose or solution at all; he was just playing around. He just wanted to see what they would do when they weren't given a clear and complete strategy, or direction.

In the absence of a clear strategy, what people tend to do—as was shown in this experiment—is try out random things and then assign causation to any actions that seem to be moving them in the desired direction. A lack of Clarity cannot only cause people to head in the wrong direction and perform the wrong actions, it can also lead to dissent between groups and individuals who share different visions. You will only gain momentum toward your desired direction when everyone in the organization understands and shares the same vision, lives the same core values and knows how they contribute to meeting strategic objectives that align with the vision. You cannot over communicate; you need to continually communicate the company's strategy so that all behaviors and actions are aimed toward a shared vision.

At times you'll be very clear about strategy, including your vision, yet no one seems to be doing what is needed to execute that strategy brilliantly. This can happen for a variety of reasons, including lack of Mastery Mindsets, an inhibitive structural context and others not yet being empowered to initiate change. The latter is quite common and easily addressed. You need to get clear about the gap between *what is* now and *what needs to be* to support brilliant execution of strategy.

GET CLEAR ABOUT THE GAP

Assess, then close the gap between what is and what's desired. One way to get clear about *what is* so that you can identify the next steps forward toward your shared vision is through assessing the gaps that have your organization stuck or off track, and closing those gaps, usually referred to as "Gap Assessment." Because I've seen major improvements, even Pivots leading to transformations, from this process, I'm going to summarize the process for you with enough detail for you to determine if Gap Assessment might prove a best next step in your Pivot.

Following is an example of how proper use of Gap Assessment led to timely regulatory compliance with the added benefits of employee performance improvements in the healthcare industry:

In the early 2000s, the U.S. healthcare system went through a transformation in order to meet requirements in the Health Insurance Portability and Accountability Act (HIPAA). The regulation defined how healthcare information was to now be protected, and provided security and electronic data interchange rules for claims. The HIPAA regulations, further customized by internal policies, defined a future "to be" state for a covered healthcare organization.

I was speaking across the nation to C-level executives who were trying to get their arms around what they had to do to be compliant with this new regulation, including by whom, at what cost and if there was a benefit to them they could not yet see.

What I heard from these leaders was that medical records experts, who understood "protected health information" (PHI), which was a critical part of this regulation, and attorneys, who could draft internal policies, another critical aspect of this regulation, were being called in to also lead the organization-wide compliance effort. But, in my view, HIPAA required *culture change.* Healthcare leaders needed to orchestrate change, with support from experts in PHI and policy. My company, Abrige Corp, stepped in with Gap Assessment software and consulting services to discover, assess, and close gaps.

Across every healthcare organization, payors, providers, health systems, administrators and more, people had to communicate and work differently. And why not leverage a process that could also bring out performance improvements as part of the transformation?

The process that got to the crux of the matter was "Gap Assessment," accomplished through phases as shown below:

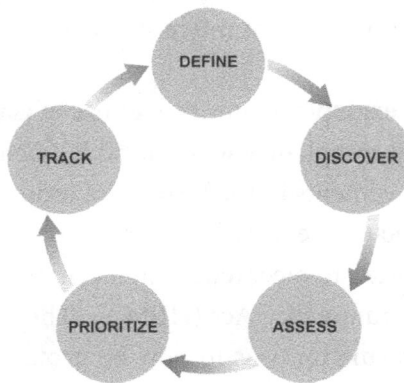

Figure 11: Gap Assessment Process: Five iterative phases

1) Define - Clearly define the new "to be" state. How will the organization and its performance differ after gaps are identified, assessed and closed? What will success look like? What will progress look like?

2) Discover - What does the organizational performance look like now? What is the "as is" state to be compared to the defined new state?

3) Assess - What are the gaps between the "as is" and "to be" states?

4) Prioritize - What are the best next steps by organizational unit, function, team and/or process so that gaps are closed in the most effective and timely manner?

5) Track - Measure progress toward the "to be" state. Is progress tracking with what was defined in the first phase?

Gap Assessment proved highly effective for the healthcare organizations that leveraged it. The process not only helped them become compliant, those we worked with also realized significant time and cost savings compared to their peers using other advice and methods. When leaders also empowered employees to initiate change, the Gap Assessment process not only spurred change to take place more quickly and at a lower cost, it further helped improve the work performance overall. Well-orchestrated readiness (change) for a new regulation became a catalyst for innovation and more effective communication.

The Gap Assessment Phases

The Define and Discover phases will get you clear about what you *want to be* and *what is*.

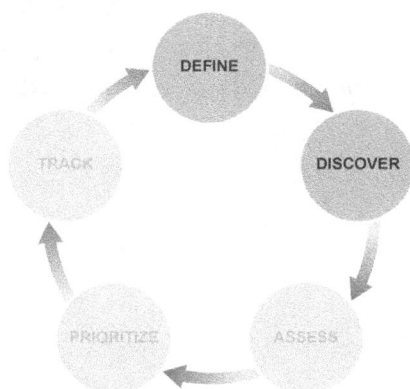

Figure 12: Define and Discover phases

Your "to be" can take many forms and fit many situations. Culture change, organizational restructuring, acquisitions, turnarounds and compliance readiness are but a few situations that Gap Assessment supports. The example in this book is about compliance readiness: to be compliant with HIPAA and to do so in a way that also improves performance over the long term.

> *If a decision considers a change or state, **from** _____ **to** _____, then the Define and Discover phases of Gap Assessment will serve you.*

Completeness and communication are important to success in using Gap Assessment. If the Define and Discover phases are not completed then Tracking will be ineffective. And, if you handle the Discover phase by trying to tell or sell your ideas to employees, neither of which connects with an employee in a way that they feel safe to speak out, you'll not likely discover the facts of what is. In fact, telling or selling can even block success, because when people are not fully engaged and paying attention they often don't hear your message and don't give themselves a chance to understand the benefit.

When employees feel safe you will receive candid and thoughtful responses for the "as is" state. You'll receive more, and more innovative, performance improvement ideas from employees during the Discover and Assess phases when they know that they are valued.

After completing the Discover phase, the next phases are Assess and Prioritize.

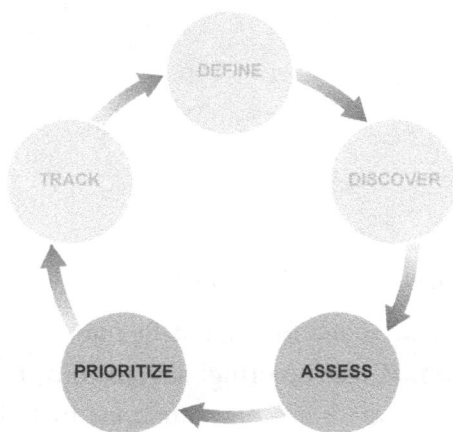

Figure 13: Assess and Prioritize phases

During these phases, you're still in active listening mode; you are listening to those who are closest to the work, assets and/or relation-ships. To Assess, you will need to examine the gap between *what is* (as uncovered during Discover), and *what needs to be* in place in order to move forward toward your vision.

Getting clear about what's possible in the future includes getting clear about "What's possible *next*?" Start by asking those closest to the work what needs to be stopped, started or changed in order to move toward the vision. Ask what will be hard. Then ask what support is needed to move through the challenges. Be open to questions about structure, flow of communication and the decision-making process.

You want all voices to be heard as you Assess. If your organization is large, at a minimum you'll want to include all the subject matter experts and managers, who in turn, can communicate with their teams and conduct similar assessments in their respective units or departments.

From the data gathered you'll be able to set priorities (the Prioritize phase) and define what progress toward those priorities looks like so that you can stay on course during the Track phase. Priorities are the "best next steps" toward your "to be" state.

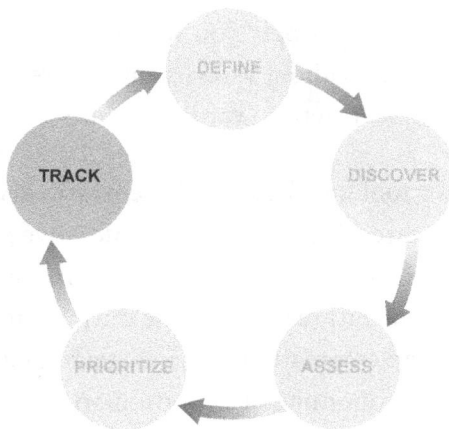

Figure 14: Track phase

Throughout this iterative process, you will Track progress toward meeting priorities.

Once you've completed all five phases, you may find that you need to reiterate one or more phases to reach the desired new state in your organization (consider using technology built for iterative Gap Assessment). Also watch out for the following missteps that can derail your Gap Assessment process:

Don't skip a step in this process (unless you are purposely only using Gap Assessment to Define and Discover before making a decision). If you skip Discover or Assess steps, for example, you may see change in the short term and even improvement, but you will not achieve a transformation.

Don't tell or sell what is or what is desired. At times the desire to move faster or assume that the leaders know best will lead to dictating change. This is a huge mistake if you have any desire for Aligned Momentum in your culture; you'd take the organization back many steps. You also will likely find your "solution" unsustainable. Well-meaning employees often work around in-place procedures (this is because most job descriptions and procedures have not kept up with what is needed to execute the current strategy).

Don't assume you know what is. In an organization comprised of more than a handful of people you will *not* know the "as-is" state without discovery. And, without assessment, you really cannot know what will be the best next steps toward the desired "to be" state.

Gap Assessment is a tool for The Pivot. It helps you discover a current state and ensures you receive feedback in an iterative process. The example of its use for HIPAA compliance was just one of many uses. I've used this to ready two cultures to combine during a merger or acquisition and for the implementation of a new technology. Compliance readiness is typically a one-time organization-wide initiative followed by ongoing onboarding of new employees and training existing employees. Gap Assessment can assist you in orchestrating change to close a wider gap such as to get you *from* where you are today to where you'll be when your vision is realized. You might use this process to ensure that your strategy, including your vision, is clear to all and shared by all.

DEFINING A CLEAR AND POWERFUL VISION

If you want your strategy to be brilliantly executed, you need to clearly communicate it, starting with your vision. Vision is your view of the business in the future. It is part of your strategic plan, your strategy, and provides direction for the business until that vision is realized. Because the vision is relied upon for direction, it needs to be clear.

Earlier we discussed Alan Mulally's Pivot, which was based on his vision of "One Ford". When Alan Mulally became president and CEO of Ford in 2006, the automaker was on the brink of bankruptcy. It was preparing to post the biggest annual loss in its 103-year history—$12.7 billion. Seven years later, Mulally was widely seen as the man behind one of the most impressive corporate turnarounds in history. Ford has posted an annual profit every year since 2009, its stock price has rebounded, and a new corporate culture has transformed the way the organization works.[69]

In a 2013 interview with *McKinsey Quarterly*, Mulally pointed to a few elements of his leadership and management style that helped change Ford's culture.[70] According to Mulally, a turnaround isn't about the executives at the top or their brilliant strategy. Rather, it's about figuring out a way to get every employee to understand the vision of the company, to inspire them to buy in to the plan and feel supported in their jobs. If people aren't optimistic, they're not going to make the sacrifices and do the work required to turn the company around. His clearly communicated vision of One Ford fulfilled each of these aims and achieved fantastic results.

Articulate your vision in a straightforward statement that all employees can understand and identify with. A vision statement describes your organization in its future successful state. It creates a mental image of what the organization wishes to achieve over time; something to become rather than something you already are.

If you're the CEO, then you probably have a vision for the organization. You may never have thought of your expectations and plans for the future of the company as being a "vision." If so, then think of the vision as being the destination on the horizon. You focus your energies on that point out there somewhere on the horizon. All your company's activities are focused on reaching that destination, even if it takes years, or a decade. A powerful vision can ignite a workforce. Properly crafted and articulated, it can become locked in the hearts and minds of every person on the team. It unites everyone behind that shared vision and gives Clarity to the company's strategic direction and to what successful progress will look like.

VISION STATEMENTS

There's often confusion about the terms "vision" and "mission." On the surface, they seem to be interchangeable.

What we most often see shared publically by any company is a mission statement, and sometimes a purpose statement. A mission statement expresses the organization's primary focus. I provide several examples below. Some companies add a purpose statement, answering why the company exists.

A vision statement, in contrast, is more internally focused and often more aspirational (everyone is not living it now; it is to be realized in the distant future). It describes your business as it would be in a future successful state of accomplishment. It creates a mental image of what the organization wishes to achieve over time; something to become rather than something the company already is. The business vision is most often communicated only internally, within the organization, while mission and purpose statements are more often also shared publically. A vision may change over time, often becoming grander, less specific to business operations and more far-reaching as a company grows and matures.

The following visions were in place near the time this book was published:

1) **Uber**
   Transportation as reliable as running water, everywhere, for everyone.

2) **Airbnb**
   To connect people all over the world in a community marketplace.

3) **Disney**
   To make people happy.

4) **Google**
   To build the perfect search engine.
   (Google's mission is "to organize the world's information and make it universally accessible and useful.")

5) **Amazon**
   To be earth's most customer-centric company; to build a place where people can come to find and discover anything they might want to buy online.

6) **Ikea**
   To create a better everyday life for many people.

7) **Nike**
   To help Nike, Inc. and our consumers thrive in a sustainable economy where people, profit and planet are in balance. (This is their corporate social responsibility vision.)
   (Nike's mission is to "bring inspiration and innovation

to every athlete* in the world. *If you have a body, you are an athlete.")

8) **Lego**
   Inventing the future of play.

9) **McDonalds**
   A little more lovin' can change a lot.

These vision statements are simple and purposeful. Also, because they can be clearly communicated, and they inspire employees to align and engage, they have helped each business step up their performance. A vision is most powerful when shared.

The power of shared visions

To create a *shared* vision, the vision created by the leader or leadership team must engage all employees. It is the *shared* view of the future that will then be brought back into the present to form part of the business's strategic objectives and quarterly priorities. When the vision is truly shared, employees will execute the company's strategic priorities well. How clearly you communicate the vision—and how well you connect to the hearts and minds of others while doing so—is vital. Your goal is to paint a picture of the future that will inspire others to contribute to its realization. Clarity around vision is a critical step toward brilliant execution of strategy. Brilliant execution of strategy is necessary to extraordinary business momentum.

> *Assess your vision statement with three criteria:*
>
> * *Is it **simple** enough to be clear to anyone?*
> * *Is it **purposeful** in a way that strengthens alignment between strategy and what people are excited to do?*
> * *Is it likely to **inspire** a step-up, even a breakthrough, in performance?*

1) **Is your vision simple?**

   Ask: Am I using simple terms that are meaningful to those I want to engage? Am I providing short phrases that are memorable and become a clear filter for making the best decisions as each individual moves through their daily work?

2) **Is your vision purposeful?**

   Does it explain "why?" for you and for each person that you want to align with this vision? In his interview with McKinsey Quarterly, *Mulally also talked about being purposeful, and for him this also means being positive:*

When people feel accountable and included, it is more fun. It is just more rewarding to do things in a supportive environment. Say, for example, an employee decides to stop production on a vehicle for some reason. In the past at Ford, someone would have jumped all over them: "What are you doing? How did this happen?" It is actually much more productive to say, "What can we do to help you out?" Because if you have *consistency of purpose across your entire organization* and you have *nurtured an environment in which people want to help each other succeed,* the problem will be fixed quickly.[71]

3) **Is your vision leading to a step-up, even a breakthrough, in overall performance?**

   Is it likely that, once inspired by this vision, the orchestration of best next steps over time will advance the company's performance? Is breakthrough performance possible? As a leader you may be a passionate communicator. But just because *you* understand the message, it doesn't mean others will. Also, even if others understand it, they may not understand how they fit. Without Clarity around fit there's no alignment and no action. Communicating your vision effectively takes planning, the right context and orchestration. You must communicate vision in a way that others will easily understand and keep top of mind.

The power of themes

One useful technique to keep your vision simple and top-of-mind is the use of a theme: a powerful phrase that sticks in one's mind and becomes a filter for better judgment calls.

> *Themes help simplify communication of the best next step closer to your vision.*

Sample themes

Fresh! Theme to orchestrate a shift in market share from third to first by Van de Kamp's.

One Ford. The theme at Ford between 2006 and 2014 (and also used as the name of their strategic plan) to bring dispersed and dysfunctional Ford global divisions together to better collaborate and share a single vision and to ultimately shift from near-bankruptcy to profitability.

There's no 'they' on the *Santa Fe*. Theme created by Captain David Marquet to cut down divisional silos and finger pointing, to create a more effectively run ship.

Victory. Theme used by Winston Churchill in his famous speech to rally the United Kingdom's citizens back into war, for World War II.

Let's revisit Mulally's "One Ford." Earlier I pointed out how his business plan bore this name. But "One Ford" also became a theme, serving as a rallying cry to get all employees working together toward a shared vision. Critics commented that this was too simple a plan, but they were wrong. Simple, repeatable, rallying, actionable, measurable—wins. The One Ford plan covered the global enterprise, from product quality and fuel efficiency to manufacturing plants, corporate culture and the company balance sheet. Mulally continuously communicated and promoted the One Ford plan and his vision.

After fixing the fundamentals, the plan through 2016 was to deliver profitable growth. Execution of the plan was completed early, by 2014. One Ford meant:

- aggressively restructure to operate profitably at the current demand and the changing model mix;
- accelerate development of new products that customers want and value;
- finance the plan and improve the balance sheet;
- work together effectively as one team.

Ford's operating units were now to work on the same agenda. Before Mulally, Ford's overseas subsidiaries were semi-independent "silos" that frequently duplicated efforts. Ford Europe and Ford North America, for example, traditionally developed separate versions of the compact Ford Focus—aimed at similar customer needs and wants, but with almost no common components.

It has been reported that before Mulally took over, internal meetings at Ford were like mortal combat. Executives regularly looked for vulnerability among their peers and practiced self-preservation over collaboration. Mulally changed all that, making executive meetings a safe environment where data could be shared without blame, improving collaboration and setting the stage for innovation success. The One Ford vision was broken down into six-month themes to rally troops. They all had catchy names, including "Back to Basics" and "The Way Forward."[72] Today, 10 different Ford models ride on the same platform, sharing about 80% common parts, often in areas customers never see. The cars and trucks are visually different, but can be built on the same assembly line—a strategy that generates huge economies of scale. And the 2016 targeted profitability? That showed up early. Ford started posting profits in 2009. By 2014 the One Ford plan was deemed a clear success.

The power of communicating an inspiring theme

Let's now look at three examples of gaining Clarity around your vision and communicating the best next step toward that vision clearly by use of a theme.

In each example below, the audience to be inspired is not under the direct authority of, or employed by, the communicator. My point is that these communicators were aiming to engage people who they had no direct hiring or firing power over.

Example 1—Victory: Winston Churchill became the Prime Minister of the United Kingdom in a period of political chaos during World War II. His words helped secure a shared commitment to creating an active opposition to the German military forces led by the Nazi dictator, Adolf Hitler. Many say that Winston Churchill carried his nation through despair after having experienced a costly defeat in World War I. His words, quoted below, provide an example of a clearly communicated theme: "Victory."

> You ask, what is our aim? I can answer in one word: victory. Victory at all costs. Victory in spite of all terror. Victory, however long and hard the road may be, for without victory there is no survival.[73]

You don't have to be Winston Churchill to communicate such a compelling theme, like "Victory," that it becomes a filter in the heads of all who share the vision and keeps them aligned long after the words are spoken.

Example 2—Nothing is impossible: The next example takes us to the 1996 Democratic Convention and to actor Christopher Reeve sharing his powerful vision for the United States of America. To inspire Americans with his theme, "Nothing is impossible," he gives examples from history when what was achieved had initially been thought impossible:

> … Now, America has a tradition that many nations probably envy. We frequently achieve the impossible. That's part of our national character. That's what got us from one coast to another. That's what got us—that's what got us the largest economy in the world. That's what got us to the moon.
>
> Now, on the wall of my room when I was at rehab, there was a picture of the Space Shuttle blasting off, and it was autographed by every astronaut now at NASA, and on the top of that picture, it says, "We found nothing is impossible."
>
> So many of our dreams—so many dreams at first seem impossible. And then they seem improbable. And then when we summon the will, they soon become inevitable.
>
> So if we can conquer outer space, we should be able to conquer inner space, too…[74]

Example 3—I have a dream. Martin Luther King provides an excellent example of Clarity in powerfully communicating a vision and theme. As he spoke at the march in Washington D.C., he didn't say, "We need to work harder!" or even "Victory at all costs!" Instead, he engaged others by sharing and clearly describing his vision: "I have a dream…" Would moving toward that vision be hard? Yes. Would making progress and creating change be a victory? Yes. This was not about combating complacency or igniting a war. He gave people hope that they could *Stride Toward Freedom*, and work against evil with dignity, pride and self-respect.[75] King aimed to clearly communicate his vision and the peaceful path toward it. He knew how important his words would be. From his words and his work he not only orchestrated a Pivot in the cultural environment for African-Americans, he also helped Pivot mindsets for people of all races.

You may see in King some qualities that you do not possess. You do possess the same ability to have Clarity—to get clear and to be clear. Eloquence helps. Yet, if you authentically care about the vision, and want others to share it with you, you will deliver your words with the energy that connects to hearts and not just minds. If you prepare yourself, by discovering what others care about, and you truly embrace the fact that your business is comprised of people and it is those people who will execute the strategy, your words will speak to them. King made clear to others the strategic direction he wanted to take as well as the current state of things, the threats and the opportunities. You can too.

Martin Luther King also made sure he was on common ground with the people he was addressing. When he had worked in Connecticut as a youth he had discovered that there he was welcome to eat anywhere he chose, without having to use a different entrance or sit in a designated area. But at the time of his activism, he was living in the same reality as those he was addressing and he actively sought input from them. He could compare what life was like for them now to his vision of the better life that could be theirs in the future. Similarly, your preparation should bring you close to the reality of those you will address. Perhaps meet with model businesses and those leaders to experience first-hand the vision you want to share.

Finally, King used simple words stated authentically. He came from a place of complete and unwavering personal commitment and by example inspired others. He gathered the resources necessary to support change, but did not dictate what each person must do. You can do this. You don't have to be Martin Luther King to inspire others to go beyond what is assumed to be possible.

The power of communicating to positively influence

I chose to use examples from the political arena because they are often the most rigorous test of communicating a vision in a way that will compel people to action. These communicators do not employ the audience they seek to inspire and they have no direct authority over the audience's actions.

> *A true leader doesn't leverage power of authority when sharing a vision, but rather seeks to positively influence others into action.*

Leveraging one's power of authority and ordering others to act is a form of short-term thinking and most often leads to short-term compliance. Reaching a vision is a long-term commitment.

BEING CLEAR

Being clear includes communicating with an aim to bring others to the same level of Clarity (of vision, theme, objectives, priorities, etc.) that you are. A passionately communicated vision won't necessarily drive action on its own. As discussed above, people must understand the vision and feel part of it. A shared vision motivates people to take action. Then, clear direction and priorities help people choose the best next actions on the path toward the vision.

A clearly communicated strategy—vision, direction and execution plan—enables the right things to be done right and in the right amount of time. How you communicate will have a significant impact on how well the strategy is executed. Consider your communication style and the completeness and frequency of your communication. You will be modeling the way for others. Then, you orchestrate The Pivot throughout your organization by first empowering more leaders, so you will have greater confidence in their ability to communicate. You've shown them, and will continue to be a model of, how to be an inspiring communicator.

An effective communication style. For Aligned Momentum to live, you must embrace a style of positive influence to gain commitment. You must stop telling, selling, commanding or controlling. Communication from the top driven by short-term thinking or a command and control leadership style can inhibit the commitment you desire from employees.

When coming from a mindset of power based on authority, one can attempt this communication as if aimed at winning in negotiations or overcoming objectives in a consultative sale. If you are applying these approaches to gain commitment from employees, you will likely find that you are not getting what you expect. Taking a negotiations or consultative sales approach in your communication with employees will bring you a mediocre outcome at best. Yes, some people in your company may be motivated simply because they feel their livelihood requires pleasing you, but others may just end up feeling frustrated and become less productive. They may not be clear about what you actually expect, how to deliver on the expectations, why they are important or what's in it for them.

Your goal when communicating, as a leader, is to inspire. You want employees, including the managers who will then work with their teams to create execution plans and priorities, to be clear about the strategy—the vision, values, direction and game plan. As you Pivot from the type of communications used in negotiations or sales to a style that will inspire and gain commitment, your best next step may be to practice the art of (win-win) persuasion. Persuasion is aimed squarely at a win for all involved. It is a type of positive influence. You present your view, including how you perceive the alignment between this view and what you've heard employees want for themselves. Employees are then likely to *choose* to adopt this strategy and act on it. It becomes a shared strategy. Persuasion is not manipulation. When you take care to ensure only positive outcomes, you are not being manipulative. The most effective leaders seek to persuade through positive influence.

To drive long term change, you want to inspire others. To inspire, you need to win your employees' hearts and minds. Inspire them to commit to a shared vision.

Create this shared vision by:

- being open to a discussion about what will be hard and giving others the authority to find the best ways to work through it (rather than being the deflector-of-objections);
- actively listening to internal and external input, including when others identify what might be in your blind spot(s);
- providing assistance or resources so that others can do their best toward achieving the vision;
- keeping track of progress, including your own;
- showing others that you truly care about their success.

Complete communication. How do you know when you've communicated effectively? The best way to know if each recipient of your communication has all that they need to execute brilliantly, is to have them communicate what they understood back to you, and to let them give you their take on the following:

- What will success look like?
- How will I track progress?
- What will be hard?
- What are my priorities and best next steps?
- What must I stop doing in order to succeed at this?
- What will I start doing, and when?
- What support do I require, and from whom?
- Who needs to be involved?

It's as simple as that, yet we often forget to do this. We see an accepting face, a nodding head, and maybe even something like "got it!" and we just leave it at that.

Frequent communication. Once the communication is clear, then, in the words of Ronald Reagan, "Trust, but verify." You'll verify through performance conversations, meetings, reports, and observation. You'll also continue to model the way. Communication is not only talking. What you do, and pointing out what others are doing or have done, also communicates a message. How might you practice and model the way to communicate what you want to see from others?

> *What "tone at the top" are you modeling? Does what you do align with what you are expecting from others?*

Any great company has a thoughtfully designed and nurtured culture. How you model acceptable communication creates a "tone at the top" that can establish the right cultural norms for your business (or help transform unhealthy communication if that exists today). By modeling, you are creating greater Clarity around what is expected in your workplace. This is a big part of your job as a leader. Clear and inspiring communication is key to bringing your vision to life.

As you move toward Aligned Momentum, your communication will touch every employee, directly or through your management team. Every person will know the direction the company intends to take and how each person should treat another.

It takes time to get this right. And it is not a one-time project; You can't just do it once and call it done. To realize your strategic vision, communicate clearly, consistently, and continuously through words and actions. You will inspire through positive influence with your words and as a role model. You will create a bold strategy and communicate it with an aim toward transformation. Transformation shows up as extraordinary business momentum and performance breakthroughs.

THE AIM OF CLARITY IS TRANSFORMATION

After David Taylor's first year as CEO of Procter & Gamble, a clearly successful, mature "grown up" company, he expressed his intention to look at the business and organization with fresh eyes, and to get clear, stating, "Once a process is deeply ingrained, a company—and, by extension, its employees—can lose sight of the fact that it's no longer achieving the desired outcome."[76] Taylor is *getting clear*. His aim is to transform the company.

Just one year after taking the helm at Procter & Gamble, David Taylor reported that the change processes and strategic thinking—internally and through communication with the customer—have led to innovation and this is leading to a Pivot toward profitability for the company. In a recent interview with CNBC, Taylor said,

> The company has streamlined its portfolio in an effort to return to growth, but new products are also helping to drive the firm's turnaround. If you go back 10 years ago, car air fresheners was a very small, quiet category. We introduced something called Febreeze car, and it is now a quarter-billion-dollar business that's growing nicely.[77]

For transformation to occur, people first need to know that it is safe to speak out and step up without recourse. They need to be clear about what they are part of and how they fit. And they need to want to be part of the transformation.

To ensure this:

1) Prepare yourself and others in leadership roles to remain open, without prejudice, to all input about how the work is performed right now.

2) Provide the authority and means by which those closest to the work, assets, and business relationships can recommend and even initiate change.

3) Communicate the vision and strategic direction in a way that inspires action. Communicate the vision or strategy in a single word or short phrase.

4) Understand what the challenges along the chosen path might look like and provide concrete examples of others who have faced similar challenges and succeeded. (This will lend credibility to your words and give hope, which inspires.)

5) Communicate frequently and openly, and from all directions to ensure Clarity about *what is* and about *what is desired.*

> *A 2015 Gallup survey of American workers found that clarity of expectations is the most important asset of a good manager and that employees who meet regularly with their boss are three times more likely to be engaged on the job.*[78]

PIVOTS THAT CAN LEAD TO GREATER CLARITY

At times, you'll encounter obstacles that block getting clear and being clear in your communication. Orchestrate a Pivot to remove each one from your culture. Aligned Momentum cannot live in a culture with these obstacles in place. The top three obstacles to greater Clarity for leaders are identified below and then followed by recommended Pivots:

Obstacle #1:
One or more managers are not aligned with the current vision and strategy.

Obstacle #2:

Leaders and managers are not in sync with their communication, such as with respect to quarterly priorities.

Obstacle #3:

The environment is not adapted to provide the support needed to execute the new vision, direction and priorities.

The best leaders motivate and inspire people through clear communication. Leading involves communicating vision, purpose, values and direction company-wide. Managing involves communicating for execution, including aiming people toward discipline, accountability and strategic alignment.

Your managers are responsible for translating the vision into actionable priorities, and doing so with individuals and teams. If managers are merely nodding their head in meetings, but not committing to executing the strategy, then you have not been clear; they have not gained Clarity. The result is that everyone under them is not going to be clear about what the "right things" are or how and when to focus on those things. To support greater Clarity consider the following Pivots:

Pivot to trust as a cultural core value or norm

You may be wondering why trust is not one of the six Aligned Momentum Key Indicators. Being worthy of trust is foundational. Trust isn't something you improve incrementally. Trust either exists or it doesn't. Once it is broken, it is hard to get it back.

That said, as Aligned Momentum is woven into the culture, business performance is likely to improve and can be in part attributed to an increase in trust in teams, across functional "boundaries," and especially between an employee and manager. But, Clarity, foundational to The Pivot and one of the Aligned Momentum Key Indicators, is not effective without trust. You may get clear about what you want, but not trust that it will ever be executed brilliantly. You may be clear about what you want, but lack the attention and engagement of those who need to ask because they don't trust you or other key individuals needed to execute the strategy, or they aren't inspired because they don't believe that what is desired will be beneficial for them.

> *Clarity is not effective without trust.*

Are you and any other top leaders trusted? Do you trust your employees? If you answered "no" to either of those questions, this is where you start. If trust is alive at the top, then focus next on managers. The recommended Pivot will focus on managers (you may also manage others).

Are you certain that every person, including managers, can name someone in the organization that "has their back and truly wants them to be successful?" Whether you use the term manager for those responsible for team building, or something else, these people are often forgotten. "They seem so confident," you might say, "they don't need someone watching out for them." You are likely right that they don't "need" it. They certainly don't need inauthentic pats on the head. But everyone flourishes when their value is recognized and appreciated. I encourage you to make sure your team builders know that their personal and professional success is important. Perhaps the person to have their back is you.

As part of trust-building, ensure that managers or team leads are part of a change process. If your team-builders don't feel safe to change what they are delivering now, they are not going to support changing team priorities. Questions to ask yourself if this is the case:

1) Did you fail to share the vision, strategic direction and overall company objectives with managers before broadcasting the plan to the whole company?

2) Did you bypass your managers when creating your strategic plan? Do they only receive a narrow view of the strategy via what Finance has translated into budgets?

3) How does each manager know which new priorities can replace the old priorities? This information is vital to stop them from assuming they must overwork to meet this growing (vs. changing) list of duties.

- **A Pivot:** To build trust, shift *from* only telling managers (directly or indirectly via their budgets) what needs to get done, *to* including managers and coaching them to identify their their fit and their team's fit. Support managers in collaborating with their peers. Not only will their personal fulfillment and effectiveness as a manager and coach improve, often this will also create a safe place amongst managers to proactively mentor and allocate talent to support each employee and the company.

- **Resources:** A couple of excellent books about building trust are *The Five Dysfunctions of a Team* (2005), by Patrick Lencioni and *The Speed of Trust* (2008), by Stephen Michael Covey.[79]

Pivot to more Effective Management Meetings

An effective management meeting brings peers together to work through challenges and opportunities with a clear agenda, facilitated (even if by a selected peer), consistently scheduled (preferably once a month) and held within an environment of trust. Cancelling meetings, which is often the first reaction when meetings are not proving effective, is not a solution to clearer communication.

- **A Pivot:** One Pivot is *from* managers battling for their share of budgets, visibility and merit pool dollars, *to* collaboration of peers who seek success for each other within and for the organization.

- **Resources:** Effective meetings are addressed also in Chapter 6: Focused and Nimble. A helpful book is *Scaling Up* (2014), by Verne Harnish.[80]

Pivot to targeted Training for Aligned Momentum

Aligned Momentum training develops Clarity, Mastery Mindset, Nimble Decision-Making, Strategic Thinking, Talent Adaptability, and Coaching. Training for these "soft" skills requires a different type of training than is typically offered to employees; this training requires powerfully facilitated interaction, preferably in a small group of non-competing peers. The more traditional classroom presentation of information with note-taking and Q&A only scratches the surface. Presentation creates awareness. Truly connecting with a person inspires action and growth. Most workplace training does not address what inspires and motivates you, and how you will choose to be with and treat others. While the more prevalent skills, knowledge and compliance training programs have their place, what is too often missed is training that prepares the person to get clear about their strengths, desires, fit and mindset.

- **A Pivot:** Pivot *from* focusing on skills and knowledge, *to* embracing and developing the whole person.

Pivot to a Coaching Culture

A great manager can deliver results year after year, even during times of rapid change. Good managers are trusted, they empower their teams and hold them accountable and communicate effectively. Great managers are also skilled performance coaches.

The requirements for a manager to be good are demanding enough. Of all the people who are moved into a management position, few are prepared to be good. You cannot expect them to be great without training. Aligned Momentum needs to be supported by great managers. The best training to grow performance-coaching skills is to be coached!

- **A Pivot:** Provide your managers with coaching so that they might Pivot *from* managing work and processes *to* managing people (and delegating the work and processes to the team). Train your managers so that they can coach their team. Remember that coaching for managers and by managers for employees is the a first step in creating a culture where everyone knows their manager cares about their success. Such a culture is one where Aligned Momentum thrives.

An early win learning the skill of coaching, and being coached, often helps managers improve in their ability to delegate. They then have more time to coach others and to think strategically. Coaching can lead to greater Clarity throughout the organization.

P&G CEO, David Taylor explained this very leadership challenge at Chief Executive's Talent Conference in October 2016 as follows, "Giving people the courage to step out and make the future different than the past is one of the biggest challenges of managing talent."[81]

Pivot to a complete, accurate and streamlined Information & Communication Flow

When was the last time you stepped back and assessed the effectiveness of how information and communication flow in your organization? Are you and other decision makers receiving timely, accurate and complete information to support decisions? Do meetings support Clarity and result in more effective action? Are communication habits and styles achieving Clarity throughout your company or are there bottlenecks, sticking points, conflicting agendas, misunderstandings, misinterpretations or other typical communication concerns?

- **A Pivot:** Pivot *from* random reporting of what was done (regardless of priority or alignment with strategy) *to* more effective meetings, performance measurement, and communication that better captures alignment and engagement, information technology that better enables collaboration, organizational structure and design that can move you more nimbly toward your vision, and reporting to close the gap between the wisdom of senior leaders and the talent all the way out at the very edges of your organization.

Pivot to a more Nimble Organizational Structure

In Chapter 3 we reviewed the most current and common organizational structures, including hierarchical, matrix, flat and open. There are several variations on these; your optimal structure is the one that best supports the execution of your strategy by others in the organization while simultaneously supporting the core values and your purpose or mission.

- **A Pivot:** Your Pivot may require you to institute a more optimal structure for your organization that is based on current needs and the foreseeable future rather than the past. Pivoting toward Aligned Momentum is a form of organizational redesign: a step-by-step methodology which identifies dysfunctional aspects of work flow, procedures, structures and systems, and realigns them to fit current business realities and goals, and then develops plans to implement the new changes.

FINAL WORD ON CLARITY

Clarity isn't spontaneous; it requires preparation. Clarity also requires commitment to consistent, complete and accurate communication throughout the organization. It is an essential indicator in Aligned Momentum. Gaining Clarity also requires focus, which we will examine next.

CHAPTER 5: KEY POINTS

---

1) Clarity, as defined for Aligned Momentum, means getting clear and being clear.

2) Clarity is the most critical Aligned Momentum Key Indicator (and merits a full chapter).

3) If well-meaning people are not clear, they will first do their best at whatever they think they are supposed to do and then they may get frustrated, create conflict, etc.

4) To take the best next steps, you need to have a clear vision and direction, and you need to get clear about where you are right now. Gap Assessment can help.

5) Leaders need to clearly communicate strategy (including the vision).

6) Managers and their teams must get clear on how to best execute the strategy.

7) You can orchestrate Pivots starting today to gain Clarity. One of the following may lead to a step up in performance for your business.
   a) Pivot to a Culture of Trust
   b) Pivot to more Effective Management Meetings
   c) Pivot to targeted Training for Aligned Momentum
   d) Pivot to a Coaching Culture
   e) Pivot to a complete, accurate and streamlined Information & Communication Flow
   f) Pivot to a more Nimble Organizational Structure

CHAPTER 6

FOCUSED and NIMBLE

---

*"The secret of change is to focus all of your energy,
not on fighting the old, but on building the new."*

— *Socrates*

*"The successful person places more attention on doing
the right thing rather than doing things right."*

— *Peter Drucker*

Focus is important. You get what you focus on, which in a business is typically what you measure. Keeping track of progress and outcomes helps with focus.

But we also need the nimbleness to adjust course. Sometimes what is being measured is not leading us toward strategic objectives. And sometimes the strategy needs to change. More often, changing circumstances render the initial objective irrelevant or not the highest priority. Change can also render roles irrelevant or in need of a major adjustment. We need to be nimble enough so that everyone is working on and thinking about priorities: the actions that remain aligned with strategy and are expected to have the greatest positive impact on business performance if focused on right now.

> *In addition to being focused, you need to be nimble.*

Being both focused and nimble ensures you are, as Drucker said, "doing the right things," and as Socrates said, "focusing on building the new."

To be both focused and nimble, employees must feel safe to step up and speak out, and strategy must be shared. And you need to be reasonably assured that the person being relied on to execute *wants* to do so brilliantly. You also need to ensure that employees work in the right context to allow for brilliance. And you need employees with the right mindsets, who are ready for performance breakthroughs (covered here and in chapter 7). To be focused in a way that also makes you nimble requires you to think strategically. I've put all of this together, and named the capability required to be both focused and nimble, "strategic focus."

> *A capability that best ensures your business is both focused and nimble is "strategic focus."*

A capability of strategic focus is a natural outcome of Aligned Momentum and particularly when Strategic Thinking and Nimble Decision-making are improved throughout the organization. Strategic Thinking rewires each employee to look forward, with strategy in mind, before coming back to the present to choose the best next step. Nimble Decision-making, which includes judgment calls and minute by minute choices, enables each employee to now concentrate with that future vision in mind and decide to take those best next steps toward brilliant execution.

I shall describe strategic focus in this chapter so that you can get a feel for it, gain the ability to explain it, and know what to look for to observe it coming alive in your business through employees. There are too few resources offering guidance on the discipline of strategic focus; add this book to that short list.

How is strategic focus different from the ability to focus? Focus is often associated with productivity in the sense of keeping your mind trained on one thought or task until it is completed, so that you accomplish it quickly and with few errors.

> *Those who are sure they know what to do can focus. But they may not be in alignment with your company or helping your company gain momentum. They are focused, yet they are not nimble.*

Only focusing on any task at hand is not what this chapter is about. Instead, this chapter is concerned with focusing on priorities and what is core, or "what matters most" (to meet strategic objectives).

Clarity, both getting clear for yourself and being clear so that communication is quickly synthesized and effectively distributed, is critical to realizing the benefits of strategic focus. The desired benefit from the capability of strategic focus is for your business to maintain momentum by being focused and nimble. And when momentum is combined with alignment, brilliantly executing a bold strategy is possible. *Business momentum is extraordinary when it is gained swiftly. Business momentum is also extraordinary when it is maintained over the long term.*

To better understand how important Clarity is to being both focused and nimble, I'll give you an example, from Vanguard, below. You may recall from the last chapter that strategic objectives, distilled into memorable themes, become filters in one's mind that help make sure the next course of action will be the best next step and aligned with the current strategy. The filters help answer questions such as: "By doing this, or by following this line of thinking, am I executing the current strategy toward our vision?" And if so, "Is this the best way?" I promised that I'd give you a feel for how to understand this concept, communicate it effectively and to know what to look for to see if your communication is indeed becoming a filter in others' minds to guide their decisions. Vanguard offers a good example.

Vanguard, one of the world's largest investment companies, created such a filter in the mind of junior analyst Mabel Yu, which held strong even during the U.S. financial crisis of 2008.[82] For Yu, the Vanguard core values aligned with her beliefs. Vanguard was founded by John ("Jack") Bogle in 1974. The company is conservative in the risk it takes on behalf of its customers. Three core values are shared on their website: Integrity, Focus and Stewardship.

"Focus" as a core value for Vanguard is described in this way:

> It's in our clients' best interests to keep a long-term perspective in every business decision we make. This approach means, for example, forsaking short-term gains if they sacrifice our fund investors' long-term interests—even if that means temporarily closing top-performing funds to better manage the volume of cash flowing in.[83]

When Yu was researching mortgage-backed securities with prime mortgage loans as assets to decide if they should remain in the Vanguard portfolio, she ran into many external roadblocks, yet was always supported by Vanguard.

Where the rest of the world seemed to feel these securities were fine, Yu found them complex and confusing. She also saw risks that others seemed to be ignoring, such as the very inexperienced people giving those securities AAA ratings.

In a 2009 interview with NPR, Yu shared, "I got names of the rating agency analysts, and I asked them lots of questions."[84] She asked them about the possibility of house prices falling, of interest rates rising, of people not being able to refinance their mortgages. "If all of those things happen at same time, what would happen to our investment? I could not get a straight answer."

Yu says she was told repeatedly that she worried too much. "I felt so dumb," she says, adding that she was told, "Don't worry about it."

As well as holding true to its core values, Vanguard encouraged a culture of candid communication, so that employees were consistently reminded that dissent was worth discussion. Yu felt valued in an environment that applauded her candor. The whole industry was pushing mortgage-backed securities and there was a general feeling that customers could make more money if they did buy into these: the returns were quite good. Nevertheless, Yu, backed by all of her research, said "no" to those securities, and Vanguard backed her up.[85]

Yu exhibited strategic focus, and Vanguard appears to have a culture with Aligned Momentum in place. Its employees, like Yu, are clear about strategy and empowered to strategically focus. Vanguard exhibits a culture where empowering employees, more than telling them what to do, will keep the company on track. And it has. As of 2015 Vanguard was *the* largest mutual fund company in the world, with over $3.4 trillion in global assets.[86]

Burt Malkiel, the Princeton economist and current chief investment officer at Wealthfront who joined Vanguard as a director when it had less than $2 billion in assets, says that "[Bogle's] values, his strategy, the culture he established are the reason Vanguard has prospered. They are clearly his and uniquely his."[87]

The values that the company was founded on have been carried forward by former CEO, Jack Brennan and current CEO, Bill McNabb. [88]

"Every one person can make a difference."
— *Jack Bogle, Chairman & CEO 1975-1996*

"Character comes first."
— *Jack Brennan, Chairman & CEO 1996-2008*

"In business, if you do the right thing you win."
— *Bill McNabb, Chairman & CEO 2008-present*

Vanguard is one of the examples in this book that show how clearly and consistently communicating strategy, attracting and retaining (and continuing to inspire) employees that align with the company values, and empowering employees to initiate change (or to not change in a way that goes against a core value, as in the case of Mabel Yu at Vanguard) leads to brilliant execution.

Vanguard's theme was, in effect, "Do the Right Thing."
Van de Kamp became #1, with "Fresh!"
Ford collaboratively turned to profitability, with "One Ford."

> *For these leaders, weaving strategic focus into their culture was their best step toward brilliant execution.*

STRATEGIC FOCUS LEADS TO BRILLIANT EXECUTION

In *Execution*, Ram Charan and Larry Bossidy state that a lack of focus on the discipline of execution is the main reason companies fall short on their promises.[89] They are referring to the execution of a business's current strategy; not to the practice of staying busy by doing more of what was done before. They comment that "Organizations don't execute unless the right people, individually and collectively, focus on the right details at the right time." This points to the gap between what leaders want and what they, through their employees, deliver.

Sometimes it is the leaders who lack Clarity about what they want and who have not played the movie forward before giving directions. This happened to Apple between 1985 and 1996.

Apple is a company to watch for its ability to focus, while being nimble. Some attribute this ability to Steve Jobs' leadership. The company lost focus when he was not there between September 1985 and December 1996. Into the 90s, Apple's brand mantra (a longer-term theme used to orchestrate change and growth for the company aligned with its vision) was still: "To keep things simple." But between 1985 and 1996, without Jobs' leadership, orchestration was not aligned with simplicity. Complexity crept in. Products proliferated. Quality slipped. When Jobs returned in December 1996 Apple was in a death spiral. Sales and market share were falling precipitously. Expenses were ballooning out of control. Departments battled one another. Some of the former CEO's top managers were in denial; many of the most talented were leaving. The outcomes of the lack of orchestration were showing up as early as 1991 with a decline in profitability.[90]

Upon Jobs' return to Apple, he immediately focused himself and prepared to orchestrate a Pivot: *from* a proliferation of products that revealed the impact of a lack of focus on design or quality, *to* a focus on fewer products built with great design and quality in mind. His message to the team, "You are bright people. You shouldn't be wasting your time on crappy products."[91] The Pivot was to a more focused strategy, which included a return to the Apple values and marketing philosophy that the company's co-founder, Mike Markulla had written in collaboration with Steve Jobs. In Jobs' absence, the company had ceased to focus on its values and philosophy. What was needed was a great leader to make it clear that these values are *core* to Apple;

they are not to be bypassed for any reason or from any role. Executive decisions were not exempt from alignment with company core values.

The **Apple Marketing Philosophy** scribed by co-founder Mike Markulla in January 1977 best describes Apple's strategic focus when the company was founded, and then again when Jobs returned in 1996 (between 1985 and 1996, focus was lost):

Empathy
We will truly understand their [the customer's]
needs better than any other company.

Focus
In order to do a good job of those things we decided to do
we must eliminate all of the unimportant opportunities.

Impute
People DO judge a book by its cover. We may have the
best product, the highest quality, the most useful software,
etc.; if we present them in a slipshod manner, they will be
perceived as slipshod; if we present them in a creative, professional manner, we will impute the desired qualities.[92]

You may recall the outcome of this return to focus; Apple enjoyed un-precedented success. The PowerBook, iMac, iPod, iPhone, and iPad each in turn took the world by storm and changed the way people interacted with technology. Apple became the largest and most valu-able company in the world.

In 1997 at MacWorld, Jobs announced a new brand mantra (theme): "Think different." Yet this didn't replace simplicity. Simplicity was woven into the culture, still nurtured with consistent communi-cation and as a core value. Current CEO Tim Cook made clear at the

2013 Apple developer's conference that Apple is well aware that competitors ship lots more products laden with many features. But Apple is Apple and simplicity will continue to be its mantra. The "Think different" theme was added so that minds carried a filter of innovation while they were also thinking of simplicity.[93] The new theme also was intended to rejuvenate interest from and create anticipation in Apple consumers.

Apple's Pivot back to simplicity with Jobs' return in 1996 was orchestrated swiftly, but not due to an attempt to turn-on-a-dime. The culture was ready to Pivot.[94,95] Clarity was needed. A leader was needed who better fit the culture, one who felt a keen responsibility to steward the culture that had been envisioned when Apple was founded, and Jobs was that leader. And a return to focus was needed. The structural context had shifted in a way that allowed silos to develop, which is what has happened when observers say that departments are battling. Under Jobs' return, a small teams structure was created with an eye toward maintaining the discipline required to stay effective, fleet, and non-bureaucratic even as Apple grew.[96] A few core values that Jobs had helped establish had not been nurtured between 1985 and 1996, including "Empathy for the users", "Quality" and what Jobs intended with the core value, "Great management." Apple's nine values are listed below.[97,98]

1) Empathy for the users
2) Aggressiveness
3) Positive social contribution
4) Innovation and vision
5) Individual performance
6) Team spirit
7) Quality
8) Individual reward
9) Great management

Jay Elliot, a senior vice president in those early days, comments on the nine values: "[The values] became a part of everyday communication, a standard by which employees could measure how they themselves and their management were performing."[99]

It is worthwhile expanding here on the ninth value, "Great management." The 1993 Apple Employee Handbook describes great management this way: *The attitudes of a manager toward employees are of primary importance. Employees should be able to trust the motives and integrity of their supervisors. It is the responsibility of management to create a productive environment where the company's values flourish.*[100]

Consider whether Apple's cultural framework of nine values and the company's Pivot back to simplicity exemplify each Aligned Momentum Key Indicator:

1) Clarity (yes)
2) Mastery Mindset (yes)
3) Nimble Decision-making (yes)
4) Strategic Thinking (yes)
5) Talent Adaptability (likely)
6) Coaching (yes)

Apple's ninth value of great management translates to the sixth Aligned Momentum Key Indicator, Coaching. Aligned Momentum emphasizes Coaching, for it is coaching that engenders a safe and productive corporate culture in which every employee knows that their manager has their back and cares about their success. Even Steve Jobs had a coach.[101]

At Apple, cultural fit and product knowledge were made a focus for every new hire. This involved an orientation program and a buddy, who was selected based on their influence in the culture. Apple University offers optional courses to teach employees about Apple's culture and style.[102] As noted after the Vanguard story, great leaders know that weaving strategic focus throughout the organization is the best step toward brilliant execution.

STRATEGIC FOCUS REQUIRES TIMELY, EFFECTIVE COMMUNICATION

As the leader, you likely practice strategic focus naturally. You have a wider view of all that is in play, and you have the benefit of being part of setting strategy. You must communicate what you know and expect to others, possibly many others through many layers or dispersed teams.

For communication to be timely and effective, it is best to communicate frequently, in many ways and through a variety of voices. Apple even set up a University. You might consider communicating your strategy in writing, in visuals, from the direct manager, from you the leader in an all-employees meeting, amongst peers and teams, through measurement, and more.

The need for more frequent and effective communication is far-reaching (if it includes your business, it is not only your business that has room for improvement). In its March 10, 2016 report Gallup stated that only 27% of workers strongly agree that the feedback they currently receive helps them do their work better. And only 17% strongly agree there's open communication throughout all levels of their company.[103]

How do you know if you've communicated strategic objectives clearly enough that employees will set the right priorities to focus on and become aware of a need to change should the need arise?

The practice of successful strategic focusing looks like this: the employee adopts a strategic viewpoint (often referred to as "the 30,000 foot view") to survey the current state of their work, which may be in the form of a goal or quota, project, task or even their part of a process; they remind themselves of the strategic objectives or goals their manager has communicated to them and the priorities set based on these; and then, they turn their thoughts back to the present to consider, "what's the best next step?"

Coach your employees to practice this automatically and with rhythmic frequency. Hold frequent performance conversations to embed this process even to the point that the employee is asking if there are new strategic objectives they should be considering. Weaving the discipline of strategic focus into your culture combats the stalls created by rigidity. It allows everyone to focus and be nimble. With practice, Aligned Momentum brings the apparently opposing concepts—focus and nimbleness—together in a powerful way.

Without Aligned Momentum in place, a lot can go wrong. To wrap this chapter, I'll take an educated guess of where you are today, your "as is" state. Then I'll conclude with a few Pivots for you to consider.

If you are: Operationally Focused (but not Strategically Nimble)

Clearly, your ability to focus on the right things has built your business into what it is today. You've done many things right! Most companies never get to $1 million in revenue. Those that move beyond that mark obviously have learned how to focus on the right things for their growth, at least at first. Yet it is easy to lose momentum, especially if the leadership team has become detached from how work actually gets done in the company. *What's next?* You can choose to be or become inflexible, or you can choose to be or become nimble.

You can remain operationally focused *and* be strategically nimble. An obvious place to start is to ask more questions of stakeholders, such as, "In your view, what should we know that we may not know?" or, "What should we be talking about (in this quarter's, or year's, strategic planning session)?" or "What is your biggest challenge (working here, with our products, etc.)?" These questions belong in *conversations throughout the year*, not just once and at the last minute. Aligned

Momentum and The Pivot involve a well-set stage, to include Clarity and strategic focus, and a leader's orchestration of change.

Great minds can bring focus and nimbleness

A loss of focus can derail your business. But how do you know what to focus on? How do you focus and also grow? Clarity is the first step and the next is to bring selected minds together to strategically focus. Who do you include to help ensure that you are focused and maintaining momentum? In *Good to Great* (2001), Jim Collins provides one approach, called The Council.[104]

The Council, which is comprised of key people—not limited to the management team, is a way to Pivot *from* a lack of Clarity *to* Clarity, and to bring in a wider and more diverse perspective, so you can make more Nimble decisions. Membership requires that individuals have deep knowledge about an aspect of the organization or its environment.

If your company isn't nimble, if execution isn't always done well, or if working in your company is not fulfilling for you and others, take a look at how you are selecting, communicating, tracking and following through on priorities. Ask the following questions (preferably of your version of The Council):

1) Are you focusing on the wrong things?
2) Are you setting too many priorities rather than focusing on the company's vision?
3) Are you losing focus on what's core?
4) Do you lose focus on priorities after they are assigned?
5) Are employees unclear about what to focus on or do they perceive that focus is not valued?
6) Are you allowing complacency to block strategic focus?

Answers to these questions may indicate one or more areas where a Pivot will serve you and the company's direction. Every situation is different. To get you started, here are a few examples of successful Pivots corresponding to the questions above:

1) A Pivot to aligning (and re-aligning) measurement with strategy

If you find you are focused, but on the wrong things, you may then find that what is being done is not meeting strategic objectives. Focus is missing or it is applied to the wrong targets. The most common Pivot for better focus and execution is to move toward re-defining measurement and tracking to align with current strategic objectives. Ask:

- Have we clearly defined our strategic objectives?
- Have measures been defined that include "leading indicators" that provide assurance that, if the measured performance is on target, then strategic objectives will be met?
- Are we tracking the leading indicators frequently enough to know if progress is being made?
- Is there a means to adjust if initially selected measures are found to be inaccurate indicators of progress?

2) A Pivot to more effective, collaborative meetings

Are you setting too many priorities rather than focusing on the few or the main thing? You may find that too many priorities are causing nothing to be a priority. This challenge may show up in the form of ineffective meetings. Perhaps the same concerns recur meeting after meeting, such as no improvements after the meeting or the attendees' lack of preparation, engagement or interaction. Likely, priorities are not clear. Often there is no shared vision.

Priorities and the strategic objectives they are tied to must be the highlight of team meetings. The shared view will naturally strengthen as priorities are made more clear. Alignment of priorities around a few strategic objectives spurs collaboration. One of two Pivots may work well for your company, and both are often needed:

i. **A Pivot *to* more effective meetings.**
Ineffective meetings are one of the first concerns a team performance coach will promptly recognize and address. The cost of an ineffective meeting exceeds the hourly cost of the people in that room. The remedy requires practice. Your team players will likely want improvement, so look to them to initiate the change.
Here's a framework to consider when training each team member to do their part in creating a more effective meeting:

a. Preparation. When preparing, aim to spend just 20% of your time compiling materials. Devote 60–70% to thinking and 10%–20% to whittling reports down to capture the crux.
b. Process questions, issues, challenges.
c. Agree on what success will look like and how to track progress.
d. Identify what will be challenging and who is available to help.
e. Prioritize next steps and assign accountability.

ii. **A Pivot *from* a group of individuals *to* a collaborative team.**
Meetings are more effective when there is collaboration. When everyone has a voice, collaboration is engaging. Compare this to a group of individuals reporting endless (boring) details of work that is already done. A collaborative team still values and measures individual accountability, but also creates a shared responsibility for team results. Pivoting toward a collaborative team

can kick-start more effective meetings. A close look at your culture will bring to the surface the incentives and disincentives of collaboration. This is the stuff of Aligned Momentum.

3) A Pivot from growth-for-growth's-sake to aligned growth

Are you losing focus on what's core? If you find that you are losing focus on what's core, first take a look at your growth strategy to ensure that growth by acquisition never harms what is core to your business purpose and performance.

Growth tends to slow over the life of a company. Many companies invigorate growth through acquisition. This works some of the time, yet not most of the time, as we've learned, including in those case studies that I've discussed in this book.

A growth-by-acquisition strategy can cause very capable business leaders to lose sight of core values, purpose or competency. Acquisitions often require the integration of different company cultures, and that integration is often expected to happen on the turn of a dime. Why? Because typically, acquisitions are held under wraps; few employees know about the acquisition until it is finalized. Turn-on-a-dime pivots rarely work. Acquisitions can severely impair focus. Momentum toward achieving objectives can stall for many months, even years, as employees adjust.

Maintaining focus on what's core while making an acquisition decision will help ensure that your growth game plan will enhance rather than slow momentum or break momentum that would otherwise lead to a breakthrough.

Orchestrate this Pivot with both culture and strategy in mind. Bringing your Council into the decision-making, for example, will improve your ability to discern the potential impact on the business's culture and on its long-term performance when executing an acquisition growth strategy. Nimble Decision-making and brilliant execution of a growth strategy must involve more than financial due diligence and modeling. People matter most to the success of your business.[105]

4) A Pivot to frequent performance conversations

Do you lose focus on priorities after they are assigned? An absence of Clarity, accountability, measurement and tracking, or reporting and check-ins could be the reason that strategic priorities aren't being focused on and why strategic objectives aren't being achieved. Often, you won't even know you are off track until it is too late to get back on track.

Information and communication must be well-designed and managed. Without a clear expectation of what you want and the discipline to sustain it, then you'll get whatever you get (and it is rarely what you want). Pivots that address a lack of focus arising after priorities are set are all about communication, specifically, style and frequency, Clarity, and candor.

- **A Pivot in communication style and frequency:** *from* telling and waiting, *to* informing and actively maintaining an open dialogue.

  Consider performance conversations
  Guidance for holding performance conversations is provided in chapter 3 when describing Pivots for a hierarchical structure. In summary: the manager clarifies the strategic objectives (which have usually been translated into goals for the quarter or year); the employee offers his or her priorities for the next period (one month or more frequently, depending on the work and speed of change) that they expect will lead to meeting their goals; then there is a conversation related to these priorities and the employee's accomplishments in the previous period.

- **A Pivot in Clarity:** *from* not being clear, leaving managers to figure out what you expect, *to* ensuring that each manager is clear on their priorities and is aligned with the strategy. Also, for communicating priorities, consider using a theme.

Theme your top priority

The top priority is the guidepost for activity in your business. All that you, your leadership team, and your employees do should point back to it and support it. The language you use for your priority is up to you. Examples are "one main thing" from George Labovitz in *Rapid Re-Alignment* (2012), "top box" from Steve McKee in *When Growth Stalls* (2009), "theme" as used in the Balanced Scorecard methodology (2010) from Robert S. Kaplan and David P. Norton, or quarterly "rocks" from Verne Harnish in *Scaling Up* (2014).[106, 107, 108,109] The point is to ensure that what is top priority for the next period becomes the constant filter through which all decisions and judgment calls are made.

This top priority is what needs to be communicated throughout the organization clearly, concisely and consistently, so everyone gains Clarity about the strategic objectives this priority is aligned with and each person's role in achieving it.

Notice how short these calls to action can be. They should be memorable and everything the organization and its employees do should point back to the strategy encapsulated by the theme. If you want your strategy or priority to be made clear and to become a filter for every decision or judgment call in your organization, you want to keep it short.

To translate strategic objectives into action, you need to create a system of continuous communication between the leaders who are accountable for ensuring the company does the right things, and the managers and their teams who are executing the priorities set to meet these objectives.

- **A Pivot in candor and accountability:** *from* discussing priorities without clear accountability, *to* candid exchange about the commitment, accountability (who-what-when) and with a process that tracks progress with a frequency that allows for timely adjustments.

5) A Pivot to more ways to gain Clarity about strategic focus

Are employees unclear about what to focus on or do they perceive that focus is not valued? What message are you sending employees about the value of strategic focus? It is fairly common for employees to be rewarded for meeting quantity and standards of quality that are the same as or incrementally improved upon what was done before. However, it is less common for employees to be rewarded for focusing on finding and setting better ways of completing their work, working together or initiating change. Aligned Momentum improves when employees know that they are valued for, and given time for, practicing strategic focus and innovation.

Consider how you are modeling the way for strategic focus to live in your culture. Have you, for example, ever encountered a senior leader who, after attending an offsite meeting or conference, comes back with a new priority? Strategic objectives suffer when priorities shift precipitously or multiply beyond control. To move toward your vision and to remain nimble, everyone must fully commit to strategically focus. If you are unclear about the progress of existing priorities, there is likely to be a lack of accountability, measurement and timely reporting and you will need to address that first. Does this mean you ignore the great ideas you've just discovered, or that potential strategic direction that struck you while you were away from the office? No! This is about timing.

Rather than turning every new idea into an urgent priority that you then have someone manage, leverage strategic focus and the orchestration of a Pivot. What is your strategic direction? What are the objectives? What is the Pivot you are orchestrating? You might start with thinking of each new idea as a scenario. Visualize the scenario in your mind and play that movie forward. How do you imagine other ideas will play out? Often the best next step shows itself. And then, you orchestrate. Maybe the new idea truly is an immediate priority or maybe the longer-term result will be grander if that idea plays into a future quarter. By practicing this discipline of taking a "best next step" you are giving yourself time to fit each great idea into a timeline that will maintain alignment with your strategy.

6) A Pivot to the discipline required to lead a great company

Are you allowing complacency to block strategic focus? Consider if the priorities you are communicating to your employees are getting the focused action that results in positive change. Complacency is not nimble. Disciplines that support Aligned Momentum are nimble. Remember, focus and nimbleness can co-exist. While discussing *Good to Great* with *Fast Company* magazine in 2001, Jim Collins pointed out the "Doom Loop" caused by a lack of discipline in leadership:

> Think about it for one minute. Why do most overhyped change programs ultimately fail? Because they lack accountability, they fail to achieve credibility and they have no authenticity. It's the opposite of the Flywheel Effect (what it feels like when you're inside a company that makes the transition from good to great); it's the Doom Loop. Companies that fall into the Doom Loop genuinely want to effect change—but they lack the quiet discipline that produces the Flywheel Effect.[110]

If your company lacks discipline, which is a fundamental requirement for Aligned Momentum, you must Pivot. Remember that a Pivot is not a quick-fix change program, which, as Collins points out, will likely fail. A Pivot is comprised of many small shifts often carried out by many people. These well thought out shifts are orchestrated carefully and precisely over time to produce an accumulative, and often significant, change. The obvious Pivot to suggest in answer to this imagined scenario is toward the discipline required to lead a great company.

DOING THE RIGHT THINGS RIGHT

When leaders set the right tone and path, work with managers to set priorities, and then communicate and follow through with managers who are skilled in execution… *the right things are done right*. That phrase was often used by Peter Drucker, possibly the most followed thought leader on business management.

Drucker reminded us for decades (*The Effective Executive* was first published in 1967) that intelligence, imagination and knowledge may all be wasted in an executive job without practicing the required discipline to mold them into results.

Jim Collins reminds leaders in *Great by Choice* (2011) that "10x" leaders, those leading companies to perform ten times better than their peers, maintain a discipline of focus.[111] Collins boils his research down to four traits, all of which tie in well with strategic focus:

1) Fanatical Discipline—being focused on priorities and consistent in their actions.

2) Empirical Creativity—leveraging facts rather than opinions to drive bold moves.

3) Productive Paranoia—staying aware, prepared and never complacent.

4) Level 5 Ambition—channeling ego and focus on the vision, not on themselves.[112]

These four traits together provide the focus that is needed from leaders to support a culture with Aligned Momentum. You likely have one or more of these traits. And you may have put in place systems and processes that support you in those areas. Yet the business you are leading may not be nimble, or as nimble as it could be. You may not have started to empower others with Clarity and the authority to initiate change. You and your business may need to Pivot *from* being held by ingrained traditions *to* being more nimble.

HOW TRADITION CAN WORK AGAINST YOU

As your company grew, you brought in people who were the right fit for your company at that time. Likely, not all have grown at the same pace at which the company has grown. As the company matured, systems were installed, processes were documented and controls were put in place. These are now woven into the fabric of your company.

Indeed, you've followed good advice for becoming more operationally efficient and less tolerant of risk. What often happens, though, as you focus on "growing up" and "acting like a real business" with an eye toward efficiency and risk management, is that the strategic focus can be lost.

Your culture is often what suffers. You may keep people not because they are a positive influence on your culture but because it is simply easier to keep them, and you think "they know how the work gets done here." You may manage risk through policy and limited delegation of authority rather than providing the training and coaching that will support more empowerment. You may relegate performance measurement to your finance and accounting department. You may put all hiring into the hands of human resources, rather than empowering your managers to build the right team. And the list goes on.

Your managers may have been promoted due to their ability to do the work. You expect that they can now manage people. Yet not all are ready or want to manage and coach people, so how will they execute brilliantly through others? All that you have in place now may not serve your business in the future. You may have lost strategic focus.

There's no need to give up on what's possible for your business. Consider The Pivot, which starts with preparing people for Aligned Momentum with Clarity and strategic focus, and moves onto addressing the context that affects their ability to brilliantly execute strategy. We've discussed the context created by your organizational structure. Next we'll address the social context in your workplace.

CHAPTER 6: KEY POINTS

---

1) Brilliant execution of strategy requires more than measuring productivity. Being better at what was done last year rarely leads to meeting strategic objectives.

2) To be both focused *and* nimble, empower employees with a clear understanding of strategy and their role in it. Give them authority to adapt work to strategy.

3) Growth strategies and focusing on what is core must co-exist.

4) Growth strategies typically require a high degree of thoughtful and broad discernment, especially with respect to any potential impact on culture.

5) Thinking you know it all is not the same as being nimble.

6) If you've lost focus consider a Pivot *to*:
   - measurement that is always aligned with strategy;
   - more effective, collaborative meetings;
   - aligned growth (to ensure that growth by acquisition never harms what is core to your purpose and performance);
   - frequent performance conversations for Clarity and accountability;
   - more ways to gain Clarity about strategic focus;
   - the discipline required to lead a *great* company.

7) If what the bulk of your employees do this year is what they have traditionally done year after year, it is time to weave nimble practices into your business.

CHAPTER 7

Change The Social Context

INTENTIONS & HABITS

"Sow a thought, reap an action; sow an action, reap a habit; sow a habit, reap a character; sow a character, reap a destiny."

— *Stephen R. Covey*

"We are what we repeatedly do. Excellence, then, is not an act, but a habit."

— *Aristotle*

Throughout this book I've recommended Pivots and best next steps toward extraordinary business momentum. The reality is: Some people will resist. What if your employees aren't ready for change? What if they don't believe that a new way will be better for them than the current way? What if those hesitant or resistant are on your leadership team? *What about you?*

Creating the context that supports change requires you to be a positive influence and to communicate, in a variety of ways, including modeling—that this is an organization where people grow. When managers know that you expect them to build up others, with you modeling the way, they will make time to be great coaches. Some will resist and may need to transition to something, or somewhere, that is a better fit for them. Some may be all-in and may perceive your clearer message about coaching as the go-ahead to finally do more of it. Great! These managers will become your champions, and role models. You may have always cared about leading an organization that builds up people. You may have assumed that managers knew that growing people was a priority. If you are not seeing in-action what you are looking for, first address a likely lack of Clarity.

Pivot *from* assumptions and misunderstandings *to* Clarity about helping all the people in your company grow.

> *You can't change a person (they must choose to change), but you can change their context at work.*

In addition to the context created by your organizational structure, there is a social context in your workplace that is created by the behavior of the people working there.

CLARITY ABOUT BEHAVIOR

To position your employees for success they need to not only be clear about what they are expected to *do*, they must also be clear about how they are expected to *behave* while at work. For example, are they being calm and curious, or frenzied and close-minded in their work and interactions with others? How do you want individuals in your workplace to be? Is your vision clear to all? How one behaves today is built on many years of learning. A person's behavior can be adjusted to fit your culture, but only with respect to their own awareness of the need for change and their willingness to change.

Think back to the meaning of the poem, *The Blind Men and The Elephant*. Every person filters what they hear through their own point of view, which is based on beliefs formed from their past experiences. Gandhi said it well:

> Your beliefs become your thoughts,
> Your thoughts become your words,
> Your words become your actions,
> Your actions become your habits,
> Your habits become your values,
> Your values become your destiny.[113]

Belief

Belief is the state of mind in which one accepts something to be the case, with or without empirical evidence to prove that something is the case with factual certainty.

> *What you believe drives how you view*
> *the world and your place in it.*

When you accept, often unconsciously, that something exists or that a statement is true, you are expressing your beliefs.

For example, if you believe that in general people want to do the right thing, then you will likely give them your trust unless they prove themselves untrustworthy. If you believe that people will take advantage of another person given the opportunity to do so, then you will not likely trust them until they have proven themselves trustworthy.

Belief and mindset are related, but they are not one and the same.

> **Belief:**
> *The state of mind in which you accept something to be the case,*
> *regardless of empirical evidence to prove that it is the case. It can be*
> *about you, or about anyone or anything else.*
>
> **Mindset:**
> *What you believe to be true about yourself and how life*
> *is, and will be, for you. It is about you and you alone.*

Mindset

How your mind is set can determine how you perceive "things are" for you. Although similar to belief, mindset is limited to you; it is about you and your place in this world, whereas something you believe in can be completely apart from you. For example, you may believe that artistic abilities are inherent and not learned, and you may have a mindset that you cannot draw now, or ever (yet learning to draw, even later in life has been proven to be possible by those who do set their minds to the task).

Carol Dweck is a psychology professor at Stanford and one of the world's leading researchers in the field of motivation. She discovered that people have either a fixed or growth mindset and this usually stems from what they were told and what they experienced while growing up.[114]

In general, a person with a growth mindset believes they can develop their abilities through dedication, hard work, and learning from others and their mistakes. In the language of Aligned Momentum we call this a Mastery Mindset.

A person with a fixed mindset views talent as innate or they view themselves today as the best they are going to get; they aren't willing to change or grow. It is more likely for a person with a fixed mindset to only get involved in work that affirms their abilities rather than stepping up and growing.

Both belief systems and mindset start forming as we grow from the blank slate of infancy. By age 14 many people maintain beliefs and have a mindset that will barely shift by ages 24, 34, 44, 54 … 84. Are you certain that the beliefs and mindset that may have served you well at age 14 are serving you well now?

> *Consider what you intend to experience over the rest of your life, and the legacy you wish to **live** (not just leave).*

Intention

An intention *mindfully* drives action—what you do, create, and generate. Compare this to hope: hope is a starting point, but does not shape your actions. Intention can generate action in how it guides you to pay attention to something or someone, and sometimes indirectly, almost as if by luck. Intentions can also be blocked by beliefs that drive behaviors that run counter to your intentions.

The first of a few sample characters illustrating the effects of different beliefs, mindsets and intentions in the workplace is Tom. At the start of the new year Tom lays out a plan of how he intends to carve out at least an hour per week for practicing a greater focus on strategy, culture and innovation. He shares his plan with others, but at first doesn't ask for help. He holds the belief that if something is to get done, he should just do it. His days become filled with doing what others could do, if they were prepared. So, he spends only an hour per week on what is meant to be a priority and it is not enough. In effect, his priority is founded on hope and not intention. Yet, he truly wants to act on priorities and achieve his goal. He realizes, with the help of a coach, that there is something more basic that is causing him to sabotage his priority; his, "I step in to do whatever needs to get done" belief is not serving him as a leader. Awareness plus intention plus realistic best next steps give him the power to start shifting his belief. Within the year he's stopped counting on sheer willpower and a do-it-all belief system. Instead, he seeks help from colleagues to address accountability and masters his delegation skills. By the end of that first year he is promoted to a more senior position, leading more people. Tom now carves out the time he needs to grow as a leader.

> *Leadership requires intention. You must hold it in your mind and take conscious action to keep it alive.*

Habit

A habit is a *mindlessly* repeated action. You want good habits. You also want to be aware of all your habits, so you can decide if they are still serving you. Repetition causes a shortcut in the brain.

> *If what you say you intend to do is not getting done, perhaps you have a habit formed from a belief that is no longer serving you.*

Consider David, who has acquired the habit of reading the paper every morning. In his younger days he believed that he needed to have something to add to every conversation. He no longer feels he must know as much or more than anyone else; instead, he wants to continue to be aware and learn so that he might serve others in his leadership. He is aware that the knowledge he gains as he reads the newspaper is often overridden by the negativity much of this news leaves him with. His intention over the next month is to shift from news to books or articles for 80% of his morning reading, and to consider diverse perspectives to add the depth and awareness he desires that keep his mind (and business) nimble, and to skim emailed news alerts, headlines and summaries for 20% of this time. Now, David remains able to participate in conversation, but he no longer carries the stress of having to know it all, and he starts his day with more positivity.

We can easily recognize physical habits, such as our habit to take a certain driving route from home to the office. However, it takes introspection, and often also someone observing us, to become aware of the habits that have formed from our beliefs. One belief I've mentioned above is about whether our traits, such as intelligence, are fixed or are capable of being developed, with effort and intention.

We might not always recognize the beliefs and mindset of a person until we get to know them better. Or perhaps we never know exactly *why* they act as they do, but we become accustomed to how they might act.

When you are in a top position it is helpful to meet with trusted peers and a coach who will help you become more aware of how your beliefs and mindset are impacting your decisions, and how others experience you.

> *Leaders can leverage a trusted advisor and/or peer group*
> *to help them become aware of, and adjust, beliefs that*
> *are showing up as habits that do not serve them.*

Brandy grew up in poverty and developed a belief that money was what mattered most in life. For her, there is never enough money. Now, as a successful business woman she's sensing that she's missed something. So, she recently joined a peer group. The leader of that group, a coach, was surprised to hear that she was considering the purchase of a business that had no connection with her current business. In fact, it undermined her professional reputation to be buying what seemed to be a randomly chosen business that did not reflect her values. However, this decision fit with her belief system: her reasoning for looking at the new business was the potential profit margin.

Ultimately, Brandy is the one who will decide if her belief that money matters most is still serving her, but to keep her momentum she has hired a coach to help her be aware of bad habits she's formed as a result of her beliefs.

> *Leaders can benefit from good habits that run in the background, almost mindlessly.*

But stay aware of what habits you operate with, because they can take over, like being on autopilot.

Value

A value is formed based on what you believe reflects the "right" behavior. Your values guide you in your personal and professional life. A company has values as well, and these are often outlined as a set of core values or as a basis for how the company, its leadership and employees will behave at work.

A true leader I've had the pleasure to work with has just two core values for his company: "Be kind" and "Be safe." Although this is not a lesson in strategic planning, I appreciate that he focuses on just two values. If there are so many values that no one remembers them, how do you expect them to be alive throughout the organization? There must be Clarity around values.

Zappos lists 10 core values on their website.[115]

1) Deliver WOW through service
2) Embrace and drive change
3) Create fun and a little weirdness
4) Be adventurous, creative, and open-minded
5) Pursue growth and learning
6) Build open and honest relationships with communication
7) Build a positive team and family spirit

8) Do more with less
9) Be passionate and determined
10) Be humble

Microsoft shares six core values.[116] The descriptions aid Clarity.

1) Integrity & honesty
   Integrity and honesty can be demonstrated in many ways. Honesty and integrity are demonstrated not just in the extraordinary, but also in the everyday decisions we make. As employees, we strive for excellence even when no one else is looking.

2) Open & respectful
   People who are open and respectful of others understand that how work is accomplished is as important as the work itself. We never act in a manner that could be perceived as threatening, intolerant, or discriminatory.

3) Passion
   Passion is everywhere you look at Microsoft. We have a zeal for technology and what it enables customers to do. We strive to meet customer and partner expectations of quality, security, privacy, reliability, and business integrity.

4) Accountable
   Accountability is about keeping your word and taking responsibility for the commitments you make. When you say you'll do something, you do it. Trust is built over time in just this way. Be honest and accountable.

5) Big challenges
   From the very beginning, Microsoft has tackled big challenges. Big challenges have little to do with a specific job and everything to do with the vision, courage,

and fortitude of our people. People just like Bill Gates. People just like you.

6) Self-critical

Our dedication to quality is not exclusive to our products. Each of us should improve over time. We must consistently ask ourselves and co-workers, "What could I have done better? How can I improve for next time?"

The values that are truly alive in a company are considered core to company culture. If values are not alive in the culture then they are merely aspirational, not core.

How can you tell if a company's stated value is core (alive every day)? First, a value is core if those who live it are willing to take a financial or personal hit in order to hold true to that value. Secondly, you and others in your organization should actually see those values in action. Although posting values on a wall can be inspiring, it is by observing and applauding the living of core values that you create the most powerful positive influence and accountability.

Each person also has personal values they live by. When they work in your organization their values need not be exactly the same as yours, but they do need to align.

Legacy

The impact or influence you have on others will determine how you make them feel and how they remember you. This is what legacy means in the language of Aligned Momentum (it is so much more than the traditional definition as the amount of money or property that you leave for someone in your will). Consider how you will show up, both intentionally and habitually, today and in the future. This will define how others remember you after you are no longer here.

Legacy, in this context, is how you will intentionally and mindfully show up in the present, based on how you want to be remembered at the end of your life. Your legacy statement creates a filter in your mind about how you will live and be with others, every day. It is personal. It should be. It is for you, and need not be shared verbally or in writing; it is *expressed* through how you live each day. I will share mine with you so that you might have an example of what a legacy statement looks like: "I am a bright light, courageous, tenacious and wise, a great mom and always true to my word." This embodies the expression of my life each day, at work, at home or at play.

You may have a personal purpose or mission statement. It's similar to a legacy statement. Oprah Winfrey's mission statement is, "To be a teacher. And to be known for inspiring my students to be more than they thought they could be."[117] Sir Richard Branson's is, "To have fun in [my] journey through life and learn from [my] mistakes."[118] You might have a purpose statement that you apply to your career. I have one. It is: "To catalyze momentum for leaders and their teams."

A legacy statement (or personal purpose or mission statement) is created mindfully, and helps us live that way. It drives intention and action, and should lead to good habits. Your leadership ensures that the vision, mission, strategy, and communication support alignment with, and the right actions from, each person in the organization.

ALIGNING PEOPLE WITH YOUR ORGANIZATION'S CULTURE

When behaviors do not align with core values, the culture, direction, mission, and vision of the company can suffer. When company core values don't align with your personal values, you'll end up feeling unhappy and unfulfilled. As such, it's important to choose a role in a company with core values that align with your own values.

Each person is unique. Beliefs, mindsets, legacies and values will vary, and that is okay. They must, however, align and not conflict with your organization's culture.

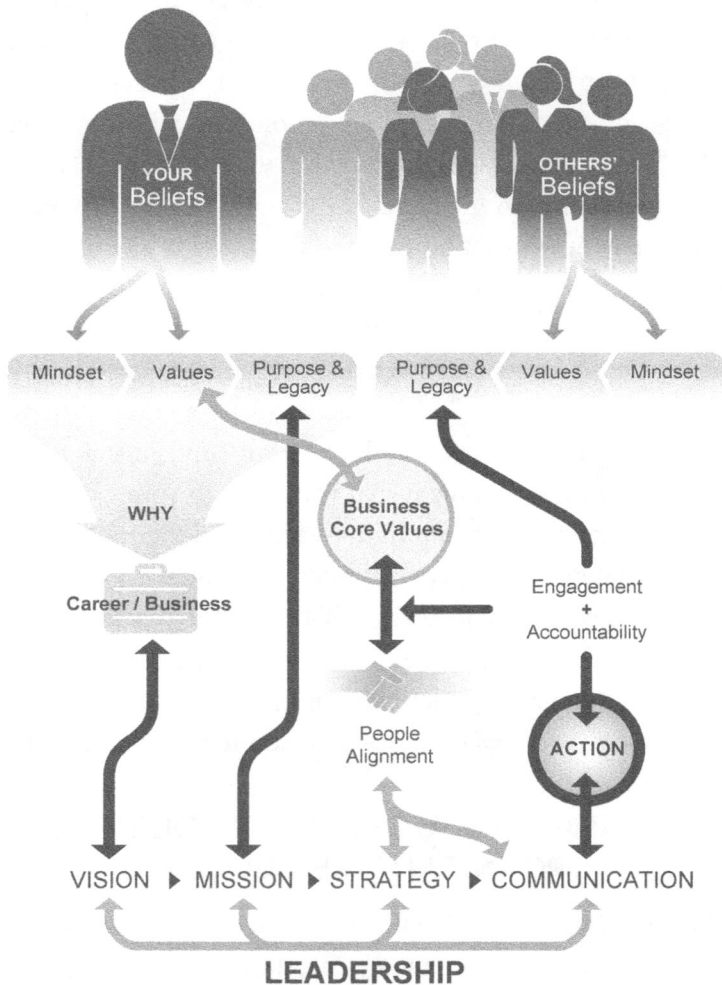

Figure 15: Leadership and Personal Alignment

How to read the Alignment infographic (Figure 15):

- Your beliefs have helped form your mindset and values.
- Each of your employee's beliefs has helped form their mindsets and values.

Great Leadership is intentional...

- Often, your values are the foundation of the business's core values (or you were clearly aligned with the values set for the company culture prior to your position at the top)
- Your legacy or purpose is closely aligned with the mission of the business.
- "Purpose" is often referred to as answering "why" the business exists. Your why and the business's why are what create an inspiring vision.
- Your strategy (including mission) is important to employees for feeling engaged, staying aligned and being accountable.
- Communication is critical to gaining the desired action from employees (for brilliant execution of strategy).
- Alignment requires intentional leadership.

Aligned Momentum will thrive in your organization when each role is aligned with strategy *and* with each person's purpose (or mission) and legacy. Jim Collins puts it this way, "Building a visionary company requires 1% vision and 99% alignment."[119]

What it means to be intentional

How an individual behaves and acts will be greatly influenced by what they believe to be true about themselves and the world around them. When aligned with what is expected of them in their role, their intentional and habitual actions and behavior fit your culture. Their performance and behavior positively influence business momentum. Satya Nadella shows that he understands this dynamic when speaking about the cultural Pivot he is orchestrating at Microsoft, "We want to push to be more of a learn-it-all culture than a know-it-all culture."[120]

When an employee is positioned to grow, they are also positioned to step up and use their initiative. When employees take the initiative to develop clearly on a path toward what matters most for your company, you are getting alignment right. The person is not merely complying with your request, they feel committed to it to the point that they live it. Compliance reads something like this in the person's mind: "Okay, I'll do what you tell me to do, but I may not like it. I'm not all in and I'll look for opportunities to get out of doing it." When what you are asking aligns with a person's purpose and values, you gain commitment. Commitment reads something like this in the person's mind: "I'm excited to do that. Just watch me give this all I've got … without you needing to ask again." Commitment is intentional; it is mindful.

Awareness is the key to changing bad habits

Changing habits, even those that no longer serve you, requires awareness that a change is needed, motivation to change, and feedback about progress. A long-held belief may need to be replaced by a better-serving belief, or adjusted to serve your intentions for the future and best next steps.

Awareness is the first step to changing a habit and the belief(s) that led to it. Often the belief and resulting habit served you at one time, but they may no longer serve you now. The moment that you are aware that you are doing things out of a habit that is no longer serving you is the moment you can start to Pivot toward a habit that will serve you now.

Mary felt held back in her career. At the time, she held beliefs that rewarded her for being "good" and "respectful." She needed to be liked. In this case, her beliefs translated into not questioning, not stepping out of turn or sharing her ideas, especially if they might run counter to the norm amongst the group. Although she has a Mastery Mindset, she allowed herself to stall. Mary had to shed her need to be liked in order to lead.

In the case of Tom, introduced earlier, he believed that he needed to do everything himself, or at least direct the work to be done. He wasn't able to delegate effectively. He was exhausted, which caused him to relegate rather than delegate what needed to be done. When relegating, he placed the work completely out of his mind, retained no accountability, and did not ensure that those now doing the work were clear about the desired outcome or even if they were on the right track. Tom was in a position of authority, but was struggling to develop into a true leader. He joined a leadership peer group, which helped him become quickly aware that there was a better way. In the group he gained support from others who had been through a similar struggle, and received customized guidance one-on-one from the coach who led the group.

Alice shifted into a top leadership spot, as the first chief executive hired from outside the company. She is forthright and personable. These strengths have helped her rise quickly within a traditional organization where top-down communication is the norm and decisions are made at the top. As she has assumed a position within an organization where she is not yet known, her strengths might be misunderstood. Her beliefs about herself project an outward sense of confidence and assertiveness. Unfortunate as it is, the prevailing perception of confident women is that they are self-serving (whereas confident men are perceived as strong leaders) and assertive women are seen as less likable than assertive men.[121, 122, 123] Alice understands this. But also understanding how to orchestrate The Pivot is critical for Alice. She intends to double the revenue of this mature, stable company. She is wired toward those hero-like, turn on a dime top-down directive changes that are rarely successful. She is building relationships with her new team, and this is a great start. Her best next steps will be to improve Clarity and Strategic Thinking throughout the organization.

Brandy, Tom, David, Mary, or Alice could be in your organization today. Each person has their own beliefs, mindset and values causing them to act in ways that may not be serving them in their work or in the workplace culture. And, these ways have likely formed into habits.

What might these habits look like? For example, before Mary became self-aware and changed, she did not step up or offer input. Because she led a team, her team took her approach as the way to model in their workplace. Collaboration didn't exist. And before Tom embraced delegation, others were not surfacing ideas or taking initiative because they figured Tom had his way of doing things and he'd just let them know. The cultural norm had become one of compliance. Tom envisioned commitment for the culture (and that change is in progress).

Another more general example of a habit is saying "yes" to anyone who asks. Tom initially had that habit. Saying "no" to any opportunity that will send you out of your comfort zone is yet another habit that rarely serves a leader. Alice is finding that many in her new company are not up to the level of candor that she is. She's learning to be more empathetic so that she can positively influence her senior team to embrace her bold new strategy.

Some of your habits, formed from beliefs that no longer serve you, may run counter to you becoming a more effective leader. Reaching high levels of power and authority does not necessarily mean you have all that it takes to be a great leader. But you *can* be a great leader. You may need to Pivot.

HOW TO STOP DOING WHAT NO LONGER SERVES YOU

The ancient philosopher, Lao Tzu taught that, "A journey of a thousand miles must begin with the first step."

While it's true that your parents had a great impact on what you physically look like, you can make *of* yourself what you will. You can change the beliefs, behaviors and habits that you have formed over time from your environment, social context or culture. You can also help others change their beliefs, behaviors and habits by providing them with a different culture and helping them become aware that the way they are being now is not serving them in their role or in realizing their desired future.

Many people still *believe* that the brain is fully formed at adulthood and can't be changed. In fact, old scientific schools of thought believed our ability to generate new pathways dropped off sharply around the age of 20, and then became permanently fixed around the age of 40. But new discoveries in science indicate that this is simply not the case.[124] Our habits can not only be changed through willpower or altering our belief systems or intentions—but we can actually "rewire" our brains. Why is this important? Two reasons relevant to Aligned Momentum and The Pivot are:

First, it is important to understand that willpower alone is typically not sustainable. You can rally your team toward a big goal, but if the results aren't quick then what they did to achieve a higher level of performance will slip. Some refer to this as "they forgot how to work!" Not exactly. One or more of your employees lost steam. If you've ever set a personal goal but just couldn't get it to stick, you know how this happens. Have you ever committed yourself to a line of action that promises you will do this or that differently, and then, in the moment, the old way of behaving is what you follow? Consider this next time you feel disappointed that an employee seems to have slipped back from a higher level of performance.

The second relevant reason to rewire rather than rely on will-power is that, with rewiring, the new way of working becomes the norm. You can take this individual change and apply it to the entire organization. But it takes continuous practice over time, so plan ahead with milestones or "quick wins" as you orchestrate people through a culture change.

Recent studies using PET and MRI brain-scanning technology show that new neural cells are generated throughout life. They also show that the brain can be rewired; new neural pathways can be formed.[125, 126] The science tells us that rewiring is physically possible. But there's more to consider for this to happen and stick.

Rewiring our brains requires:

1) **Awareness** of our beliefs that created the existing wiring that has led us to learn behaviors and develop habits
2) **Understanding** of what triggers our behaviors
3) **Motivation** to change
4) **A concerted effort** to change underlying beliefs and to form new behaviors and habits
5) **A supportive environment**, including social context and workplace culture

Each of these five components that support change are potential Pivots. You can affect these five components for everyone you lead. And for you, personally, you can change by putting all five components into place. As you read through the examples below, consider your organizational culture and what you might do to create a ripple of change—changing the social context—allowing brains to rewire, leading to improvement of performance.

Awareness

As you drive, are you aware of what you quickly pass by? We miss most of what we see. Yet, sometimes something catches our eye and we truly become aware of it, even if we have previously passed it by. Or perhaps you are in a crowded room and the voices are just a mumble, until you hear your name mentioned or a shocking word stated. You become aware of it above the din. It is the same with becoming aware of holding a belief that is no longer serving you.

Ask yourself, "Which one of my beliefs is allowing (this situation that I don't want)?" You can do this right now. Pause and ask yourself, "What do I believe?" and start capturing your list.

If it doesn't flow, here are a few prompts from Ari Weinzweig, co-founder of Zingerman's and author of *A Lapsed Anarchist's Approach To The Power of Beliefs in Business* (2010), to get you started.[127]

1) What things mean or don't mean
2) Who we are or are not
3) Why things have happened or not happened
4) What's possible or not possible
5) What's important or not important
6) Why we care or don't care
7) What matters and what doesn't
8) How we should be living our lives
9) What it means to be successful
10) The nature of authority
11) Business in general
12) The nature of our own organization in particular

We all find that one or more of our beliefs no longer serve us. Again, be kind to yourself. A belief was formed to serve you at some point in your life.

> *You behave according to your beliefs, but your*
> *beliefs are not you. You can change.*

Understanding

Once you are aware that you are acting (habits) or presuming and filtering (mindset) in a non-serving way, your next step is to understand your triggers. Be kind to yourself on this self-discovery. *It's not your fault; it's your default.*

> *Seek to be aware of, and to understand, what triggers you to act*
> *in a way that no longer serves you. Only you can change you.*

For example, when I started my business, I found that what I could do so well for my corporate employers and consulting clients, I was not doing for myself; I was not at all times using my discernment expertise and patience to properly vet prospective partners and suppliers before committing. I too quickly bestowed trustworthiness and capability on them if they were already working with or had investment from someone I respected. I stayed committed to what I said I would do, even when all the facts I'd relied on had been proven false. Certain situations were triggering beliefs that perhaps served me at one time, but were not serving me now. The results were personal pain and financial loss.

After becoming aware that I was getting in the way of my own success, I had to *get clear* about what I wanted, *become aware* of what was in the way, and then *understand* the changes I needed to make and what triggers might challenge me. My Pivot, like every Pivot I describe in this book, required Clarity, preparation, focus, nimbleness, tenacity and accountability to maintain momentum over the long term. My Pivot led to extraordinary momentum. Within 18 months I changed and rebuilt my inner circle to be comprised only of people who align with my values; lowered my ego to accept help, guidance and accountability from others including a coach; and strengthened my discernment in all situations. My business is more fulfilling for me in every way. My biggest reward continues to be realized through catalyzing momentum for leaders and their teams.

Motivation

Motivation is a willingness to do something. You want to do it.

The strongest motivation is available when one has drawn the idea or conclusion themselves, rather than when they have been told what to do. Stephen King offers an excellent take on motivation in *On Writing* (2000), "There are lots of would-be censors out there, and although they may have different agendas, they all want basically the same thing: for you to see the world they see... or at least to shut up about what you do see that's different. They are the agents of the status quo."[128] Intrinsic motivation is much stronger than compliance with someone else's agenda or expectation, and intrinsic motivation will lead you to your unique rewards.

A motivation to change is critical to gaining momentum.

Effort

Changing a behavior or a habit does not happen without concerted effort. The effort is mostly yours and the responsibility is all yours. That said, others may help you during this change and that's why I describe the effort as "concerted." You may benefit from support to impede non-serving behaviors. Choose people who you know care about you and want you to be successful. You also may benefit from support in forming new behaviors and better habits. Choose people who are with you often enough to see the change. To help your good intentions gain momentum, build in ample opportunities for repetition of these new behaviors and habits.

Supportive context

While you can't change the culture by changing people, you can change the culture by changing the context within which people are working.

In *Everybody Matters* (2016), Bob Chapman, CEO of Barry-Wehmiller, speaks about doing exactly that—changing the context within companies his company has acquired. I encourage you to read all of his stories.[129] Here, I've drawn out a couple "best next step" Pivots that worked for him and will most likely work for you:

1. Clearly define values and be serious about keeping them alive in your culture. Scenarios in which short-term decisions harm long-term strategy, politics thrive, silos develop, gossip pervades, and stress affects everyone are created or fueled by the way people read the environment they are in. Unless those scenarios express your values (and I hope they don't), then it is likely that your intention to have a culture living your core values is being blocked by your own modeling (including not consistently upholding values), or by a lack of clarity around those values. Visit your values often, such as in conversation, meetings and while walking around. Do so in a meaningful way—get specific with what was done or said, and how that expresses a core value.

2. Learn to inspire people to solve problems. Chapman shares his story about meeting with a customer service team of a newly acquired company. The team was highly dysfunctional, being protective of doing only what fell directly into their job description, avoiding anything hard, and tolerating unproductive behavior. When he asked their manager about the team, the manager was sure that he just had a poor performing team and needed to "weed a few out."

Chapman proceeded to inspire the team to carry out a higher level of performance and collaboration. He offered $100 to the individual who sold the most parts in a week. This required each person to answer the phone, which had been an issue previously. He also offered everyone on the team $100 if the team made their weekly sales goal. Thirteen weeks later sales had gone up 20%. The manager's reaction was, "I didn't know they had it in them."

Coach your managers so that they might grow as leaders. Learn to inspire people to solve problems and provide them with the authority and resources to do so, or at least to initiate the solution. Rather than trying to manage people out of problems, learn to inspire them to solve problems on their own.

3. Remove barriers to communication and smart work. Look at your organizational structure and how communication and information flow. Is your structure bogging people down when they try to solve problems? Does your structure discourage open communication between functional units? Are there aspects of your incentives that may be emphasizing individual performance and discouraging team work? Are performance reviews and the means by which bonuses, merit pools, or promotions are determined undermining the motivation and engagement of your people? Are there open and frequent conversations about individual and team performance, and how the team's work and behavior influences organizational performance? Do you have obsolete rules that are not serving anyone or any initiative now? Do you have policies that devalue human intelligence and two-way trust?

Pick one barrier, check its alignment with core values, and then test an alternative way that is in better alignment. Chapman gives us an example. After creating a more open dialogue with all company staff, he received feedback from the people working on the shop floor who felt that the break policies, in which a bell would ring signaling that each worker had to drop what he or she was doing no matter what, implied they were not trusted to do what's best. Chapman ordered the time clocks and break bells to be removed.

CONCLUDING ON SOCIAL CONTEXT

I bet that somewhere in your career you have experienced a supportive environment and social context where you felt both safe and accountable. Perhaps that was in a leadership peer group, or with a mastermind or a coach, or at a workshop led by skilled context-creators.

Over the years I've seen even the most serious professional dance in front of others, share vulnerabilities, stay highly-engaged for long days, and walk across burning hot coals during a workshop. At all times everyone was mindful of others, participants generated positive energy, and everyone worked together to create success for something that was bigger than any one of us.

I'm not proposing that you bring this into your workplace. What I am proposing is that you make a Pivot toward creating a workplace where people feel safe to speak up and accountable for their words and actions. Culture, including transformation of culture from what is now to what is possible, is not a one-time undertaking. Culture, like the world today, is dynamic.

It's never too late to reinvent either your business or yourself. It's never too late to Pivot on any number of levels to achieve greatness. What may be even more exciting, since this is about an organization full of people, and not solely about you, is that you can change the structural and social context in the workplace. You can positively influence performance and even improve lives.

You have the ultimate power to take your business to the next level. The choice is yours, no matter what stage your company is at or how you have chosen to lead it towards greatness. How do you define a great business? That becomes your bottom line.

CHAPTER 7: KEY POINTS

---

1) You can't change a person (they must choose to change), but you can change their context at work.

2) To position your employees for success they need to not only be clear about what they are expected to do, they must also be clear about how they are expected to behave while at work.

3) Understanding that each person has entered your workplace with their own belief system, values, mind-set and habits will help you be clear about what you expect of them in your organization.
   - Your beliefs become your thoughts,
   - Your thoughts become your words,
   - Your words become your actions,
   - Your actions become your habits,
   - Your habits become your values,
   - Your values become your destiny.

4) You may have habits created from beliefs that no longer serve you. Self-discovery will help you become aware of these beliefs and habits. Then there are steps to take to replace those habits with ones that better serve you. You may need to shed a long-held belief.

5) It's never too late to reinvent either your business or yourself.

CHAPTER 8

The Bottom Line

"Helping people to reach their highest potential and purpose, naturally, has a positive impact on the bottom line of business."

— *Sir Richard Branson*

"Overall advantage or disadvantage results from all of a company's activities, not only a few."

— *Michael Porter*

What's your bottom line? The traditional measure of business success is "the (financial) bottom line," expressed in terms of net earnings or profits. Too often the bottom-line result just happens, without a clear understanding of why. If the result was lower than expected, for example, you determine a variety of reasons such as: "The team was not focused enough. Waste needs to be reduced. Customers are taking too long to close. There's just not enough time for managers to coach," etc.

If the result is better than expected you may presume that, internally, everything is going well. Although, the improvement may be mostly due to external factors. Or maybe some best steps were taken, but not learned, so may not be repeated. While all of the identified problems may be worth solving, and the wins worth celebrating, perhaps you never get to the crux of what is happening in your business. Everyone is happy when the end result is good, and unhappy when it is not good. No leader can orchestrate a Pivot without employees who care about best next steps, Clarity about what is desired and what actually is the state right now or a drive by all to get to the crux of the matter.

The financial result at the end of a year, or even each quarter, doesn't tell you a lot about what might happen next year.

> *Great leaders have their eye on more than financial results.*

Looking now or ahead at yourself as a *great* leader, you have key indicators in place, such as Aligned Momentum Key Indicators, and track them with the level of frequency that allows for small shifts to stay on track. You remain, in Jim Collins' words, "productively paranoid." No significant surprises push you off track. You set a foundation for innovation. You empower people and inspire them to keep their eye out for the facts, inside and outside the business, that could lead to a significant change, good or bad. You value people and, although you will always put people before profits even when it is hard to do so, you also know that doing so will result in a long-term healthier company. A healthy business is healthy in its culture and on the business's (financial) bottom line.

With Aligned Momentum the bottom line is the result from all that you do to move toward your vision:

1) Your bold and clearly communicated strategy
2) Employees who are ready to adapt, shift and innovate

3) Pivots orchestrated to stay aligned with strategy
4) Well-chosen best next steps taken
5) Priorities that align with strategy and are brilliantly executed

You want extraordinary business momentum and to be positioned for performance breakthroughs. You've learned that neither will happen without preparing with Clarity, strategic focus (being focused *and* nimble), and a supportive context. You must prepare to Pivot.

Southwest is a good example of Aligned Momentum in action. Southwest has built a successful business as a reliable low-cost airline with great customer service. They define "The Southwest Way" in the following statements: Have fun, don't take yourself too seriously, maintain perspective, celebrate successes, enjoy your work and be a passionate team-player.[130] One of my favorite stories about Southwest is from co-founder and former CEO, Herb Kelleher.[131] The story goes like this:

Herb Kelleher received a letter from a disgruntled customer who felt that using humor to illustrate safety points was highly inappropriate (The flight announcement said something like "In the event of a landing on water we will bring round fresh towels and cocktails!"). Most companies would have apologized to the customer, given them some form of gift or compensation and chastised the flight team for their poor and inappropriate behavior. Herb didn't—he sent a short, three-word response to the lady. It said simply, "We'll miss you!"

Having fun is so central to Southwest, it is part of their culture. Its people thrive. And, it is so important to Southwest to live core values that they will take a financial hit to do so.

Herb Kelleher once said, "We tell our people, 'Don't worry about profit. Think about customer service.' Profit is a by-product of customer service. It's not an end in and of itself."[132] Southwest has found that sticking to its core values, even if it results in losing a customer, is good for business over the long-run. As it finished out the year 2015, Southwest reported that it had achieved its 43rd consecutive year of profitability and a record 4th quarter net income of $591 million ($2.2 billion for the year).

GROW PEOPLE AND WATCH GREATER PROFITABILITY FOLLOW

People drive results. The measurements related to people are the leading indicators to bottom-line performance results.

Aligned Momentum Key Indicators are people-oriented. To help discover and define in a measurable way those (not-easily-quantified) "people" measures, ask, "What will success look like?" and then, based on that vision, "What will progress look like?" And then, based on that view of progress, "What needs to stop?" "What needs to start?" "Who needs to be part of this?"

Capture not just the financial results but also the indicators that lead to the results you seek. For example, more frequent performance conversations and employee empowerment may lead to higher employee engagement and Nimble Decision-making, which may lead to on-time delivery *and* higher quality, which could lead to attracting larger volume orders from a customer who has greater trust in you, which would then bring about the financial bottom-line result desired. From this state of mind, The Pivot comes more naturally.

Profit, at best, is a lagging indicator of business performance; it is an outcome of your progress or lack of progress.

Financial statements are a history lesson. If you measure success by the financial bottom line alone, you will always be behind in knowing whether or not you are meeting your strategic objectives. And you may find it is too late to reap the full advantage of a Pivot that was actually needed a month or more ago.

This isn't to say that you will ignore profitability and focus on your people alone. Pause, gain Clarity, practice strategic focus, and then consider what you want to measure and the timing of each measurement. To gain and sustain momentum, you must measure progress, not just outcomes.

Techniques for reducing the risk of innovation

You want to innovate. You may know you need to innovate. The risk, mostly in terms of time and cost, that innovation takes may be deterring you. Even as a company, when you are grown up you anticipate a harder fall than when you were young. What do you do when you are in the process of growing people and innovating, but must show favorable financial bottom-line results quarterly? Both growing people and innovating can put pressure on short-term profitability. Innovation especially requires smart timing.

A meaningful way to envision innovation timing that can reduce your risk is the "S-Curve" of innovation, designed by Everett M. Rogers.[133] Successful companies purposively disrupt themselves with a continuous flow of innovation, resulting in momentum and even breakthrough business performance. Although Rogers' model is aimed at product innovation, it can be adapted to business performance, as depicted below:[134]

The Growth & Innovation "S" Curve

Are you stalled here?

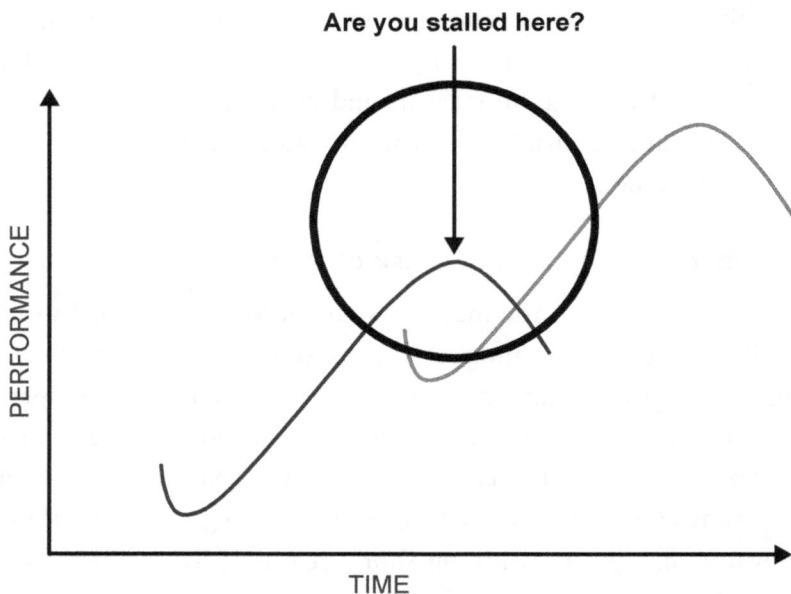

Figure 16: The Growth "S" Curve

The "S-Curve" (the plotted data creates a curve that looks like an "S") shows us that the innovation lifecycle, from idea to implementation, will require you to plan for a likely dip in business performance at the start of each cycle. It takes time for people to get on board and for the innovation to take shape.

Innovation is too often deferred for short-term thinking and fixed mindsets that have little patience for dips and do not tolerate failure. Plan innovation according to the "S-Curve" model, timing the start of a new innovation before the last one hits its peak to minimize the pain. Better, yet, do this and Pivot your mindset toward Aligned Momentum, which will allow for many small shifts that are initiated by those closest to the work. You'll see that it takes much less time for people to get on board—because they initiate the change. If there is a dip in business performance, it will be less drastic, because you are not trying to force ideas, effort or change on a turn-of-a-dime.

A SAFE CULTURE AND INNOVATION WORK TOGETHER

The leader who creates a safe place for ideas, a culture of Aligned Momentum, and does not expect innovations to be perfect will reap the benefits of more engaged employees and a successful company by every measure. One way to create this safe place is to share your own innovations or decisions that may not have worked out so well. For example:

Managers at 3M routinely reinforce the company's mistake-tolerant atmosphere by freely admitting their own goofs. In the *Harvard Business Review*, Richard Farson and Ralph Keyes discuss case studies of "successful failures." One study is of 3M and their "successful failure," Thinsulate®, a synthetic fiber thermal insulation used in clothing.

> Former CEO, L.D. DeSimone never hesitated to recount how he repeatedly tried to stop the development of Thinsulate. Luckily, DeSimone failed, and Thinsulate became one of the company's most successful products. By being so candid about his near blunder, DeSimone powerfully conveyed that it's okay to be wrong and to admit it when you are.[135]

Far from revealing weakness, admitting mistakes demonstrates a leader's self-confidence and openness. It helps forge closer ties with employees and colleagues. A blunder admitted is empathy earned.

> *Leaders who don't cover up their errors, and instead learn and share their learning, reveal themselves as human—they become people whom others can admire and identify with.*

To move forward as a company, innovation must be continual and it must become part of the culture.[136]

Success is about so much more than the financial bottom line

Whether you lead a mature business or a start-up, you must allow the qualities of being nimble and being focused to coexist. By now, it should be apparent that you get the best results, including financial bottom-line results, when you have these pieces in place:

- a bold, inspiring strategy (vision, direction, etc.);
- clearly communicating strategy;
- empowering employees, with clear alignment of their role with strategy, and authority to initiate change;
- a safe culture where everyone knows their manager wants them to be successful;
- creating supportive structural and social contexts;
- being focused *and* nimble;
- *valuing more than the financial bottom-line.*

People are critical to business success. In this book I have paid a lot of attention to people, for good reason. You won't experience the business momentum that is possible, and you'll struggle to orchestrate a Pivot, without valuing people. Create a safe place where each employee knows that their success is important, particularly to their manager. Safety doesn't mean complacency. Employees also must do their part to fit the level of performance required for the role, and in how they live company core values at work. Performance conversations and reviews, and assessing talent for purposes of having the right people positioned to execute a new strategy and for leadership succession, will prove more helpful to business performance and momentum when employees feel safe to speak out and step up.

Adapt talent to stay nimble

With every change in strategy, assess the people—the talent—in place to execute that strategy. Then train, promote and adjust in order to maintain alignment between each role and strategy and between each person's brand and the role they fill.

One of the most effective methods to identify the readiness of employees (your business's talent) for the future is talent assessment. In recent years, talent assessment, performance review, performance ratings and even the title of "manager" have all come under fire. Some companies, such as GE and Deloitte, have publically announced that they have dropped one or all of these.[137, 138, 139] Just like any communication, though, any of these methods of assessing people does not have to be negative. They can be used to build individual and team performance. Talent assessment, for example, does not need to pit one person against the next or result in the "rank and yank" that may have served GE and other companies well in the 1980s and 90s, and no longer serves them today. GE and other smart companies continue to assess talent, only now it's done without the ranking used for the purposes of cutting. Talent assessment is used to aid Talent Adaptability and leadership succession for the future. For the right fit, a company might assess an individual on a matrix with others, something like shown in Figure 17.

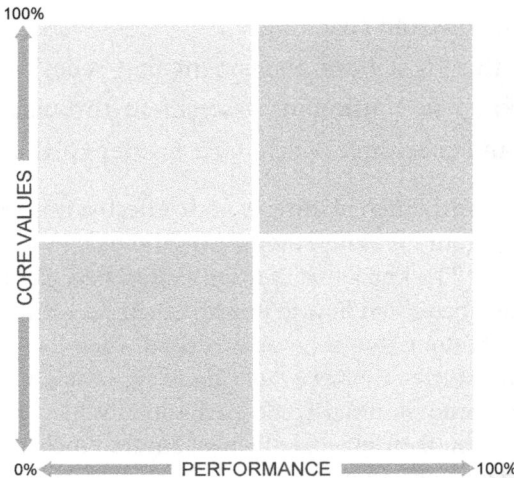

Figure 17: Sample Talent Assessment Matrix for Talent Adaptability/Right Fit

For succession the vertical axis might instead read "Potential," defined as motivation plus commitment plus ability (for the more advanced position).

What's different today is that the assessment leads to a plan of action aimed at growing people, not eliminating them (that said, if a person is not the right fit in your business they are likely better off in a business where they do. Talent assessment and performance reviews are most effective, and win-win, when done frequently over time. Frequent performance conversations, aimed at clear alignment with strategy, and empowerment to take best next steps, build momentum!

> *Pivot* **from** *traditional performance management*
> **to** *performance momentum.*

Great leaders understand that growth in performance happens through ongoing conversations with managers, teams, experts and a diverse group of peers, if possible.

GE has even changed the name of their assessment process to emphasize their Pivot toward Aligned Momentum. They now call the assessment "Differentiation" and the process includes ongoing performance conversations and coaching.[140]

Regarding the Pivot *from* assessment that relies on annual performance ranking, *to* continuous assessment through performance conversations and coaching, Welch, GE's former CEO, shares:

> [What makes] differentiation work so effectively is feedback and coaching. Your stars know they are loved and rarely leave. Those in the middle 70% know that they are appreciated, and they receive clear guidance about how to improve their performance.
> And the bottom 10% is never surprised when the conversation sometimes turns, after a year of candid appraisals, to moving on. No, they are not summarily shown the door. When differentiation is done right, their manager helps them find their next job with compassion and respect.[141]

The main aim of GE's new performance assessment process is to unlock constant improvement and real-time feedback from managers and employees.

Managers at GE are expected to have frequent conversations, named "touchpoints," with their employees on how far they are from their goals. Technology, and in particular a mobile app, supports both managers and employees with these touchpoints.

Now, by relying on frequent feedback rather than an annual rating, managers have a much richer set of data regarding an employee's unique contributions and impact throughout the year. For example, engineering executive, Leonardo Baldassarre and operations executive, Brian Finken reported to the *Harvard Business Review*, that "As a result, the year-end discussions are more meaningful and future-focused—and less fraught with expectations because they are simply part of an ongoing dialogue."[142] Be clear about the performance progress and results you expect from each role, again individually and as part of a team. Over time, seek Clarity about the future of the individual, regardless of what role they are in right now.

> *Performance conversations are best started even before you hire an individual to fill a role.*

To hire for talent and cultural fit, it is critical to prepare well for each new hire. This means assessing not only how a prospective employee is likely to perform individually, but assessing what the team dynamic might look like with the addition of this new person. Be clear about the performance you expect from them, the values you expect them to live and what they can expect will be communicated or done to help them succeed in their role and in your culture.

People change roles, but what is expected from a role should also change, based on what best serves the strategy. Once job descriptions are created, it's too easy to institutionalize them in the name of efficiency, freezing them in time, and hire new employees based on the needs stated in an outdated job description.

Revisit job descriptions for all roles affected by a change in strategy.

Do this well before hiring for the role and even when the role, as previously described, is filled.

Once you've hired and placed a person in their best-fitting role, then the most important component of having people positioned to execute brilliantly is frequent performance conversations, observation and measurement. The manager is the performance coach—the person who clearly cares about the individual employee's success, as well as the success of the team and company. This generates a win-win-win-win; the company, manager, team and individual employee all benefit.

MAINTAINING ALIGNMENT WHEN THE FACTS CHANGE

Maintaining alignment of roles with strategy makes no sense when your strategy is not (or is no longer) moving you toward your vision. Yet, it is a common leadership oversight. Either the strategy has not been updated, or it has not been communicated clearly.

Too often, Strategic Thinking about internal and external strengths, weaknesses, opportunities, threats and trends is performed, at most, once a year by the leadership team. Today, for most companies, the significant influences on their growth and performance change more frequently. At minimum, that means priorities for each quarter should be revisited and then communicated clearly before that quarter starts. Successful, growing companies revisit their strategy and plans at least once per quarter. They also have a well-orchestrated means to gather enough information to Pivot (to determine their best next moves) and to brilliantly execute (to move quickly from words to actions through their teams).

Fearing change, believing you are insulated from the changes around you, and doing nothing as a result, do not play forward toward success. Nokia stumbled for this reason.

Nokia did not maintain alignment when the facts changed. In fact they didn't adjust to facts, it seems, because they felt they knew better. Nokia's biggest mistake was in not making any change—for fear it might prove to be a mistake. If you are not familiar with Nokia, the company was a respected manufacturer of cellular phones. They held the number one position in this market for 14 years until Samsung took over the number one spot in the first quarter of 2012.

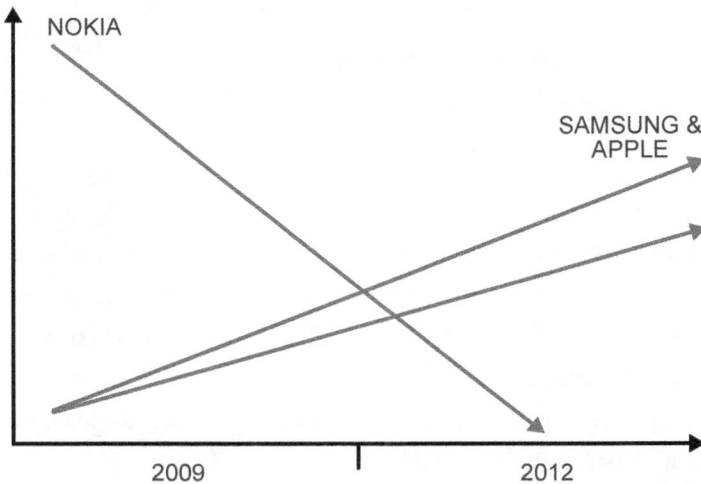

Figure 18: Global market share held by smartphone vendors since 2009 [143]

Here's what the smartphone market looks like today, but by operating system:

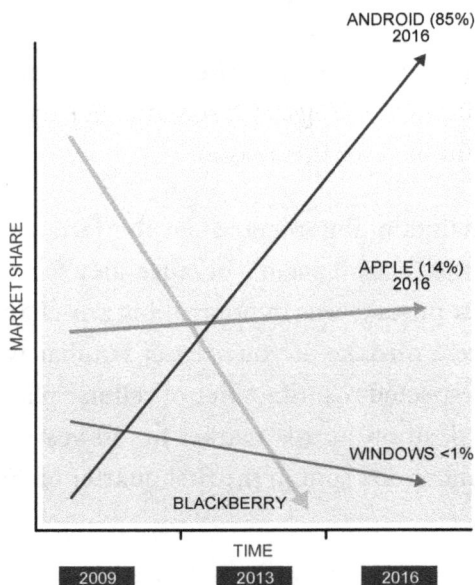

Figure 19: Worldwide smartphone operating system market share [144]

Nokia's strategy was to stay the course and do nothing, even as their market share continued to shrink. They chose not to adopt the Android operating system. Instead, the Nokia Lumia ran Microsoft's phone operating system, which was not well-adopted in the market and had a very small developer community. In the end, staying the course and avoiding change to avoid mistakes cost them everything because Apple and Android continued to adapt and change as market opportunities presented themselves.

Said Stephen Elop, former Nokia CEO, "We didn't do anything wrong, but somehow, we lost."[145] Nokia's huge stumble led to the acquisition of the company's phone assets by Microsoft for $7.9 billion in 2013. Over the next two years, Microsoft took a financial write-off of $7.6 billion and removed thousands of Nokia-related jobs.

If your vision is not clear, if you aren't seeing how you might innovate in your market or how you might become irrelevant if you don't innovate, take a look at a few models. The companies you look at do not have to be in your specific industry. Start with an aspect of your business that is most obvious to you.

Often, a winning innovation will simplify the experience for your customer. For a model of making the buying transaction simpler, look at Amazon.[146] For a model of making the product simpler for the buyer to use, look at Apple.[147] Do you aim to create more ease and speed in accessing a service? Look at Uber.[148] For a model of moving from a hierarchy to a more open structure of small teams in order to speed customer relationship and service communication, look to American Airlines and its social marketing control center. For a model of high employee retention and teamwork in a traditional industry, look to Nucor Steel.[149, 150] There are other models for these areas of innovation. For any other innovative idea there is also likely a model. And often the models are in another industry, so that when you implement your change you put yourself well ahead of your direct competitors.

Successful companies challenge their own status quo. They master staying relevant. Their every employee is empowered to discover facts and speak out to gain or maintain momentum for the company. As a successful leader you stay aware and never complacent. You are highly attuned to changes that impact your company or industry, even when—especially when—all's going well. You are always orchestrating a Pivot.

CHAPTER 8: KEY POINTS

1) The traditional measure of business success is "the bottom line," expressed in terms of net earnings or profits.

2) Too often the bottom-line result just happens, without a clear understanding of why.

3) Grow people and watch greater profitability follow.

4) People drive results. The measurements related to people are the leading indicators to bottom-line performance results.

5) To move forward as a company, innovation must be continual and it must become part of the culture.

6) Value more than the financial bottom line to reap performance and momentum benefits.

7) Adapt talent to stay nimble.

8) Successful companies challenge their own status quo.

9) Leaders are always orchestrating a Pivot.

PART 3

Take Action

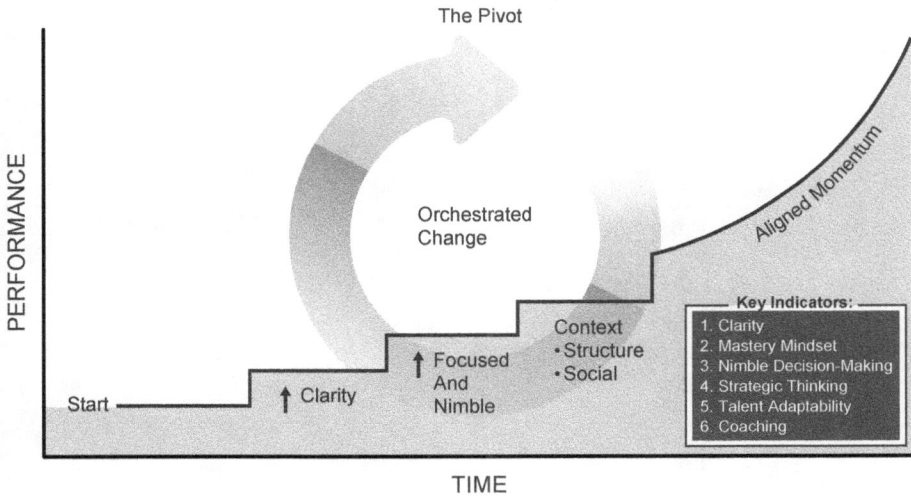

The Pivot

Orchestrated
Change

Aligned Momentum

PERFORMANCE

↑ Clarity

↑ Focused
And
Nimble

Context
• Structure
• Social

Start

TIME

Key Indicators:
1. Clarity
2. Mastery Mindset
3. Nimble Decision-Making
4. Strategic Thinking
5. Talent Adaptability
6. Coaching

CHAPTER 9

Aligned Momentum Pivots

---

*"We all have a sense of what is happening, a deep uneasiness.
But we have become habituated to the modern artifacts
of successful living, so we keep ourselves distracted and
entertained -- so we don't pay much attention."*

— *Peter Senge*

In this chapter I recommend Pivots to move your organization's culture toward Aligned Momentum. Scan these recommendations and then come back to them for support as you move forward. Take the assessment offered with this book to find your starting point. You'll find examples below based on typical results from a first assessment, and the recommendations for Pivots so that you can also take action right away. Prepare your business now so that you don't get disrupted or stalled in the future.

Disruption is now the norm in the world of business. And, so, you want to orchestrate change—to disrupt yourself in a planned and positive way—rather than be blindsided, stalled or eliminated.

Stalls are becoming more prevalent, typically of businesses that have lost their nimbleness. A September 2013 article in the *MIT Technology Review* noted that companies are bumped off the S&P 500 list more quickly now than in the past: in 1958, companies remained on that list for an average of 61 years, while today the average is only 18 years.[151]

Businesses of any size or type are at risk of a stall from complacency, or even going out of business due to becoming irrelevant. Perhaps you picture stalls happening only to a large, complex, public and bureaucratic global organization. You may be wearing "that doesn't apply to us" blinders.

It is the nimble business that stays in business—and grows.

ALIGNED MOMENTUM READINESS ASSESSMENT

The radar chart below displays typical readiness on a scale of 0–10 for the six Aligned Momentum Key Indicators, from a sample of companies grouped by size. While company size does not strictly dictate the results there are differences that make this grouping relevant. For example, a small company will not have many layers of management.

Reference this book often as you grow. Remember the advice given in the Introduction: there is a code in the Appendix that will give you access to an online Pivot/Aligned Momentum Assessment to take for your business.

The rest of this chapter walks you through the sample assessment results and provides recommended Pivots. There are sections within this chapter for each Aligned Momentum Key Indicator. Skim the material and then come back to it when you are ready to move forward. The recommendations are based on findings and observations that have served other companies. They may also serve you, now or in the future.

Aligned Momentum Readiness

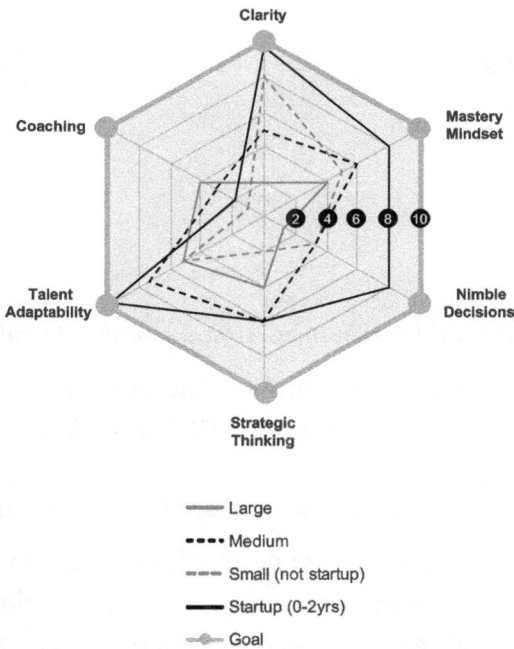

Figure 20: Sample Aligned Momentum Readiness Assessment chart

Business sizes reflected in this chart by number of employees are as follows:

1) large: over 1000 employees;
2) medium: from 101 to 1000 employees;
3) small (not a startup): up to 100 employees;
4) startup (0–2 years from start): 5 to 500 employees.

Large business: typical assessment results

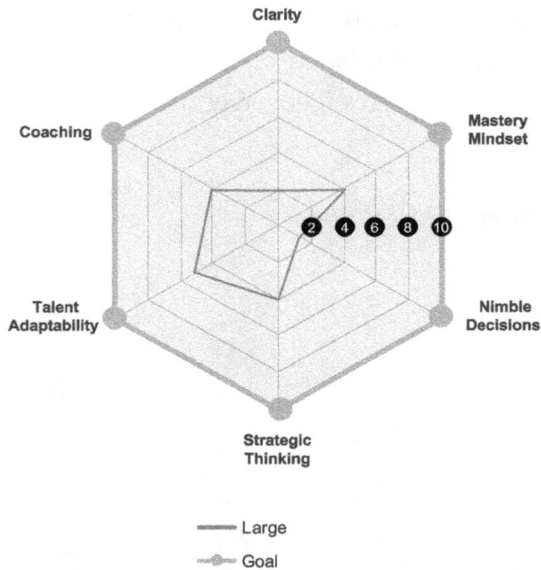

Figure 21: Large business: typical assessment results

The weakest Aligned Momentum Key Indicators for a large business tend to be Nimble Decision-making (2/10) and Clarity (2/10).

Will your results be similar? Assess to see if you and your team are:

1) maintaining curiosity; never allowing egos to close off awareness or personal and professional development;
2) staying ahead of advancements in technology that may lower the barrier to competitors in your industry or completely disrupt your industry and company;
3) keeping communication channels open in all directions.

Create a plan to Pivot toward or improve in these areas, as needed. When well-orchestrated by you, these small shifts and Pivots will accumulate with other Pivots described later in this chapter to build Aligned Momentum, and position your business for breakthroughs.

Medium-sized business: typical assessment results

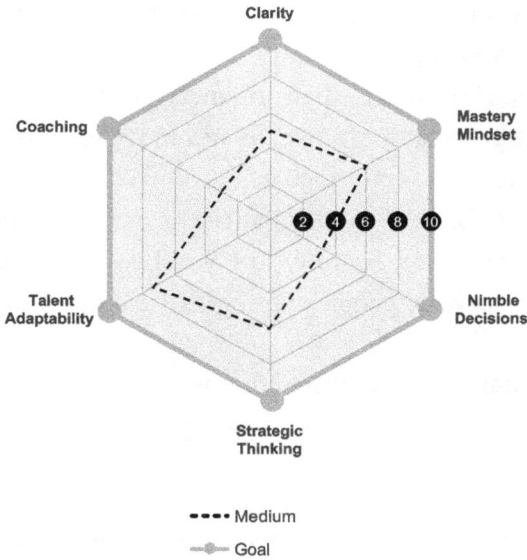

Figure 22: Medium-sized business: typical assessment results

The weakest Aligned Momentum Key Indicators for the typical medium-sized business are Nimble Decision-making (3/10) and Coaching (3/10).

It is not uncommon for a medium-sized business to experience a stall. Stalls happen when you aren't nimble. Stalls can also happen when your people aren't coached (rather than commanded or managed) to higher levels of performance. Revenues may remain flat for years or rise briefly then fall back. Or perhaps your revenue rises and falls with the cycle dictated by your local economy. Your business's bottom line may also suffer from complacency and other internal challenges, similarly to a larger enterprise, especially if your business has been operating for five years or more. Assess if you and your team are consistently:

1) valuing awareness, strategic focus and all voices, and allowing for mistakes during practice, so that innovation can happen;

2) measuring more than financial outcomes. Define what progress looks like, as you move toward Aligned Momentum—and track it;

3) holding ongoing performance conversations individually and as a team to ensure you have positioned and adapted your people's strengths (talent) to their best role;

4) maintaining the discipline to pause, gather facts, choose influencers wisely, and "play the movie" to support better decisions.

Small businesses: typical assessment results

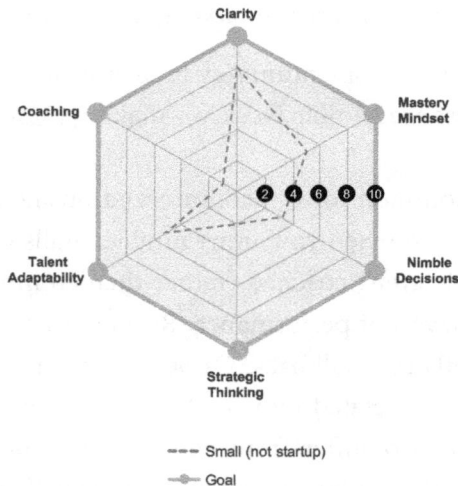

Figure 23: Small business: typical assessment results

The weakest Aligned Momentum Key Indicators for small businesses that are not startups are Coaching (1/10) Strategic Thinking (2/10), and Nimble Decision-making (3/10) Assess if you are:

1) clearly communicating the strategy;

2) creating quarterly themes to improve execution;
3) mutually defining priorities with the team, assigning accountability, and defining how progress will be tracked (and tracking frequently enough to adjust as needed);
4) visiting your company core values often. Ensuring you have the right people in the right seats, and are transforming a group of individuals performing separate tasks into a team in which they all share the same vision of the workplace culture;
5) establishing ongoing performance conversations.
   Your employees may be clear about the work they do. They may not be clear about the full value that their strengths can offer in their role and beyond their role. Pivot, as needed.

Startups: typical assessment results

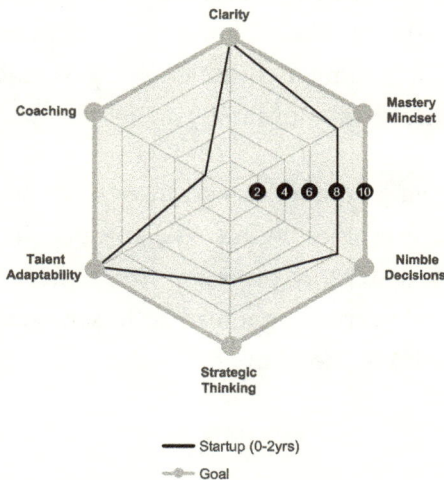

Figure 24: Startups: typical assessment results

The weakest Aligned Momentum Key Indicator in startups is Coaching (2/10). Startups typically have a core team that has a Mastery Mindset and is highly adaptable. As the team grows, especially if it is growing fast or pressured to bring in more experienced management, Aligned Momentum can suffer. Assess how you are doing with the following:

1) defining core values and weaving them into every aspect of your culture, including your hiring process;
2) including every person in performance conversations (coaching the founders and executives aids them and the organization);
3) ensuring accountability.

Prioritizing Aligned Momentum

With Aligned Momentum in place, you, your leadership team and all employees are ready for long-term success, extraordinary business momentum and the possibility of performance breakthroughs. But, prioritizing those strategic objectives that are aimed at people, with financial results likely not being realized immediately, can be a challenge to commit to. It takes a great leader.

Aligned Momentum allows your employees to best support your business's health. It is similar to the choice you make for your own health or for the health of your family.

Each of the following subsections addresses one of the six Aligned Momentum Key Indicators. While I've grouped the recommended Pivots and best next steps by company size, I encourage you to read through every section, reading ahead to lessen challenges and reap greater opportunities in the future.

PIVOT TO CLARITY

"Leaders communicate, however, as much through deeds as words."

— *Carnes Lord*

Clarity—getting clear, being clear, and ensuring that everyone else is also clear—is an art that great leaders master. The market changes swiftly, making *getting clear* a challenge. The organization's structure and composition also changes, making *being clear* a challenge. Ensuring that managers are adept at Clarity and willing to frequently and clearly communicate effectively may also be a challenge.

Too often a lack of progress toward strategic objectives can be traced back to a lack of Clarity.

- What do you want? Why?
- What will reaching for what you want do for you (and, in this case, the company)?
- How does what you want align with your role?
- What behavior from you and what performance in your role will best align with the company's strategic objectives, purpose, values and vision?
- How does what each employee wants align with the role they are in (or moving into)?
- What behavior from them and performance in their role will best align with the company's strategic objectives, purpose, values and vision?

A lack of Clarity results in misunderstanding. Misunderstandings can all too often cause unnecessary and sometimes debilitating pain or loss. If people do not understand what "We" (everyone in the company) are trying to achieve, and their part in that, they will not make the right choices, judgments or decisions.

As you Pivot toward achieving Aligned Momentum, misunderstandings will still inevitably occur, but you can prepare for these. People may have grown accustomed to certain ways and many will not yet be adaptable to, or trust, change. This is one reason why during any change you must communicate more than you may be accustomed to. As you communicate, check that your employees have the current strategy and priorities securely in mind, perhaps by a simple method of seeing if they can repeat key messages back to you. If you are told that others are mimicking you saying these words, it is a good thing. It means those words are now clear and running through their heads. When people are clear not only about what is expected *of* them but also about what's in it *for* them, you've hit the jackpot. Patrick Lencioni refers to Clarity as a key element of organizational health:

> Organizational health is about making a company function effectively by building a cohesive leadership team, establishing real clarity among those leaders, communicating that clarity to everyone within the organization and putting in place just enough structure to reinforce that clarity going forward.[152]

You cannot achieve Aligned Momentum when there is a lack of Clarity. You need to Pivot.

Pivots to greater Clarity, by company size

Two Clarity Pivots for large businesses

With 1,000 or more employees, cascading a message through hierarchical levels or broadcasting that message out to the edges of your open organization often doesn't accomplish the desired result. Achieving Clarity takes more than a single, one-way broadcast to all: it requires each employee to be open and ready to receive that communication. It also requires that the employee feels safe to work with their manager.

With Clarity, each employee knows what outputs, level of performance and teamwork is expected from the role they are in; what values and behaviors they are expected to live at work; who cares about them and their work; and what's in it for them.

> *As you master Clarity, also Pivot managers **from** managing work **to** building on the strengths of their employees and empowering them to deliver great work.*

Model the way for managers, train them, coach them or provide a coach, and reward them for growing the people they manage.

> *Another Pivot is **from** an "us" vs."them" dynamic between units, divisions, departments or teams, **to** a "we" mindset that reaches all areas of the organization.*

Many organizations find themselves with an "us vs. them" cultural stalemate, indicating that silos have cropped up within the company. In *Turn This Ship Around!* (2013), L. David Marquet talks about this challenge and his solution.[153] When Marquet was Captain of the *USS Santa Fe* he faced the issue of departmental silos along with "us vs. them" finger-pointing. If a part did not arrive on time, it was "they" (the parts department) that were blamed by "us" (the service crew).

Captain Marquet created a new policy that was made clear by its theme: "There is no 'they' on the *Santa Fe*." Everyone on the submarine was required to use only the term "we", if what they were communicating was to be heard and acted upon. The *Santa Fe* moved from ranking at the bottom of well-operating crews to the top, achieving the highest retention and operational standings in the Navy, and became a model for others. According to Captain Marquet, "building trust and taking care of your people is a mechanism for clarity."

A Clarity Pivot for medium-sized businesses

Clarity is critical to getting the right things executed brilliantly. You have less wiggle room and typically lower cash reserves than a large business. Poor execution can create a stall, or worse. You may struggle to hold onto your stars with the larger companies wooing them.

> *Each employee must be very clear about what is expected, who cares, and what's in it for them. Pivot* **from** *only annual reviews that aren't effective and often deferred (then deferred again),* **to** *more frequent performance conversations.*

When Clarity has been achieved, you'll better engage your best people and grow, move or replace those who are pulling down the team.

Performance conversations work like this:

- Every month or week—depending on the nature of the work—each employee sends a message to their manager listing their top 1–5 accomplishments (addressing previously set priorities) and the top 1–5 priorities they propose for this next period.[154]
- The manager then reviews and responds within 24 hours. The manager may have a brief "all good!" response, if the employee's stated accomplishments and priorities are right on track, or else set up some one-on-one time with the employee to explore best next steps.
- Leverage a communication technology that is appropriate for your company, creates a set deadline, and offers reminders. Even if a one-on-one session is required to ensure Clarity, this can be done via technology if meeting live is not possible.

Performance conversations improve Clarity. There are also other benefits, not the least of which is better execution of strategy. The employee is setting up an intention, which builds their sense of responsibility and commitment to what they said they would do. The manager grows as a coach and more effectively executes strategy through their team.

A Clarity Pivot for small businesses

In a small business, it's common to presume that all your employees are clear about what is most important. Still, there may be a lack of Clarity. Employees may be doing their best, but not doing what matters. Their work may not be aligned with strategic objectives. Or what they are doing could be more efficient or effective with innovation. Employees may be relying on what seemed to work for them in the past or following exactly what was done by the person before them. There may be a lack of collaboration and teamwork.

> For employees to be clear about how they can best align with strategy, Pivot **from** individuals doing their work in isolation, **to** a team aimed at continuous improvement or even the next breakthrough.

Many companies reap huge gains in Clarity from a simple, short daily meeting, most often called a "huddle." (I describe huddles in detail in the Nimble Decision-making section of this chapter.) A daily huddle will encourage collaboration related to what work is to be done and how it is to be done. It can also be a venue for sharing values, and appreciating how they show up at work.

Clarity grows for you, the leader, as you prepare to communicate with your team. Clarity becomes available to employees as they feel safe to speak out and ask for clarification or support.

Two Clarity Pivots for startups

In a startup, there are two main obstacles to Clarity. One obstacle is the speed of change, which creates a challenge in getting current, relevant facts out to every employee swiftly.

> *To get current, relevant information to each employee, Pivot* **from** *each person operating on the basis of what they feel is the shared strategy,* **to** *a daily huddle that brings new facts to light.*

Sharing facts daily allows everyone to regroup around a new strategy or priority. Daily huddles also help you build and sustain the work culture that you want.

Another obstacle for Clarity in a startup is a leadership team that is not cohesive. Especially as the business grows and adds more people, executive mindsets, actions, and communications can be at odds. Is every active decision-maker and influencer on the same page? Or do you have a variety of values and objectives made by decision-makers and influencers who only share the financial outcome portion of the vision?

> *Pivot to Clarity* **from** *individual executives aimed at different priorities,* **to** *a leadership team with a shared commitment to strategy and quarterly priorities.*

PIVOT TO MASTERY MINDSET

*"Everyone thinks of changing the world, but
no one thinks about changing himself."*

— *Leo Tolstoy*

A Mastery Mindset is present when one is continuously seeking to increase their contribution at work, in how they are behaving, and through the work they do.

In *Mindset* (2006), Carol Dweck refers to a Mastery Mindset as a "Growth Mindset" and compares this to a "Fixed Mindset."[155] (The value of these ideas for your business's social context was discussed in Chapter 7.) The table below will give you an idea of what to look for and where a Pivot might be needed:

FIXED MINDSET	GROWTH MINDSET
Intelligence is static	**Intelligence can be developed**
Leads to a desire to *look smart* and therefore a tendency to	Leads to a desire to *learn* and therefore a tendency to
• Avoid challenges	• Embrace challenges
• Give up easily due to obstacles	• Persist despite obstacles
• See effort as fruitless	• See effort as path to mastery
• Ignore useful feedback	• Learn from criticism
• Be threatened by others' success	• Be inspired by others' success

*Figure 25: Fixed vs Growth Mindset, adapted from
Carol Dweck's book, Mindset (2006)*

Aligned Momentum helps people step up, speak out, and build their Mastery Mindsets even if their minds have been fixed in previous environments.

For some of us, a Mastery Mindset begins in childhood when an environment supports learning, choosing, trying, and making mistakes.

Most of us, however, have been so exposed to rules, ratings, and reprimands that we have learned how to stay comfortable, and especially how to never look bad. Luckily, it is never too late to Pivot toward a Mastery Mindset. Pivoting *to* a Mastery Mindset later in life can be a rewarding experience, even at the point of initial awareness and choice to change. This will require many small shifts over time, and patience. In *Mastery* (2013), Robert Greene points out the following:

> With those who stand out by their later mastery, they experience this inclination more deeply and clearly than others. They experience it as an inner calling. It tends to dominate their thoughts and dreams. They find their way, by accident or sheer effort, to a career path in which this inclination can flourish. This intense connection and desire allows them to withstand the pain and the process—the tedious hours of practice and study, the inevitable setbacks, the endless barbs from the envious. They develop a resiliency and confidence that others lack.[156]

Greene is referring to the experience of developing a Mastery Mindset later in life. Becoming aware and more clear about what you want is inspiring. A powerful desire to Pivot from what you are experiencing today and what you expect to experience with a Mastery Mindset aids you as you grow. As momentum builds, the desire gets stronger and although, typically, your biggest challenges happen right before your goal is met, your developing Mastery Mindset can pull you through. You now have the mindset that helps you break through any resistance.

It is while in a Mastery Mindset that breakthroughs can occur.

Pivots to Mastery Mindsets, by company size

A Mastery Mindset Pivot for large businesses

In a large business, especially one with many hierarchical layers, people sometimes lose their sense of value, saying they feel like "cogs in a machine." A person who has become resigned to being a "cog" is not in a Mastery Mindset at work. They may have entered the company eager to excel, and then have become complacent or even engaged. They are not performing at their best and they may be weighing down the team.

Those who have a Mastery Mindset cannot flourish in such a culture. They will leave a workplace rather than become complacent. They seek ways to better their contribution every day. They feel that the work they do is meaningful for their lives and for the company. They are both competent and engaged when in a culture where mastery is alive. That is, a culture with Aligned Momentum.

What makes the difference between a person who is uninspired and feeling like a "cog" and one who is inspired and upping their contribution every day and in every way available to them? The number one difference is their manager. You've probably heard the phrase: "People join a company, and leave a person." That person is often their manager.

When managers also have a Mastery Mindset, they are more likely to express appreciation for the value others bring to the company. They also live the company core values. And they do what it takes to help each person grow, and execute brilliantly so that everyone succeeds.

> *Pivot* **from** *fixed mindsets* **to** *Mastery Mindsets,*
> *throughout the organization.*

Two best next steps toward building Mastery Mindsets throughout your organization could be:

1) Take the pulse of managers—all managers, including those on the leadership team who likely manage managers. If they too started out engaged and over time have become complacent or disengaged, then this is a cultural issue that starts with the tone at the top and what has been rewarded or tolerated over time.

2) Coach, train and measure the performance of managers, not just for managing work, but also for core values and their ability to be the person who helps others grow.

Without a Mastery Mindset helping each individual hold themselves accountable for living the company core values, your organization can suffer. The Wells Fargo scandal in 2016 lends an example of what happens when Mastery Mindsets are not in place and when Fixed Mindsets allow people to do or tolerate unethical actions that only accomplish one thing: to make that person look good (in this case, by meeting quotas for the number of accounts per bank customer, being a team player, etc.). Momentum toward financial outcomes at any cost was the game plan and core values were ignored.[157, 158]

Wells Fargo's stated core values are:

1) People as a competitive advantage
2) Ethics
3) What's right for customers
4) Diversity and inclusion
5) Leadership

Yet, to gain momentum toward financial outcomes (clearly, at any cost), employees were told to meet quotas that were not reasonable. Specifically, employees were expected to reach an "eight is great" quota, which meant reaching eight accounts per account holder (when the average across all banks is three accounts per account holder). To reach this level, employees were asked to create fraudulent accounts. In a letter to employees, CEO John Stumpf called the employees' actions "inconsistent with the values and culture we strive to live up to every day." Stumpf held the position of top leadership. An individual who is not orchestrating toward strategy (which includes core values) is not leading.

Over a five-year period 5,300 people were let go for these acts. This included branch and regional managers—but no senior leaders under Stumpf were negatively impacted immediately (repercussions are still unfolding as this book is going to publication). They kept their salaries, bonuses and shares, which had increased in value buoyed by the revenues from fraudulent cross-selling. Stumpf was not fired, but he did retire from his roles of CEO and Chairman. The board, at Mr. Stumpf's own recommendation, had previously decided he should relinquish $41million in unvested equity, one of the biggest-ever forfeitures of pay by a bank chief. He still retires with tens of millions of dollars earned during roughly 35 years at the bank.

The negative outcomes from this lack of Mastery Mindset include a culture that is damaged and broken consumer trust.

Two Mastery Mindset Pivots for medium-sized businesses

A medium-sized business often has yet to identify and build up those employees with Mastery Mindsets. These are the people who are ready to step up to mentor others, innovate, and more.

> Pivot **from** *no attention to mindsets,* **to** *tapping the power of employees with a Mastery Mindset to mentor others and innovate.*

To nurture a Mastery Mindset it is also important to equalize the rewards for achievement and advancement. Achievement in this context means to excel as a subject matter expert and as a mentor to others. Advancement is also rewarded. The difference when compared to a traditional approach is that advancement is not required to realize greater reward within the company.

> *Pivot **from** promotion only with positional advancement, **to** career paths that reward achievement and advancement equally.*

A Mastery Mindset at all levels also removes the risks of stalls caused by perfectionism or holding oneself out as a flawless know-it-all (also known as "CEO Disease").[159] *Nimble leaders grow themselves, not just their businesses.*

To orchestrate these Pivots consider these three best next steps:

1) Build leadership capabilities at all levels.
2) Reward achievements as one masters what matters in your company; be careful to not only reward positional advancement.
3) Practice the patience and humility required to give people at every level the space to grow and make mistakes as they do so.

A Mastery Mindset Pivot for small businesses

You've likely hired for skill and your employees do care about mastering that skill. Now, consider how a collaborative Mastery Mindset grows not only the individual but also each individual's contribution as a member of the team, a mentor, and even a coach to peers.

A Pivot *to* Mastery Mindsets in a small business involves greater investment in team building and focusing on how individuals are *being* and not just on how they are *performing* the work. This includes you, the owner or CEO.

> *Pivot **from** a focus only on talent **to** also nurturing and rewarding desired behavior.*

A great example of a small business with a strong Mastery Mindset is The World Famous Pikes Place Fish Market in Seattle.[160] After coming close to bankruptcy in 1986, the fish market owner, John Yokoyama and his employees, with guidance from consultant Jim Bergquist, decided to become "world famous." They did so by changing their way of doing business. Their Pivot was in how they were *being*, individually, with team members and with prospective customers.

The team created a culture with Aligned Momentum, including daily communication of targets and their intentions to meet them (Clarity), coaching moments between any two employees including the owner (Coaching), and a weekly meeting that included declarations of their path toward mastery both professionally and personally (Mastery Mindset).

Four years later, they were featured repeatedly in the national media and television shows and members of the team are asked to speak at conferences around the world, for a handsome fee. The store is now a popular tourist destination in Seattle, attracting up to 10,000 daily visitors. While the size of the store has not grown, its revenue and profits have grown significantly.[161]

Many team members have been with the company for years. While highly skilled, they maintain a Mastery Mindset. If you watch them set up (or join them in setting up, as I did), you will see them mastering the presentation of fish in cases, the speed of set up, cutting fish, interacting with prospective customers and team members, and more. For more than a decade they have met weekly to share what professional and personal mastery they are focused on that week. They also share appreciation freely, and ask for help or offer help openly. A Mastery Mindset is the key factor in their continued success.

Two Mastery Mindset Pivots for startups
As new people enter a startup, especially if they are well-experienced in other environments...

> *Pivot* **from** *relying on how it was done where I worked before* **to** *"what will work best here?"*

Adopting a Mastery Mindset will help them be successful.

It is also critical for all key decision makers in a startup to be on a path toward mastering business and leadership.

––––––––––––––––

No matter what size of business you lead, nurturing a Mastery Mindset in your culture requires that you establish milestones for quick wins as mastery improves, and celebrate meeting each milestone. The team at The World Famous Pikes Place Fish Market observes, supports and celebrates each individual's improvement in the personal and professional mastery they've declared just the week before.

Tom Peters and Robert Waterman found while researching *In Search of Excellence* (2004) that setting really high "stretch" targets and rewarding only the ultimate goal led to under-performance.[162] The absence of quick wins or any acknowledgment of effort toward a stretch goal caused the employee to "feel like a loser."

> *Pivot* **from** *unrealistic stretch goals,* **to** *performance systems that support people with more opportunities to feel they are winners, and reinforce winning with celebration.*

Peter's and Waterman's findings support the old adage, "Nothing succeeds like success."

PIVOT TO NIMBLE DECISION-MAKING

"The inflection point.. [is] the point at which a curve stops one way and starts curving the other way. So it is with strategic business matters, too. An inflection point occurs where the old strategic picture dissolves and gives way to the new, allowing the business to ascend to new heights."

— *Andrew S. Grove*

Decisions and judgment calls are nimble when you are clear about strategy, have gathered the minimum necessary information, consulted people with expertise to offer, and coordinated with those who can influence or who will be impacted by that decision or call.

Here, I will use the word "decisions" to cover fully researched and modeled decisions as well as real-time judgment calls.

Both types of decisions can be made "too fast," missing the minimum necessary depth, prep, future-look and collaboration. Even when the call includes just you, not having the depth or prep you need to play the movie forward can result in bad, and certainly not nimble, decisions.[163]

Pivots to more Nimble Decision-making, by company size

A Nimble Decision-making Pivot for large businesses
Two common obstacles that hinder or block nimble decisions in large businesses are employees who are not clear about strategic objective(s) and little, poor or conflicting communication between business units and functional departments (aka "silos").

A few questions to ask if you think you are facing these obstacles include:

- Are there critical dynamics that only those closest to the situation are seeing right now, and are not incorporated into decision-support models?
- Do the data and assumptions presented in models support decisions only on the basis that the past is an accurate predictor of the future?
- Do those compiling the data that supports decision-making understand the company's vision and strategic objectives and have it incorporated into the data?
- Do those supplying support know that you value objectivity and are not looking for them to massage the numbers so that you see what they perceive you want to see?
- Regarding judgment calls, which happen instantly without modeling or compilation, are you or others making these calls missing the benefit of quick collaboration and strategic focus?

*Pivot **from** meetings that reinforce silos in thought or function **to** meetings that bring more heads and more diverse minds together collaboratively to expand both awareness and decision-making support.*

Your best next step may be a daily huddle. A daily huddle is a meeting of 15 minutes or less and provides awareness, strategic alignment, and some collaboration.

Daily huddle (or daily scrum)

If you are not running a quick daily meeting, you are missing an opportunity for greater momentum. It seems counterintuitive to expect that adding a team meeting of 15 minutes or less every day will increase productivity. Done right, a daily huddle will not only reduce the time to delivery, it will also increase awareness, alignment and often improves engagement. There are, in general, two types of daily meetings: A daily scrum relevant to project-based work such as software development, and a daily huddle relevant to all roles.

A daily *scrum*, facilitated by the Scrum Master, requires every person to answer the following three questions when it is their turn and without prompting:

1) What did you do since the last meeting?
2) What will you do today?
3) What impediments are you facing?

A daily *huddle* requires every person to answer these three questions when it is their turn and without prompting:

1) What's up?
2) KPI (progress metrics, critical numbers) progress?
3) Stucks?

Each attendee's "KPIs" ("Key Performance Indicators") are those 1–3 progress metrics relevant to one's goals typically for a quarter or year, prioritized for this week or month, and aligned with the company's strategic objectives. Use the terminology that fits your company. A "Stuck" is any obstacle, bottleneck or issue getting in the way of progress. These are called "impediments" in a daily scrum.

High-performing teams may incorporate values into their huddles, such as through shout-outs and stories about a team member exhibiting core values the prior day. Huddles are short—no longer than 15 minutes—and no problems are solved during these meetings. If an issue arises, those who need to get together after the meeting to solve it are identified, and then the huddle keeps moving.

You'll want the huddle facilitated, at least to start. The facilitator is there to keep the meeting moving along, note those who are in follow-up meetings to solve problems that have arisen, and if possible, record progress.

Huddles move along at a crisp pace, so consider leveraging technology to capture details. Each person can input their answers to the huddle questions prior to the actual huddle and an audio recording of the meeting itself can be used to capture the details.

A live meeting is always best, when possible. Huddles can also be held via conference call or webcam sharing. In larger organizations, these meetings consist of teams of no more than 20 people, and then a delegate from each team joins a cross-team or managers' huddle held later that day. The benefits for organizations with a daily huddle discipline are proven, not just in productivity (including significantly fewer interruptions throughout the day and avoiding unnecessary "fires" that can be started by a simple misunderstanding), but also in connection, inclusion, learning, preparation, appreciation, and engagement. A quick daily meeting could be the one main Pivot you need to make to become more nimble.

I recommend a daily huddle for any size and type of organization. The Ritz Carlton Leadership Center maintains a discipline of huddles and says, "Can you imagine an American football team making it to the Super Bowl without ever having a huddle? The huddle is a critical part of the game. It's used to communicate strategy, to make sure players understand their role, and to inspire a winning attitude. Players huddle many times throughout the game in order to keep the team informed and unified."[164]

A Nimble Decision-making Pivot for medium-sized businesses

A common obstacle to Nimble Decision-making is access to complete, accurate and timely information. Often even your business intelligence technology is not helping you, because the data is not there or data is presented in a way that you can't rely on.

The crux of the issue is not likely your technology, it is how people are using it (or not using it). If people understood how correct use of technology would lead to more Nimble Decision-making and how more Nimble Decision-making will help the company, and them in it, then they would likely make the changes needed. They, too, would be committed to everyone in the company having access to complete, accurate and timely information relevant to their roles.

Do your employees know what information is needed? Do they understand how to transform the data they've collected into more meaningful information, or have access to someone who can help with that? Do they have a clear channel to communicate information, and can they get the information out to all who would be influenced or impacted by it, rather than having to (try and) reach someone closer to the top of an organizational hierarchy?

> Pivot **from** *decision-quality information only at the top,* **to** *leaders throughout the organization being empowered to initiate change and to understand how the data they are responsible for fits into brilliant execution of strategy.*

To be clear, "leaders throughout the organization" are those employees who others follow, who live the company core values and who are aligned with strategy. This does not mean that you are granting final decision-making authority to those who aren't positioned to set strategic direction for the company. What this Pivot will do, though, is support Clarity and sophistication in decision-making. Questions being asked will become more strategically focused, and judgment calls will improve.

Best next steps in this Pivot include:

- *Talent assessment, training and mentoring*
  Even if you hire consultants for your more complex decisions, ensure that you have employees involved in the work and mentored in how these decisions are made.

- *Communication plan for strategic objectives*
  Too many companies still strategically assess and plan at the top, but only communicate the budget to those

closest to the work. Until you more clearly communicate strategy, employees are really given no option other than to do "more of what we did before that seemed to be okay—at least we didn't fail." That mentality does not enable Nimble Decision-making.

A Nimble Decision-making Pivot for small businesses

A small business owner may be the only *strategic* decision maker. But you are not the only one making judgment calls, and these also impact on your business's health.

> Pivot **from** *the presumption that the judgment calls made by every employee during their day only need to be addressed if something goes wrong,* **to** *empowering your employees with the strategic focus to make better calls.*

Empowering employees so that they are making better judgment calls or supporting more Nimble Decision-making requires you to clearly communicate the strategy and not only task-level priorities for the day or week.

A Nimble Decision-making Pivot for startups

Nimble does not simply mean acting quickly in the context of decisions.

> Pivot **from** *doing everything in the immediate, including how you make decisions,* **to** *a more disciplined approach that includes slowing down for better decision-making.*

Nimble Decision-making requires pausing long enough, asking enough questions, and considering diverse points of view to gain awareness and perspective. You will look forward into the future to remember the strategy, before coming back to the present and choosing the best next step. Also, strengthen discernment through learning who to have near you to influence you or to provide expertise. *Know-it-alls are not Nimble Decision-makers.*

PIVOT TO STRATEGIC THINKING

"Myth: A Manager's job is to come up with answers."

— *Jack Stack*

Strategic Thinking is a skill used in strategic focus. Strategic Thinking is also an Aligned Momentum Key Indicator. I sum it up as: "play the movie" before choosing the best next step in the present. While Strategic Thinking is a skill used in strategic focus, strategic focus is a method to stay nimble while also being focused, and was discussed in Chapter 6: Focused and Nimble. Both the skill of Strategic Thinking and the strategic focus methodology require that strategy becomes a filter in one's mind to support them in taking the best next step.

If you search for definitions of Strategic Thinking in business you'll find something like these: "The ability to come up with effective plans in line with an organization's objectives within a particular economic situation" and "To help business managers review policy issues, perform long term planning, set goals and determine priorities, and identify potential risks and opportunities."[165] These are not wrong, per se, yet they imply that this type of thinking happens only at the top.

Strategic Thinking will serve you and your business if it is a skill that empowers every employee. It can help any person make better decisions (including judgment calls and day-to-day choices), to innovate and to initiate change. Strategic Thinking becomes part of doing one's best work.

Not everyone is in a strategic role, but everyone can improve their proficiency in Strategic Thinking. The table below provides a few reasons why doing so will shift your organization toward the more nimble ways of Aligned Momentum:

Why Strategic Thinking

STRATEGIC THINKING	
Leads to	**Avoids**
• Future-based	• Reactive
• Curious	• Isolated
• Steward resources	• No investment in future
• Take risks	• Maintain status quo
• Prioritize what's most important	• No priorities
• Nimble	• Rigid
• Learning & growing	• Complacent or knows it all
• Innovative	• Stick with what's been done before

Figure 26: Strategic Thinking: Leads to and Avoids

Pivots to effective Strategic Thinking, by company size

Two Strategic Thinking Pivots for large businesses
You can weave Strategic Thinking into your training efforts that are aimed at being more innovative. Include all leaders and managers. When the leaders or managers that employees trust are undergoing training, and modeling the way, training transforms into knowledge sharing, and can reap benefits throughout the organization. Training leaders and managers, who then share this knowledge in all their communications, especially with their teams, is often referred to as a "train-the-trainer" process. To make this effective for weaving Strategic Thinking through your culture consider the following Pivots:

> *Pivot **from** believing that strategic thinking is only done by senior executives, **to** committing to Strategic Thinking training for all employees.*

Your best next step will be to start planning for Strategic Thinking training and identifying the leaders and managers who will be the best models.

> *Pivot **from** tapping every minute of managers' and experts' time with problems, **to** engaging managers and experts in the train-the-trainer program.*

This will help managers delegate more problem solving to employees and will free up managers and experts to be more proactive.

Why train managers first? Because managers, in a culture committed to Aligned Momentum, create the safe place where any individual on their team knows that their manager has their back and cares about their success.

A Strategic Thinking Pivot for medium-sized businesses.

Usually a lack of Strategic Thinking shows up in poor execution. Yes, this happens in large businesses too, but usually there is someone ready to step up right below them—those executing also think strategically and ask questions about strategy if they are not clear.

In medium-sized businesses a gap in communication between those with knowledge of strategy and those without will bring your business to a stall. In some cases, senior executives, especially if previously from a larger enterprise, may be too used to staying on the strategic level. They are clear about the strategy, but are not clear enough about how work is executed in your business. They are not using Strategic Thinking, which requires awareness and curiosity, and looking to the future with the express intention of taking the best next step now. Instead they are stuck in the big picture. They may also be stuck in a know-it-all state based on what they've learned elsewhere. As such, they may be failing at execution of your business strategy.

Why mention execution when our focus is on Strategic Thinking? Because if there is a significant gap between those with the strategy in mind (but not yet shared in an actionable way) and those needing to execute it, then it can be difficult to effectively communicate strategy.

> *Pivot* **from** *too wide a communication gap between those in the know about strategy and those who execute it,* **to** *empowering all with Strategic Thinking and the knowledge that is needed to ensure brilliant execution of strategy.*

Best next steps include:

- Train and model the way for more effective communication, aiming toward Clarity throughout the organization.
- Measure individual (e.g. each executive) and company progress toward better execution.
- Ask questions, and be open to receive questions, in meetings that will develop Strategic Thinking and reinforce the connection between strategy and execution.

With Strategic Thinking available to every employee you'll narrow the gap between strategy and execution, and be poised for brilliant execution of strategy.

A Strategic Thinking Pivot for small businesses

In a small business, the most effective step toward improved Strategic Thinking starts with you. Are you taking the time to think both strategically and with execution in mind to determine the best next step?

> *Pivot* **from** *separating strategy and execution* **to** *consistently linking them together in every thought before every action.*

Whether you use the phrase "play the movie," or start with a process that requires thinking forward, such as when you want to innovate, you want to slow down to first look forward before making a hasty decision or judgment call. Once you have this down pat you can model the way for your employees.

Two Strategic Thinking Pivots for startups

As you've learned, I am not referring to a turn-on-a-dime pivot in strategy when I speak of The Pivot or Strategic Thinking. Now is the time to weave Strategic Thinking, and every aspect of Aligned Momentum, into your culture.

You are likely already following a proven process to gain traction for your product or service.

> *Pivot **from** a mindset of turn-on-a-dime pivots, **to** a mindset of Aligned Momentum—including Strategic Thinking and The Pivot.*

Create and nurture an intentional culture; a culture that has the look and feel you desire, and that you want to work in. When considering who to select to be on your team, you may start with your funding sources and others with a vested voice in your company's strategic direction. But there's so much more that matters to meeting strategic objectives and realizing your vision. To "not grow up ugly," you must be intentional about culture. You want to attract and retain people who will be an active part of building a company that you continue to be excited about.

> *Pivot **from** inattention to culture, **to** intentionally creating and nurturing the culture that has the qualities you desire, and that you want to work in.*

Frequently revisit talent assessment, making sure an employee's core values and performance contribution align with your company's strategy.

If used incorrectly, assessments and reviews can become part of what you may refer to as "becoming a corporate bureaucracy" and I refer to as "growing up ugly." This happens when one or more of the following are true:

1) The only purpose of HR is (litigation-protection) record-keeping.
2) The manager is out of touch with all of the employees they manage.
3) A manager is misaligned with corporate core values or strategic direction.
4) An employee does not trust that their manager cares about their success.
5) The manager has no manager or outside coach developing them.
6) There is no Clarity or consistency in the review or assessment process.
7) The employee is not clear about what is (or was) expected of them.
8) The process has become more like an audit—focused on weaknesses.
9) Ratings are shared in a counterproductive way, demotivating employees.

Used correctly, assessment and review tools, processes and models support Nimble Decision-making about talent. This is a great way to weave Strategic Thinking into the minds of all hiring managers, as well as all employees.

PIVOT TO TALENT ADAPTABILITY

"The difficulty lies not in developing new ideas, but in escaping the old ones, which ramify, for those brought up as most of us have been, into every corner of our minds."

— *John Maynard Keynes*

Talent Adaptability applies to individuals and teams; both must be open and flexible to change. Great companies align strengths based on what is needed to best execute strategy, which means the needs of the future and not necessarily what led to the present.

In the most nimble organizations it is easy and natural to move people to new roles or switch up their job descriptions and expectations within a team, or move them to a new team. The changes are based on where they will best serve the company's strategy.

It is worth reminding ourselves of Zingerman's change process, "Bottom-line Change®," discussed in Chapter 2. Leveraging this process, and simultaneously supporting the development of leadership capabilities, benefits all employees in the company. In co-founder Ari Weinzweig's words:

> People are comfortable with the reality that change will be with us every day of our organizational lives... We have saved and continue to save time, money and resources, which we then spend more wisely elsewhere with a much more effective implementation of change. [166, 167]

Another example, discussed in Chapter 3 for its flat structure, is Zappos, which for many years has given people an opportunity to fit into new roles and teams, and has now Pivoted to a holacracy.[168] Holacracy is designed for full self-management, and to remove impediments to day-to-day progress in everyone's work. In fact, an employee can initiate change that includes redesigning their own role, even shedding the tasks they feel keep them from doing their best for the company. Of course, roles can be redesigned in other organizations. At Zappos, Talent Adaptability is a natural part of the culture.

Talent Adaptability requires having a change process in place so that change is not so disruptive. Talent Adaptability also requires that every employee is safe, even to initiate change.

Pivots to Talent Adaptability, by company size

A Talent Adaptability Pivot for large businesses
Without even changing the structure of your organization, you can Pivot toward Talent Adaptability.

> *Pivot* **from** *business unit or departmental silos, where managers protect their turf,* **to** *collaboration between managers. Managers embrace other managers as peers on the same team.*

Are all managers, including senior executives who manage other execs or managers, openly working with their peers to place talent where it best fits the needs of the organization? Best next steps include:

- Bring greater Clarity to managers, including how they and their teams fit with strategy. Then they have the awareness to ensure the right people are in the right seats for the future.
- Offer Coaching to your managers, and consider how you can show them that their attention to team-building and collaboration is valued. As employees themselves, your managers need to know that their manager has their back and wants them to be successful.

A Talent Adaptability Pivot for medium-sized businesses

If your business growth has plateaued in an industry that demonstrates continued growth potential, then improving Talent Adaptability could be just what you need to kick-start growth.

Often, each employee has settled into a role that they repeat day after day, month after month. They get the work done, but the ability for the company to improve is restricted, sometimes severely, when each individual has set their mindset on how the work is done and what they are capable of. Just as often, teams become inseparable either because they feel safest or most rewarded when on that team or because managers are not considering where else in the organization an employee might fit; they are either on their team under their management, or out.

> Pivot **from** *inflexible ways such as authority based on power and control, protection of turf, competing for talent, and experience always trumping possibility,* **to** *a more nimble, adaptable culture.*

When mindsets are fixed and power and control are the most influential motives for communication, then even special projects intended to support discovery don't lead to a needed change. For example, documenting workflow processes based on the assumption that improvements should jump out may simply reinforce what is already being done, even if what "is" is not effective. When well-intended projects to spur change fail, it is time to step back and address mindsets and the workplace environment.

A team that is respectful and tolerant, even though these are good traits, can cause weakness in the business if the traits themselves need to be redefined. Showing respect should not translate to "ask no questions." Being tolerant should not translate to being complacent. Neither of these support Talent Adaptability.

The idea of creating a workplace where everyone feels safe can also be misinterpreted. Safety should not translate to lack of change. Tolerating an unwillingness to adapt one's skill set and way of being to better suit the company is like adding weights to your company. It is not the way to become more nimble.

Even leaders are susceptible to entrenched thinking, a conditioned response that occurs when people are blinded to new ways of thinking by the perspectives they acquired through past experience, training, and success.

You can create a culture that ensures employees feel safe without creating complacency. In fact, creating the "we care about your success" mindset throughout the organization fuels a Mastery Mindset, supports Talent Adaptability as a cultural norm, and makes complacency unacceptable.

If your company is not keeping up with industry growth rates (in terms of revenue, profit, or another benefit that matters to you)—or with the growth opportunity you know you could realize if the team felt a greater desire to achieve it—then it is time to create a sense of urgency to change, starting with you.

Best next steps include:

- Put these questions to the leadership team, first individually and then discuss together:
  - What can you start doing to create a sense of urgency?
  - What can you stop doing that might be getting in the way of others stepping up or speaking out?
  - What can you start doing to be more clear about the new vision?
- Coach and model for your managers this new, more adaptable way of being. Be careful to clearly communicate that Adaptability does not necessitate working harder or working more hours. Talent Adaptability is

about stopping what is not working and creating more effective ways to leverage talent for growth.

• Reach throughout your entire organization to Pivot fully away from complacency. Complacency is contentment with "what is." It creates blindness to internal and external dynamics that may impact your business. Complacency blocks meaningful achievement. Complacency compels us to overlook what is right in front of us, while we bask in the warmth of our own ignorance—until we are blindsided.

A Talent Adaptability Pivot for small businesses

Often in a small business that is no longer a startup, strategy is not given much thought. There may be no bold strategy to adapt talent to. Of the few roles to consider, most have been filled for some time and the individuals in the roles consider themselves the expert already and too busy to consider changes. The entry-level roles that require training may seem like revolving doors because no one has time to train them and there is no strategy they can feel part of; the work to be done is the work that has always been done by that role. Coming together to revisit and possibly redesign work, and weaving this naturally into your culture, may be a rewarding Pivot.

> Pivot **from** overfilling days with work that may not be advancing your company, **to** a culture that regularly revisits strategy and the work to be done.

While you Pivot, also address mindsets that may be hindering Talent Adaptability. You'll get the right things done right by the right people—those who adapt to execute a bold strategy.

A Talent Adaptability Pivot for startups

The individuals attracted to working in a startup are typically nimble, and ready to adapt. Talent Adaptability may need to be strengthened if you are slipping in two critical areas: mentoring of new hires and sharing talent resources.

You may also need to address Adaptability of newly hired executives who bring an inflexible, know-it-all mindset or values that are at odds with your company's core values. If your company faces these challenges, first address how you hire.

> *Pivot* **from** *a hiring process that only seeks the strongest talent and assumes they will adapt,* **to** *the culture you envision and include Talent Adaptability—fitting your strategy—before hiring even the most talented person.*

PIVOT TO COACHING

"A candle loses nothing by lighting another candle."

—*James Keller*

Every person wanting to perform at their best can benefit from a coach. Coaching is the sixth and final Aligned Momentum Key Indicator. All the Key Indicators preceding it can improve with Coaching.

Coaching naturally increases alignment between what employees want for themselves and what the company needs from them.

Coaching helps shifts mindsets, which is an important step in opening people up to change. Early Coaching wins begin with the development of leaders at the top of the organization. Consider engaging a performance coach who facilitates offsite strategy and execution planning sessions and who develops the leaders as needed on a one-on-one basis.

Managers who are also leaders benefit from developing their Coaching skills and creating a plan to coach on a more consistent basis. Eventually you'll want all managers to coach people to higher levels of performance and also to live the company's core values. Groups of individuals benefit from Coaching in terms of gelling as a team—developing the trust, collaboration, and accountability that together generate breakthrough results.

Pivots to Coaching, by company size

A Coaching Pivot for large businesses
Individuals who are determined to achieve breakthrough performance have a coach. Now that you are committed to breakthrough performance for your business, Coaching is necessary. And not just for you. Everyone deserves a coach.

> *Pivot* **from** *managers who are managing work and responsible solely for managing the outputs of their team,* **to** *managers who coach people to their best performance.*

In a culture with Aligned Momentum, managers are the coaches of the employees on their team. They are responsible for building the team and building up every person on the team. Someone needs to coach the managers, starting with Coaching that will prepare them to coach, and that is likely best done by a professional coach. That someone also will assess readiness for Coaching and provide recommendations and a Coaching plan for your organization. A plan that includes a train-the-trainer program will be most effective.

The natural result of great Coaching is that people self-manage their performance, and their behavior, while they receive support for their growth individually, as a team member and as a valued part of the company.

You do not have to be organizationally structured for complete self-management in order to benefit from people taking accountability for their performance.

You also do not have to turn managers soft or into assistants for their employees. However, managers do serve the individuals on their team as a performance coach. Coaching is a service. Coaching is not therapy. A great performance coach, manager, or leader does not tolerate poor performance due to complacency or resistance, or bad behavior.

A performance coach wants each individual to be successful, and when the individual knows this, then performance breakthroughs can happen. This is exactly how an employee should view their manager. Being accommodating of poor performance, including behavior that impacts their performance or their team's performance, is not in the role description of a coach; in fact the opposite is true. A coach is caring, and demanding.

A Coaching Pivot for medium-sized businesses

You seek alignment and performance breakthroughs just as much as a larger business does. Your managers may be more hands-on, making it hard for them to get started with Coaching employees, even though you all agree that better delegation would solve this. So, time is an issue. Budget may be an issue, as well. A powerful Coaching option for businesses with smaller budgets is through a peer group. This may also include one-on-one Coaching.

> *Pivot* **from** *no time or budget for Coaching,* **to** *a training-sized budget for peer group Coaching to get you started.*

Plan for greater trust and collaboration between managers, and between managers and the individuals on their team. Leverage the skills of a professional performance Coach to support each manager. It can be beneficial to the manager to continue with their Coach. This Coaching will also help them be a better Coach for their team.

A manager with improved Coaching skills will find they are much better at delegation, which shifts the "how to" to the direct reports, typically creating more engagement. It's a win all around. The managers' day, then, allows them time for team alignment with strategy, Coaching, team communication such as via meetings, measurement, and follow-through.

A Coaching Pivot for small businesses

For a small business, the quickest win will be to find the alignment between each employee's personal goals and what the company strategically needs from them in their role. Coaching will help.

> *Pivot* **from** *employees in j-o-b-s,* **to** *Coaching to expand skill and to align personal goals with company strategy.*

Leverage the coach's wisdom first with a few key people, especially if you are on a tight budget. The coach can model great team facilitation and coaching, and then train your leaders.

Because time may also be tight, Coaching on a consistent basis is a concern. But consistency in your culture is critical. You must weave Coaching into the culture. Regular touch-bases with your coach throughout the year will help ensure your team doesn't revert to its old ways, and so your company doesn't stall.

A Coaching Pivot for startups

Gaining traction in the market can be so exhilarating and all-consuming that development of culture is deferred to "someday soon." This "someday," then, either doesn't happen at all or doesn't happen before unwanted habits and behaviors become norms, creating a de facto culture, that may not be the culture you envisioned.

> Pivot **from** *creating a culture unintentionally due to a lack of time to focus on that,* **to** *bringing in a performance coach to help you bring your envisioned culture to life.*

A great performance coach won't assume power of authority; they remain a trusted advisor, wise guide and skilled facilitator. What happens, happens because of what you and your team do. Coaching will help ensure you maintain the discipline to grow your company—people and profits—in a way that serves your vision, mission and values. For startups, I've come to call this "serving fast-growth startups who don't want to grow up ugly."

CHAPTER 9: KEY POINTS

1) To get nimble enough to "jump the S-Curve" and avoid a stall, you need to ready your business internally.[169]

2) Take a Pivot/Aligned Momentum Assessment. You'll find a code in the Appendix that will give you online access to the assessment.

3) Find sample findings, Pivot recommendations, and a few best next steps in the subsections of Chapter 9 per each of the six Aligned Momentum Key Indicators: Clarity, Mastery Mindset, Nimble Decision-making, Strategic Thinking, Talent Adaptability, and Coaching.

4) On average, and considering the readiness rating from 0–10 (10 is fully ready) for each Aligned Momentum Key Indicator, the areas for improvement listed by company size are as follows:
   a. Large: Nimble Decision-making & Clarity;
   b. Medium: Nimble Decision-making & Coaching;
   c. Small: Coaching, Strategic Thinking & Nimble Decision-making;
   d. Startup: Coaching.

5) Recommended Pivots include:
   a. Short daily meetings, most commonly called Huddles;
   b. Frequent performance conversations between a manager and the employees on their team;
   c. Training managers to be coaches.

CHAPTER 10

◡

Your Best Next Step

———————

"Your instinct tells you that by moving forward you will 'fall off the bike.' But it is only in letting go, and trusting that somehow some force will appear that will keep you upright, that you can ever learn to ride. Trusting the orchestra feels that way at the beginning. You must create the flow of the music, and leave to the musicians the playing of the notes."

— *Maestro Roger Nierenberg*

To brilliantly execute your business strategy, and transform via The Pivot, there will be many people who must work together toward a shared vision. You, the leader, are critical to ensuring a shared vision. And, you are accountable for that brilliant execution, even though you are not 100% in control of the results.

Ineffective meetings, poor judgment calls, interruptions in momentum (typically due to poor handovers) … these issues lead to poor execution, and even to bad strategy if they become tradition: the "way things are done" in your workplace. Sometimes traditions that create rigidity have the cumulative effect that creates a major jolt! Or when so many small jolts are missed, the accumulative result is a major jolt.

To clarify my point, I'm going to revisit the case of one company that was not in a state of Aligned Momentum, and fell short of brilliance because of it.

Nokia experienced rigidity, and lost significant market share in the smartphone market. An article in the digital magazine, *Aeon* addressed what happens when unwanted variables are ignored. They penned the term "collective stupidity" and used Nokia as the example:

> At Nokia, between 2007 and 2013, managers at the telecommunications firm were encouraged to be relentlessly positive. One middle-manager described how "if you were too negative, it would be your head on the block."
> As a result, employees wanted to give senior managers only "good news" but "not a reality check." Naysayers found their divisions starved of resources, while upbeat corporate yes-men were given ever more responsibility. When there was a genuine problem with Nokia's new smartphones, developed to compete with Apple's iPhone, few dared to speak up. This meant that senior management took more than a year to realize they were on a losing streak. By that time, Apple and Samsung were well on their way to dominating the smartphone market.[170]

Of course someone at Nokia must have noticed the smaller jolts. The loss in momentum due to a cultural norm of not asking questions led in part to the company's demise, as described earlier.

Rigidity will not result in brilliant execution of strategy. Nor will commanding or controlling others to attempt to achieve the results you want, creating an environment where it is not safe to speak out, or sticking with the thought that you know best, regardless of changing facts. This is not about you. As Don Miguel Ruiz shares in his classic

The Four Agreements (1997), "Don't take anything personally."[171] He also means by this statement to not *make* it personal. Let the passion for your vision, and the entire strategy, be steered by your instinct not to be a hero or inventor, but rather to be in alignment with your passion for the vision. In this way, you are truly "sharing the vision," "sharing strategy," and "sharing a single version of the truth" with everyone in the business you lead.

You are part of the shared vision and as the leader you are the person to be very clear about what you are looking for, and to communicate it clearly. Your employees, now sharing strategy, will define best next steps and initiate change. You will bow to the encore (from business success) knowing that this success results from the accumulation, and the orchestration, of many small shifts and right actions made by many people.

WHAT YOU DO NEXT IS IMPORTANT, EVEN PIVOTAL!

Bottom-line results will be an accumulation, and preferably an orchestration, of what you (and everyone in your company) do next, and next, and next.

> *Are you taking the time to smartly choose what to do next? Have you empowered employees to do the same? Are you maintaining alignment and momentum?*

Choose, define and commit to a best next step frequently. Recall the S-Curve and the importance of preparing for the next innovation before the rewards of the previous innovation wear off. Mastering this can be pivotal. You will require more people to be prepared and empowered to also be choosing, defining and committing to best next steps. *What is holding you back?*

Most leaders point to ineffective meetings, poor judgment calls, and breaks or interruptions in momentum as the obstacles to performance they are most challenged with. Getting better at "What's next?" will improve momentum and performance. Weave "What's next?" into your Pivot.

1) Weave "What's next?" into meetings

You can get a good idea of the best next step simply by asking "what's next?" before a meeting ends, and then assigning accountability. Effective weekly status and monthly management meetings end with next steps.

> Pivot **from** *meetings that are ineffective because they lead to no action or improvement,* **to** *meetings that are effective...*

...because they include the disciplines of preparation, facilitation, concise and measurable progress reporting, check-in on priorities, identification of next steps, and assignment of accountability.

2) Consider "What's next?" before a judgment call

Everyone in the organization with all levels of authority makes judgment calls throughout the day.

> Pivot **from** *making judgment calls only based on what seemed to work before,* **to** *better judgment calls...*

...because they are based on looking into the future and then returning to the present to choose the best next step. Making better judgment calls is a key part of Nimble Decision-making.

Train people to "Play the movie," as you move to a culture that has empowered every person with Strategic Thinking.

Also improve Clarity, so that every employee can determine his or her "best next step" in meeting priorities and strategic objectives.

3) Ask "What's next?" and "Who is next?" to improve momentum in hand-offs

Each employee is part of a process; their work is connected to the work of others in some way. When work stalls or communication is not flowing smoothly and openly from hand-to-hand, or ear-to-ear so to speak, momentum is lost.

> *Pivot* **from** *processes having different owners based on team or function,* **to** *single accountability for each process...*

...and a clear line-of-sight for each employee with responsibility in that process.

When Aligned Momentum grows, each employee will know the best response to *"What's next?", "Who's next?"* and *"Who cares?"* This includes you. There's nothing to fix. There is somewhere to go. So, for your best next steps, begin with answering these questions for yourself. You can be nimble, not rigid. So too can your business can be nimble, not rigid! Even as you grow. You are back in, and it will be extraordinary.

Last words. You and your business are unique. No one can pre-scribe the perfect solution to your situation without spending time with you and learning about your business. What is shared is that Aligned Momentum will serve all leaders and their businesses, in-cluding you and yours.

GLOSSARY

The Pivot includes the author's proprietary words and phrases that may not be familiar to every reader and may have more than one meaning, depending on the context. This Glossary serves to clarify the meaning of such words and phrases used in this book.

Alignment Commitment from every employee throughout the organization to strategic business objectives and, ultimately, toward a shared vision.

Aligned Momentum Alignment combined with uninterrupted forward movement. When associated with a bold business strategy, Aligned Momentum can lead to business performance breakthroughs.

Aligned Momentum Key Indicator A measurable characteristic of a workplace culture that, when it exists, indicates that aligned momentum is alive in that culture. *The Pivot* introduces six Aligned Momentum Key Indicators: Clarity, Mastery Mindset, Nimble Decision-making, Strategic Thinking, Talent Adaptability, and Coaching.

As-is state The current state of a person, business, or situation. "As-is" differentiates the current state from the desired "To-be" state. (See: *To-be state.*)

Assessment A method used to evaluate, measure, and document the current "as-is" state, readiness for a desired "to be" state, progress, needs, and the best next step(s).

Best next step The first move chosen, concluded, or decided after assessing a situation.

Bottom-line Change® Zingerman's recipe for effective organizational change. The process starts with an employee and their written proposal for change, which should include the vision of the future they wish to realize through the change. Their plan for change is put to and addressed by a relevant group of people, who are selected to be the messengers of the proposed change. Everyone who will be impacted by the change is informed of the proposal and is invited to write an action plan. Once the plan is agreed, the change process is begun.

Breakthrough performance A significant improvement on a prior level of performance, achieved through the orchestration of consistent, focused, and aligned execution of a bold strategy, and typically involving a Pivot.

Business Used synonymously with "company" to mean an organizational entity that sells goods or services for profit. Also used synonymously with "organization"; the term, "organization" is often used in *The Pivot* to refer to the structure or social norms inside a business. This book uses the term, "business" more often than "company" because non-profit organizations can better relate to operating "like a business," and those that do could benefit from reading *The Pivot*.

Business vibrancy A vigorous and lively performance level in business; a great place for people to work; a high market value of a business.

Clarity Getting clear and being clear when communicating a message. In *The Pivot*, Clarity is often associated with clear communication of strategy, including vision, purpose, values, and direction, as well as priorities, themes, goals, and initiatives. Clarity is a foundational step in orchestrating change and readying the workplace culture for a Pivot. Clarity is also the first of six Aligned Momentum Key Indicators. (See: *Aligned Momentum Key Indicators*).

Coaching In the context of business performance and individual performance in their business career, coaching is the art of unlocking potential to maximize performance. In *The Pivot*, coaching is crucial to catalyzing momentum. Coaching is performed through (vs. to) a person, individually and/or as part of a team, with the intention of helping them help themselves to learn and grow. Coaching is the final of six Aligned Momentum Key Indicators. (See: *Aligned Momentum Key Indicators*).

Company A commercial business. In *The Pivot*, company and business are used synonymously. (See: *Business*).

Decision-making A systematic approach to selecting "yes" or "no", which may include a course of action. In *The Pivot*, decision-making typically refers to such being performed using models and methods, and involving a group, as differentiated from quicker and more individual judgment calls and choices. In some cases, decision-making covers decisions, judgment calls, and choices.

Discover In *The Pivot*, "Discover" is one of the phases of Gap Assessment.

Employee An individual who works part-time or full-time under a contract of employment, whether oral or written, express or implied, and has recognized rights and duties. In *The Pivot* it is implied that independent contractors with recognized rights and duties, and especially if assigned to a manager, are part of the workplace culture and the orchestration of a Pivot.

Employee engagement The emotional commitment to do one's best at work. Fully engaged employees truly care about their work, the people they work with, and the company they work for. When both alignment and engagement exist, there is an emotional commitment to shared vision, values, objectives, goals, and priorities. *The Pivot* references Gallup's Q12 employee engagement measurement, stated as the proportion of engaged, non-engaged, and disengaged employees.

Empowerment The act of delegating authority to one or more employees, which includes the training, coaching, and resources to be prepared for the responsibility delegated.

Extraordinary business momentum Ordinary momentum is incremental. Extraordinary momentum reaches new heights. *The Pivot* describes a method for readying many people to initiate changes that are in alignment with the organization's strategy, and that, over time, and when well-orchestrated, generate extraordinary business momentum—even performance breakthroughs.

Fixed mindset A perception that qualities such as intelligence and talent are innate and unalterable. People with a fixed mindset may document their qualities rather than grow them. They may also believe that talent alone leads to success, without effort. Psychologist, Carol Dweck in her book Mindset, compares a fixed mindset to a growth mindset. In *The Pivot* what is termed, "Mastery Mindset" is similar to a growth mindset. (See: ***Growth mindset***).

Focus To pay close attention to, without distraction.

Goal A desired result.

Grown-up business An organization formed over two years ago, and that has been in operation since formation.

Growth mindset A perception that, with effort, intelligence and talent can be improved. (See: *Fixed mindset*).

Hero A person who is admired or idealized for courage, outstanding achievements, or noble qualities. Although someone may call a role model of admired traits or abilities their hero, *The Pivot* is using the more traditional "saves the day" definition of a hero. The term as used is gender neutral.

Huddle Also referred to as a team huddle or daily huddle. A peer-to-peer discussion, lasting no more than 15 minutes daily or weekly, designed to support awareness, collaboration, and the early identification of opportunities and challenges.

Initiating change Starting the process of change with a defined purpose for the change and for your vision of the future after the change (Also see: *Bottom-line Change*).

Key Indicator A shared definition (and metric) that marks progress toward a desired strategic objective, goal, or priority. Similar terms are KPI (Key Performance Indicator). And, as used in combination with strategy objectives it is similar to an OKR (Objective and Key Result). A Key Indicator offers a means to track progress. It answers, "How will we know we are making progress?" A definition of the destination, i.e., the vision and strategic objectives (or goals or priorities), is required before you can recognize the destination, and answer, "What will success look like, and how will we know we are there?" (Also see: *Aligned Momentum Key Indicators*).

Large business In *The Pivot*, and The Pivot/Aligned Momentum Business Assessment, a large business is defined as one having over 1000 employees.

Leader A person whom others follow. In *The Pivot*, when "leader" is stated with no further description, it is referring to the person at the top of an organization. Other definitions of "leader" include those people throughout the organization that other employees look to for advice, guidance, or to model the way of the business and workplace culture. These are typically referred to as "leaders throughout the organization."

Level Position in a hierarchical organization.

Mastery Mindset An open, growing mind. A perception that one can improve, even significantly with effort. Mastery Mindset is the second of six Aligned Momentum Key Indicators. The indicator helps you coach employees to approach their work, interact with others, and engage in training in such a manner that they continuously improve their strengths. Employees with a Mastery Mindset step up to apply their strengths, even when it will require learning something new, to best serve the organization's goals, purpose and values. (See: *Aligned Momentum Key Indicators*).

Medium-sized business In *The Pivot*, and The Pivot/Aligned Momentum Business Assessment, a medium-sized business is defined as one having 101–1000 employees.

Mission statement An expression, written or verbal, of the organization's current primary focus in terms of the business they do and the industry or market they serve.

Momentum A continuous state of forward movement in business.

Nimble The ability to act quickly and easily.

Nimble Decision-making The ability to select the best next step(s) when making decisions, judgments calls, or choices. Nimble Decision-making is the third of six Aligned Momentum Key Indicators. (See: *Aligned Momentum Key Indicators*).

Orchestrate From a position that affords observation of all the component parts (mainly your people and their words and actions), communicate via respectful guidance that empowers those closest to the action to make the proper changes for the betterment of the whole organization.

Ordinary business momentum Incremental improvement, with occasional breakdowns, delays, and stalls

Organization A group of people who work together in an organized way for a shared purpose. Often used in *The Pivot* to refer to the organizational structure and social norms at work.

Personal Brand Alignment A method of ensuring alignment between a person and their role, and between each role and the business's strategy. Personal Brand Alignment helps establish: awareness of one's personal vision, values, and strengths (personal brand); alignment of personal brand with a definition of success; and alignment of personal brand with the definition of success in one's role at work.

pivot A term to describe a quick turn, usually in response to changing external variables: turning away from one customer segment and focusing on a new one, for example. Or, changing a government policy; an unplanned career change; going for the big, quick win (being the hero); and so on. A turn-on-a-dime pivot may prove successful for an individual or a small startup. This type of pivot is rarely a successful route to positive, sustainable change for a grown-up business. *The Pivot* presents a turn-on-a-dime pivot in lower case and a well-orchestrated Pivot in upper case. (Compare: *The Pivot*).

Purpose Why the business exists. May also be used by an individual to express their calling in life.

Purpose statement A means to communicate, usually in writing, the reason the business exists. It answers the question, "Why are we (this business) needed?" Or for an individual "What is our unique gift that we are called to express or share?"

Scrum A framework for project management that emphasizes iterative progress toward a defined goal and leverages a discipline of daily team meetings, similar to huddles (see *Huddle*). Usually associated with agile software development.

Small business In *The Pivot*, and The Pivot/Aligned Momentum Business Assessment, a small business is defined as one that has been operating for over two years and has up to 100 employees.

Silo A closed structure that allows communication to move up and down within the structure, but not into or out of the structure. In an organization, units, divisions, and departments can become siloed. This silo mentality is similar to a person having a fixed mindset (see *Fixed mindset*). A silo inhibits collaboration and in most cases this also inhibits the growth of individuals and the momentum of the business.

Startup In *The Pivot*, and The Pivot/Aligned Momentum Business Assessment, a startup is defined as one having been in business for two years or less and having 5–500 employees.

Strategic direction The selected path and strategy toward achieving the business vision.

Strategic focus A capability that best ensures your business is (and people are) both focused and nimble. Strategic focus requires understanding the business strategy, or at least how that strategy translates to one's role.

Strategic objective A long-term (usually for a year or longer) desired, measurable achievement that helps to translate a vision into more specific team and individual goals, priorities and initiatives. Broadly stated, strategic objectives must be achieved to remain or become competitive.

Strategic plan An expression, usually in writing, of business vision, mission and/or purpose, values, strategic objectives, and game plan, supported by research, assessment, and analytics.

Strategic Thinking The ability to look forward with a clear understanding of what is needed to brilliantly execute strategy, and then come back to the present to take the best next step. Strategic Thinking is the fourth of six Aligned Momentum Key Indicators. (See: *Aligned Momentum Key Indicators*).

Strategy All aspects of the strategic plan that need to be understood and acted on to move forward toward the vision, as planned (see: *Strategic plan*). Strategy is sometimes referred to as only the game plan. In *The Pivot*, strategy is the concise term for the whole strategic plan, including vision, values, strategic objectives, direction, game plan, etc.

Talent Adaptability Fitting roles to strategy. A state or mindset of readiness in an employee that affords a business the flexibility to fit the best talent into a role where they are most needed. Talent Adaptability is the fifth of six Aligned Momentum Key Indicators. (See: *Aligned Momentum Key Indicators*).

Talent assessment A method of determining if the current workforce holds the right talent for the current strategy, with the aim of training, adapting, and hiring the right talent if required. Talent assessment is also used for succession planning.

To-be state The desired state, after improving from the current state. (See: *As-is state*).

The Pivot A well-orchestrated change over time, comprised of smaller changes or shifts initiated by many people. Mastering *The Pivot* is critical to extraordinary business momentum and makes performance breakthroughs possible. (Compare: *pivot*).

Turn-on-a-dime To turn direction quickly; in some contexts, too quickly.

Vision A desired future state of the business, so clear in one's mind that it can be "seen," and forms the basis for strategy. (See: *Strategy*).

Vision statement An expression used in internal business communication, usually in writing, of a desired future state of the business, made so clear that it can be "seen" in one's mind.

APPENDIX

THE PIVOT/ALIGNED MOMENTUM ASSESSMENT

Use the code below at www.thepivotbook.com to access The Pivot/ Aligned Momentum Assessment. If you misplace your code you can still register for the assessment. The code provides at least one additional resource.

Your ACCESS CODE is:

0617PIVOTAM

Find more resources at www.thepivotbook.com. Join the mailing list and receive new resources and special access to articles, webcasts, podcasts, and Lori's next book, already in progress. Learn more about Lori and LML Services at www.lorimicheleleavitt.com.

NOTES

Introduction

---

1. Cloud, Henry. *9 Things You Simply Must Do to Succeed in Love and Life* (Nashville, TN: Thomas Nelson, 2004).

Chapter 1: Aligned Momentum

---

2. Case, John. *The Open-Book Management: Coming Business Revolution* (New York: Harper Business, 1996).

3. Stack, Jack and Bo Burlingham. *The Great Game Of Business, Expanded and Updated: The Only Sensible Way to Run a Company, Revised, 20th Anniversary edn* (New York: Crown Business, 2013).

4. Case, John. *The Open-Book Management: Coming Business Revolution* (New York: Harper Business, 1996).

5. Ibid.

6. Kurtzman, Joel & Michael Distefano. *"Alan Mulally: The man who saved Ford"*, Korn Ferry Institute, August 11, 2014. Available at: http://www.kornferry.com/institute/alan-mulally-man-who-saved-ford [Accessed: February 26, 2017].

7. Caldicott, Sarah Miller. *"Why Ford's Alan Mulally is an innovation CEO for the record books"*, Forbes, June 25, 2014. Available at: https://www.forbes.com/sites/sarahcaldicott/2014/06/25/why-fords-alan-mulally-is-an-innovation-ceo-for-the-record-books/#502755a37c04 [Accessed: March 27, 2017].

8. Rogers, Christina *"CEO Mark Fields sets Ford on a dual track"*, The Wall Street Journal, Updated October 17, 2016. Available at: http://www.wsj.com/articles/ceo-fields-sets-ford-on-a-dual-track-1476696604 [Accessed: February 26, 2017].

9. Dan Barnett was President of Van de Kamp's, a division of Pillsbury (a leading food company) from February 1979 – October 1988 (9 years and 9 months).

See his profile on LinkedIn: https://www.linkedin.com/in/dan-barnett-a39301/ [Accessed: February 27, 2017].

Chapter 2: Mastering The Pivot

10. Barnett, Dan. Public lecture on the subject of increasing market share. Available at: http://www.abrige.com/PillsburyVandeKampsMarketShareStory.mp3 [Accessed: February 27, 2017].

11. Southern, Mike. *"Describe the pivot turn in the golf swing"*, Golfswing, [n.d.]. Available at: http://golftips.golfsmith.com/describe-pivot-turn-golf-swing-20214. html [Accessed: February 26, 2017].

12. Reporter interviewing Julie Sapan, *"What I learned from developing branding for Airbnb, Dropbox and Thumbtack"*, FirstRound Interview, [n.d.]. Available at: http://firstround.com/review/what-i-learned-from-developing-branding-for-airbnb-dropbox-and-thumbtack/ [Accessed: February 26, 2017].

13. Yeung, Ken. *"FlightCar revamps airport car-sharing service after major shakeup"*, VentureBeat, May 18, 2016. Available at: http://venturebeat.com/2016/05/18/ flightcar-revamps-car-sharing-service-after-being-told-to-get-out-of-its-own-way/ [Accessed: February 26, 2017].

14. Reporter interviewing Julie Sapan, *"What I learned from developing branding for Airbnb, Dropbox and Thumbtack"*, FirstRound Interview, [n.d.]. Available at: http://firstround.com/review/what-i-learned-from-developing-branding-for-airbnb-dropbox-and-thumbtack/ [Accessed: February 26, 2017].

15. Oremus, Will. *"The poisonous employee-ranking system that helps explain Microsoft's decline"*, Future Tense, August 23, 2013. Available at: http://www.slate. com/blogs/future_tense/2013/08/23/stack_ranking_steve_ballmer_s_employee_ evaluation_system_and_microsoft_s.html [Accessed: February 27, 2017].

16. Eichenwald, Kurt. *"Microsoft's lost decade"*, Vanity Fair, August 2012. Available at: http://www.vanityfair.com/business/2012/08/microsoft-lost-mojo-steve-ballmer [Accessed: February 27, 2017].

17. Dua, Kunal. *"How Satya Nadella rebooted Microsoft's corporate culture"*, Gadgets360, May 14, 2016. Available at: http://gadgets.ndtv.com/laptops/features/ how-satya-nadella-rebooted-microsofts-corporate-culture-837363 [Accessed: February 27, 2017].

18. Ibid.

19. Christensen, Clayton M., Richard Alton, Curtis Rising and Andrew Waldeck. *"The big idea: The new M&A playbook"*, Harvard Business Review, March

2011. Available at: https://hbr.org/2011/03/the-big-idea-the-new-ma-playbook [Accessed: March 4, 2017].

20. Finance reporter, *"Why do 90% of acquisitions and mergers fail?"*, Business Review Europe, Jan 28, 2015. Available at: http://www.businessrevieweurope. eu/finance/390/Why-do-up-to-90-of-Mergers-and-Acquisitions-Fail [Accessed: February 27, 2017].

21. Cook, John. *"After the writedown: How Microsoft squandered its $6.3B buy of ad giant aQuantive"*, GeekWire, July 12, 2012. Available at: http://www.geekwire. com/2012/writedown-microsoft-squandered-62b-purchase-ad-giant-aquantive/ [Accessed: February 27, 2017].

22. Wilhelm, Alex. *"Microsoft's lesson from the aQuantive disaster: Acquisitions require autonomy"*, The Next Web, July 12, 2012. Available at: http://thenextweb. com/microsoft/2012/07/12/microsofts-lesson-from-the-aquantive-disaster-acquisitions-require-autonomy/#gref [Accessed: February 27, 2017].

23. See also: Jacobsen, Darcy, *"6 big mergers that were killed by culture (and how to stop it from killing yours)"*, Globoforce, September 6, 2012. Available at: http:// www.globoforce.com/gfblog/2012/6-big-mergers-that-were-killed-by-culture/ [Accessed: February 27, 2017].

24. Alain, Patrick. Quote No. 2 at: http://www.patrickalain.com/why-leader-phrases/ leader-quotes/ [Accessed: February 27, 2017].

25. Cloud, Henry. *9 Things You Simply Must Do to Succeed in Love and Life* (Nashville, TN: Thomas Nelson, 2004).

26. Weinzweig, Ari. *Zingerman's Effective Organizational Change Process: Bottom-line Change* * (Zingtrain, 2016) Available at: https://gazelles.com/static/resources/ conf-materials/scaleup-2016/ari-weinzweig-opp.pdf [Accessed: February 27, 2017]. PDF.

27. Weinzweig, Ari. *"Changing the way we change: Zingerman's approach to organizational change"*, The Great Game of Business, July 17, 2015. Available at: http:// greatgame.com/annual-gathering-of-games/changing-way-change-zingermans-approach-organizational-change/ [Accessed: February 27, 2017].

28. Weinzweig, Ari. *"Zingerman's Bottom-line Change recipe"*, Zingerman's effective organizational change process, 2016, p.5. Available at: https://gazelles.com/static/ resources/conf-materials/scaleup-2016/ari-weinzweig-opp.pdf [Accessed: April 13, 2017].

29. Nierenberg, Roger. *The Music Paradigm*. Available at: http://www.musicparadigm. com [Accessed: March 9, 2017].

30. Nierenberg, Roger. *Maestro: A Surprising Story About Leading by Listening.* (New York, USA: Portfolio, 2009).

31. Oestreich, James R. *"There's a lesson here; all you have to do is listen: Roger Nierenberg and the Music Paradigm Program"*, The New York Times, September 17, 2014. Available at: https://www.nytimes.com/2014/09/18/arts/music/roger-nierenberg-and-the-music-paradigm-program.html [Accessed: March 9, 2017].

Chapter 3: Change The Context

32. Laloux, Frederic. *Reinventing Organizations: A Guide to Creating Organizations Inspired by the Next Stage of Human Consciousness* (Brussels, Belgium: Nelson Parker, 2014).

33. Kotter, John P. *Accelerate: Building Strategic Agility for a Faster-moving World* (Mass., USA: Harvard Business School Publishing, 2014).

34. Ari Weinzweig interviewed by Lori Michele Leavitt for a gathering of leaders from Whatcom and Skagit County WA leaders, April 19, 2017.

35. Stayer, Ralph. *"How I Learned to Let My Workers Lead"*, Harvard Business Review, November-December 1990.

36. Jack Stack interviewed by Peter Day, "Unlimited Company", In Business, BBC Radio 4, November 29, 2009. See the program's overview archived at: http://www.bbc.co.uk/radio4/features/in-business/peter-days-comment/20091126/ [Accessed: March 10, 2017]. The audio file is archived at: http://www.bbc.co.uk/programmes/b00nz005 [Accessed: March 10, 2017].

37. Marlier, Didier. *"How the janitor saved our company"*, Enablers Network, November 14, 2010. Available at: http://enablersnetwork.com/2010/%E2%80%9Chow-the-janitor-saved-our-company%E2%80%9D/ [Accessed: April 19, 2017].

38. Case, John. *"The open-book managers. Why many CEOs are adopting open-book management styles"*, Inc.com, September 1, 1990. Available at: https://www.inc.com/magazine/19900901/5332.html [Accessed: April 28, 2017].

39. Rockwood, Kate. *"This startup launched without a titles or a traditional business structure. Here's what it's doing now."* Entrepreneur, November 1, 2016. Available at: https://www.entrepreneur.com/article/284068 [Accessed: March 10, 2017].

40. Sathe, Vijay. *Corporate Entrepreneurship: Top Managers and New Business Creation* (Cambridge, UK: CUP, 2007).

41. Belasen, Alan T. *Leading the Learning Organization: Communication and Competencies for Managing Change* (New York: SUNY Press, 2000).

42. *"Zappos is a weird company — and it's happy that way"* PBS Newshour, March 3, 2017. Available at: http://www.pbs.org/newshour/bb/zappos-weird-company-happy-way [Accessed: April 22, 2017].

43. Guzman, Zac. *"Zappos CEO Tony Hsieh on getting rid of managers: What I wish I'd done differently"*, CNBC, September 13, 2016. Available at: http://www.cnbc.com/2016/09/13/zappos-ceo-tony-hsieh-the-thing-i-regret-about-getting-rid-of-managers.html [Accessed: February 27, 2017].

44. Eckel, Bruce. *"Holacracy vs. Teal"*, Reinventing Business, April 6, 2015. Available at: http://www.reinventing-business.com/2015/04/holacracy-vs-teal.html [Accessed: February 27, 2017].

45. Hsieh, Tony. *"Holacracy and self-organization"*, Zappos Insights, 2016. Available at: https://www.zapposinsights.com/about/holacracy [Accessed: February 27, 2017].

46. Johnston, Casey. *"Amazon offers workers $2000 to quit, but the incentive is nothing like Zappos"*, ArsTechnica, April 11, 2014. Available at: http://arstechnica.com/business/2014/04/amazon-offer-workers-2000-to-quit-but-the-incentive-is-nothing-like-zappos/ [Accessed: February 27, 2017].

47. Whitehurst, Jim. *The Open Organization: Igniting Passion and Performance.* (Boston, Massachusetts: Harvard Business Review Press, 2015).

48. McChrystal, Stanley A. *Team of Teams: New Rules of Engagement for a Complex World.* (New York: Portfolio, Penguin, 2015).

49. Suddath, Claire. *"What makes Valve Software the best office ever?"*, Bloomberg, April 26, 2012. Available at: https://www.bloomberg.com/news/articles/2012-04-25/what-makes-valve-software-the-best-office-ever [Accessed: February 27, 2017].

50. "Gallup Q12 Employee Engagement Survey" Available at: https://q12.gallup.com/public/en-us/Features [Accessed: April 14, 2017].

51. "Understanding your Gallup Q12 Results: A guide for sponsors, managers and consultants", Learning and Development, University of California, Berkeley. Available at: http://sa.berkeley.edu/sites/default/files/Gallup%20L%26D%207-16-2014%20.pdf [Accessed: April 14, 2017].

52. *"Gallup Q12 Employee Engagement Survey"*. Available at: https://q12.gallup.com/public/en-us/Features [Accessed: April 14, 2017].

53. "Understanding your Gallup Q12 Results: A guide for sponsors, managers and consultants", Learning and Development, University of California, Berkeley. Available at: http://sa.berkeley.edu/sites/default/files/Gallup%20L%26D%207-16-2014%20.pdf [Accessed: April 14, 2017].

Chapter 4: Gaining Momentum

54. Sathe, Vijay. *Corporate Entrepreneurship: Top Managers and New Business Creation* (Cambridge, UK: CUP, 2007).

55. Belasen, Alan T. *Leading the Learning Organization: Communication and Competencies for Managing Change* (New York: SUNY Press, 2000).

56. Drucker, Peter Ferdinand. *Management challenges for the 21st century* (New York: Harper Business, 2001 [1999]).

57. Gawande, Atul. *The Checklist Manifesto: How to Get Things Right* (London: Profile, 2011).

58. Gawande, Atul. *"The heroism of incremental care"*, The New Yorker, January 23, 2017. Available at: http://www.newyorker.com/magazine/2017/01/23/the-heroism-of-incremental-care [Accessed: February 27, 2017].

59. Ibid.

60. Ibid.

61. Sorenson, Susan. *"How employee engagement drives growth"*, Gallup, June 20, 2013. Available at: http://www.gallup.com/businessjournal/163130/employee-engagement-drives-growth.aspx [Accessed: February 27, 2017].

62. Mann, Annamarie and Jim Harter. *"The worldwide employee engagement crisis"*, Gallup, January 7, 2016. Available at: http://www.gallup.com/businessjournal/188033/worldwide-employee-engagement-crisis.aspx [Accessed: March 21, 2017].

63. Blanton, Brad. *Radical Honesty, the New Revised Edition: How to Transform Your Life by Telling the Truth* (Stanley, Virginia: Sparrowhawk Publications, 2005).

64. George, B., Peter Sims, Andrew N. McLean, and Diana Mayer. *"Discovering Your Authentic Leadership"*, Harvard Business Review, February 2007. Available at: https://hbr.org/2007/02/discovering-your-authentic-leadership [Accessed: February 27, 2017].

65. Ibid.

66. Ibid.

Chapter 5: Clarity

67. Saxe, John Godfrey. *"The blind men and the elephant"*. (c.1873). See: https://www.commonlit.org/texts/the-blind-men-and-the-elephant [Accessed: February 27, 2017].

68. Koen Smets interviewed by Lori Michele Leavitt for a gathering of leaders from Whatcom and Skagit County WA leaders, 16 November 2016.

69. *"Ford Motor Company"* Available at: https://en.wikipedia.org/wiki/Ford_Motor_Company [Accessed: February 27, 2017].

70. Kirkland, Rik. *"Leading in the 21st century: An interview with Ford's Alan Mulally"*, McKinsey Publishing, November 2013. Available at: http://www.mckinsey.com/

business-functions/strategy-and-corporate-finance/our-insights/leading-in-the-21st-century-an-interview-with-fords-alan-mulally [Accessed: February 27, 2017].

71. Ibid.

72. Stallard, Michael Lee. *"7 practices Alan Mulally helped Ford pass competitors"*, Michael Lee Stallard, January 22, 2014. Available at: http://www.michaelleestallard.com/7-practices-alan-mulally-helped-ford-pass-competitors [Accessed: February 27, 2017].

73. Churchill, Winston. *First speech given to His Majesty's Government on May 13, 1940. HC Deb May 13, 1940,* vol. 360, cc.1501–25. Available at: http://hansard.millbanksystems.com/commons/1940/may/13/his-majestys-government-1 [Accessed: February 27, 2017].

74. Reeve, Christopher. *1996 Democratic National Convention Address.* August 26, 1996. Chicago, Illinois. Available at: http://www.americanrhetoric.com/speeches/christopherreeve1996dnc.htm [Accessed: February 27, 2017]. Text and audio recording.

75. King, Jr., Martin Luther. *Stride Toward Freedom: The Montgomery story, King Legacy* (rev. repr., Boston, Mass.: Beacon Press, 2010 [Harper & Brothers, 1958]).

76. Pellet, Jennifer. "P&G CEO David Taylor talks about how to unlock employee innovation", Chief Executive, October 17, 2016. Available at: http://chiefexecutive.net/talking-talent-pg-ceo-david-taylor/ [Accessed: February 28, 2017].

77. Pitt, Sofia. *"One year later: How P&G has changed under new CEO David Taylor"*, CNBC, October 27, 2016. Available at: http://www.cnbc.com/2016/10/27/one-year-later-how-pg-has-changed-under-new-ceo-david-taylor.html [Accessed: February 28, 2017].

78. Rigoni, Brandon and Bailey Nelson. *"Do employees know what's really expected of them?"*, Gallup Business Journal, September 27, 2016. Available at: http://www.gallup.com/businessjournal/195803/employees-really-know-expected.aspx? [Accessed: March 14, 2017].

79. Lencioni, Patrick. *The Five Dysfunctions of a Team: A Field Guide for Leaders, Managers and Facilitators* (U.S.A.: John Wiley & Sons; Jossey-Bass Inc., 2005); R M Stephen Covey and R Rebecca Merrill. *The Speed of Trust: The One Thing That Changes Everything* (U.S.A.: Free PR, 2008).

80. Harnish, Verne. *Scaling Up: How a Few Companies Make It...And Why the Rest Don't* (Ashburn, Virginia: Gazelles Inc., 2014).

81. Pellet, Jennifer. *"P&G CEO David Taylor talks about how to unlock employee innovation"*, Chief Executive, October 17, 2016. Available at: http://chiefexecutive.net/talking-talent-pg-ceo-david-taylor/ [Accessed: February 28, 2017].

Chapter 6: Focused and Nimble

---

82. Fast Facts about Vanguard, *Vanguard*, [n.d.]. Available at: https://about.vanguard.com/who-we-are/fast-facts/ [Accessed: March 19, 2017].

83. Core Values, *Vanguard*, [n.d.]. Available at: https://about.vanguard.com/what-sets-vanguard-apart/why-character-counts/ [Accessed: March 15, 2017].

84. Blumberg, Alex and David Kestenbaum. *"Economy got you down? Many blame ratings firms"*, NPR, June 5, 2009. Available at: http://www.npr.org/templates/story/story.php?storyId=104962188 [Accessed: March 15, 2017].

85. Green, Sarah. *"Making Decisions in Groups"*, HBR Ideacast, Harvard Business Review, March 22, 2012. Available at: https://hbr.org/ideacast/2012/03/making-decisions-in-groups.html [Accessed: March 15, 2017].

86. MacBride, Elizabeth. *"The eight success principles Jack Bogle lives by"*, CNBC, March 15, 2016. Available at: http://www.cnbc.com/2015/02/17/jack-bogles-success-principles-to-live-by.html [Accessed: March 15, 2017].

87. Ibid.

88. Core Values, *Vanguard*, [n.d.]. Available at: https://about.vanguard.com/what-sets-vanguard-apart/why-character-counts/ [Accessed: March 15, 2017].

89. Bossidy, Larry, Ram Charan and Charles Burck. *Execution: The Discipline of Getting Things Done* (New York: Crown Business, 2002).

90. Kirkpatrick, David. *"The second coming of Apple through a magical fusion of man—Steve Jobs—and company, Apple is becoming itself again: the little anticompany that could"*, Fortune, November 9, 1998. Available at: http://archive.fortune.com/magazines/fortune/fortune_archive/1998/11/09/250834/index.htm [Accessed: April 17, 2017].

91. Smith, Dave. *"Apple is losing its focus again—and this time, there's no Steve Jobs coming to the rescue"*, Business Insider: Nordic, December 21, 2016. Available at: http://nordic.businessinsider.com/apple-is-losing-its-focus-again-steve-jobs-2016-12/ [Accessed: February 28, 2017].

92. Fell, Jason. *"Apple's simple marketing manifesto"*, Entrepreneur, October 26, 2011. Available at: https://www.entrepreneur.com/article/220603 [Accessed: February 28, 2017].

93. Rogowsky, Mark. *"Apple WWDC: iOS7 to keep things simple"*, Forbes, June 10, 2013. Available at: https://www.forbes.com/sites/markrogowsky/2013/06/10/apple-wwdc-ios7-to-keep-things-simple/#2229a7092229 [Accessed: April 17, 2017].

94. Showing a desire for change: Kirkpatrick, David. *"The second coming of Apple through a magical fusion of man—Steve Jobs—and company, Apple is*

becoming itself again: the little anticompany that could", Fortune, November 9, 1998. Available at: http://archive.fortune.com/magazines/fortune/fortune_archive/1998/11/09/250834/index.htm [Accessed: April 17, 2017].

95. Showing a culture built on the Apple values: *"A chat with Jay Elliot"*, Stories of Apple, December 8, 2011. Available at: http://www.storiesofapple.net/a-chat-with-jay-elliot.html [Accessed: April 17, 2017].

96. Tetzeli, Rick. *"Tim Cook on Apple's future: Everything can change except values"*, Fast Company, March 18, 2015. Available at: https://www.fastcompany.com/3042435/steves-legacy-tim-looks-ahead [Accessed: April 17, 2017].

97. Moisescot, Romaine. "Timeline", *All About Steve Jobs*, 2017. Available at: http://allaboutstevejobs.com/bio/timeline.php [Accessed: February 28, 2017].

98. Fell, Jason. *"Apple's simple marketing manifesto"*, Entrepreneur, October 26, 2011. Available at: https://www.entrepreneur.com/article/220603 [Accessed: February 28, 2017].

99. Elliot, Jay. *Leading Apple with Steve Jobs: Management Lessons from a Controversial Genius* (Hoboken, N.J.: Wiley, 2012).

100. Apple Computer, *Apple Employee Handbook* (Cupertino, CA: Apple Computer, 1993), 1. 31. Anonymous employee, quoted in Apple Computer, *"Human Resource Policies and Practices at Apple Computer,"* May 20, 1994, 18. 32. Ibid, 19. 33.

101. Reporter. *"Bill Campbell, management coach to Steve Jobs and other Silicon Valley leaders, dies at 75"*, Washington Post, April 18, 2016. Available at: https://www.washingtonpost.com/business/bill-campbell-management-coach-to-steve-jobs-and-othersilicon-valley-leaders-dies-at-75/2016/04/18/8f339532-05d8-11e6-b283-e79d81c63c1b_story.html [Accessed: February 28, 2017].

102. Chen, Brian X. *"Simplifying the bull: how Picasso helps to teach Apple's style"*, The New York Times, August 10, 2014. Available at: https://www.nytimes.com/2014/08/11/technology/-inside-apples-internal-training-program-.html [Accessed: February 28, 2017].

103. Mann, Annamarie and Jim Harter. *"Amid rapid-fire workplace change, Pulse Surveys emerge"*, Gallup Business Journal, March 10, 2016. Available at: http://www.gallup.com/businessjournal/189875/amid-rapid-fire-workplace-change-pulse-surveys-emerge.aspx [Accessed: April 17, 2017].

104. Collins, Jim. *Good to Great: Why Some Companies Make the Leap—and Others Don't* (New York: HarperBusiness, 2001).

105. There are a number of authors who have written on this topic. In alphabetical order, I recommend the following articles and books: Bob Chapman and Raj Sisodia's *Everybody Matters: The Extraordinary Power of Caring for Your People Like Family* (New York, USA: Penguin Random House, 2015) and related podcasts are available here: http://www.trulyhumanleadership.com/?p=2852; Ed Johnson, *"Merger and acquisition success: People count more than numbers"*, Cerius Executives, April 9, 2014, available at: https://ceriusexecutives.com/people-count-more-than-numbers-in-merger-and-acquisition-success/ [Accessed: April 17, 2017]; Bruce Kasanoff, *"People are what matters most in business"*, Forbes, July

21, 2014, available at: https://www.forbes.com/sites/brucekasanoff/2014/07/21/ people-are-what-matter-most-in-business/#6bcfffbc7647 [Accessed: April 17, 2017]; Darnal Lattal, *"Achieving the promise of acquisition success: Designing the human factor"*, PM eZine [n.d.], available at: http://aubreydaniels.com/pmezine/ Promise-of-Acquisition-Success [Accessed: April 17, 2017]; Harriet Rubin's article on The Female Vision by Sally Helgesen and Julie Johnson: *"Where were the women?"*, strategy + business, July 30, 2010, available at: https:// www.strategy-business.com/article/ac00015?gko=a7c05 [Accessed: April 17, 2017];

106. Labovitz, George and Victor Rosansky. *Rapid Realignment: How to Quickly Integrate People, Processes and Strategy for Unbeatable Performance* (New York, NY: McGraw-Hill, 2012).

107. McKee, Steve. *When Growth Stalls: How It Happens, Why You're Stuck and What To Do About It* (San Francisco, CA: Jossey-Bass [Wiley & Sons], 2009).

108. Kaplan, Robert S. *"Conceptual foundations of the balanced scorecard (working paper 10-074)"* (Harvard Business School, 2010). Available at: http://www.hbs. edu/faculty/Publication%20Files/10-074.pdf [Accessed: February 28, 2017].

109. Harnish, Verne. Scaling Up: How a Few Companies Make It…And Why the Rest Don't (Ashburn, Virginia: Gazelles Inc., 2014).

110. Collins, Jim. *"Good to Great"*, Jim Collins, October 2001. Available at: http://www. jimcollins.com/article_topics/articles/good-to-great.html [Accessed: February 28, 2017].

111. Collins, Jim and Morten T. Hansen. *Great by Choice: Uncertainty, Chaos, and Luck—Why Some Thrive Despite Them All* (New York: HarperBusiness, 2011).

112. Ibid.

Chapter 7: Change The Social Context

---

113. Quotation. Mahatma Ghandi ["Your beliefs become your thoughts"] Available at: http://www.goodreads.com/quotes/50584-your-beliefs-become-your-thoughts- your-thoughts-becomeyour-words [Accessed: February 28, 2017].

114. Dweck, Carol S. *Mindset: The New Psychology of Success* (New York: Ballantine books, 2016 [2006]).

115. "Zappos' core values", *Delivering Happiness*, [n.d.]. Available at: http://deliveringhappiness.com/book/zappos-core-values/ [Accessed: February 28, 2017].

116. "Core values", Microsoft, [n.d.]. Available at: https://www.microsoft.com/en-us/legal/compliance/buscond/overview.aspx [Accessed: February 28, 2017].

117. Vozza, Stephanie. *"Personal Mission Statements Of 5 Famous CEOs (And Why You Should Write One Too)"*, April 25, 2014. Available at: https://www.fastcompany.com/3026791/dialed/personal-mission-statements-of-5-famous-ceos-andwhy-you-should-write-one-too [Accessed: February 28, 2017].

118. Ibid.

119. Stack, Laura. *"The execution continuum: your means of spinning victory from chaos"*, The Productivity Pro, August 28, 2013. Available at: http://theproductivitypro.com/blog/2013/08/the-execution-continuum-your-means-of-spinning-victory-from-chaos/ [Accessed: February 28, 2017].

120. Greene, Jay. *"CEO Satya Nadella seeks to change Microsoft's image"*, The Wall Street Journal, October 25, 2016. Available at: https://www.wsj.com/articles/ceo-satya-nadella-seeks-to-change-microsofts-image-1477368916 [Accessed: February 28, 2017].

121. Kay, Katty and Claire Shipman. *"The confidence gap"*, The Atlantic, May 2014. Available at: http://www.theatlantic.com/features/archive/2014/04/the-confidence-gap/359815/ [Accessed: March 19, 2017].

122. Sandberg, Sheryl. *Lean in: Women, Work and the Will to Lead* (New York, NY: Alfred A. Knopf, 2013).

123. Brzezinski, Mika. *Knowing Your Value: Women, Money and Getting What You're Worth* (New York, NY: Weinstein Books, 2012).

124. *"Medical definition of neuroplasticity"*, MedicineNet, updated January 24, 2017. Available at: http://www.medicinenet.com/script/main/art.asp?articlekey=40362 [Accessed: February 28, 2017].

125. Lee B. Reid et al., *"Interpreting intervention induced neuroplasticity with fMRI: The case for multimodal imaging strategies,"* Neural Plasticity, 2016, doi:10.1155/2016/2643491 [Accessed: March 20, 2017].

126. Christine Lucas Tardif et al., *"Advanced MRI techniques to improve our understanding of experience-induced neuroplasticity"*, NeuroImage, vol. 131, 1 May 2016, pp.55-72, ISSN 1053-8119, http://dx.doi.org/10.1016/j.neuroimage.2015.08.047 [Accessed: March 20, 2017].

127. Weinzweig, Ari, Ian Nagy and Ryan Stiner. A Lapsed Anarchist's Approach to Building a Great Business, Zingerman's Guide to Good Leading, Part One (Ann Arbor: Zingerman's Press, 2010).

128. King, Stephen. *On Writing: A Memoir of the Craft* (London: Hodder & Stoughton, 2000).

129. Chapman, Bob and Raj Sisodia. *Everybody Matters: The Extraordinary Power of Caring for Your People Like Family* (London: Portfolio Penguin, 2016).

130. *"Culture"*, Southwest, [n.d.]. Available at: https://www.southwest.com/html/about-southwest/careers/culture.html [Accessed: February 28, 2017].

Chapter 8: The Bottom Line

131. For examples of similar stories, I recommend the following. Michael Hyatt interviews Patrick Lencioni about corporate culture: https://michaelhyatt.com/videos/an-interview-with-patrick-lencioni [Accessed: April 18, 2017]. Ken Blanchard discusses getting employees to care at Southwest: http://www.inc.com/articles/2010/12/ken-blanchard-on-getting-employees-to-care.html [Accessed: April 18, 2017]. Also see the book, *Lead with Luv* (2011) that Ken Blanchard co-wrote with Southwest's President Emeritus, Colleen Barrett: http://www.kenblanchard.com/leadwithluv/.

132. Gallo, Carmine. *"How Southwest and Virginia win by putting people before profit"*, Forbes, September 10, 2013. Available at: http://www.forbes.com/sites/carminegallo/2013/09/10/how-southwest-and-virgin-america-win-by-putting-people-before-profit/#29c5261b7b22 [Accessed: February 28, 2017].

133. Rogers, Everett M. *Diffusion of Innovations* (New York: Free Press, 2003 [1962]).

134. I may also use this version of the "S" Curve when speaking about momentum: Nunes, Paul and Tim Breene. *"Jumping the S-Curve"* Accenture, [n.d.]. Available at: https://www.accenture.com/us-en/insight-jumping-s-curve [Accessed: February 28, 2017]; and this version of the "S" Curve when working with individuals who are aligning their growth needs to their role: Johnston, Whitney. *"Surfing the S-Curve: How to disrupt yourself and why"*, Lean In, January 5, 2016. Available at:http://leanin.org/news-inspiration/surfing-the-s-curve-how-to-disrupt-yourself-and-why/ [Accessed: February 28, 2017].

135. Farson, Richard and Ralph Keyes. *"The failure-tolerant leader"*, Harvard Business Review, August 2002. Available at: https://hbr.org/2002/08/the-failure-tolerant-leader [Accessed: February 28, 2017].

136. Also see: Donnelly, Tim. *"9 brilliant inventions made by mistake"* Inc. , August 15, 2012. Available at: http://www.inc.com/tim-donnelly/brilliant-failures/9-inventions-made-by-mistake.html [Accessed: February 28, 2017]; Google Enterprise, *"Creating a culture of innovation"*, G Suite, [n.d.]. Available at: https://gsuite.google.com/learn-more/creating_a_culture_of_innovation.html [Accessed: February 28, 2017].

137. Silverman, Rachel Emma. *"GE does away with employee ratings"*, The Wall Street Journal, July 26, 2016 [updated]. Available at: https://www.wsj.com/articles/ge-does-away-with-employee-ratings-1469541602 [Accessed: March 20, 2017].

138. Cappelli, Peter and Anna Tavis. *"The performance management revolution"*, Harvard Business Review, October 2016. Available at: https://hbr.org/2016/10/the-performance-management-revolution [Accessed: March 20, 2017].

139. Bank, Erica. *"Reinventing performance management at Deloitte"*, Senior Leaders & Executives Blog, Association for Talent Development, January 13, 2016. Available at: https://www.td.org/Publications/Blogs/Learning-Executive-Blog/2016/01/Reinventing-Performance-Management-at-Deloitte [Accessed: March 20, 2017].

140. Nisen, Max. *"Why GE had to kill its annual performance reviews after more than three decades"*, Quartz, August 13, 2015. Available at: https://qz.com/428813/ge-performance-review-strategy-shift/ [Accessed: February 28, 2017].

141. Welch, Jack. *"Yank-and-Rank? That's not how it's done"*, Wall Street Journal, November 14, 2013. Available at: https://www.wsj.com/articles/SB10001424052702303789604579198281053673534 [Accessed: April 18, 2017].

142. Baldassarre, Leonardo and Brian Finken. *"GE's real-time performance development"*, Harvard Business Review, August 12, 2015. Available at: https://hbr.org/2015/08/ges-real-time-performance-development [Accessed: March 20, 2017].

143. *"Global market share held by leading smartphone vendors from 4th quarter 2009 to 4th quarter 2016"*, Statista, [n.d.]. Available at: http://www.statista.com/statistics/271496/global-market-share-held-by-smartphone-vendors-since-4thquarter-2009/ [Subscription required: accessed February 28, 2017].

144. Worldwide smartphone operating system market share (based on unit sales) *"The smartphone platform war is over"*, Statista, [n.d.]. Available at: https://www.statista.com/chart/4112/smartphone-platform-market-share/ [Accessed: March 20, 2017].

145. Hartung, Adam. "A $7.6 billion write-off is never a good sign, Microsoft", Forbes, July 8, 2015. Available at: https://www.forbes.com/sites/adamhartung/2015/07/08/a-7-6b-write-off-is-never-a-good-sign-microsoft/#147d79022eff [Accessed: April 18, 2017].

146. Davis, Scott. *"How Amazon's brand and customer experience became synonymous"*, Forbes, July 14, 2016. Available at: https://www.forbes.com/sites/scottdavis/2016/07/14/how-amazons-brand-and-customer-experience-became-synonymous/#287cc6db3cd5 [Accessed: March 20, 2017].

147. Bajarin, Tim. *"Six reasons why Apple is successful"*, Techland, May 7, 2012. Available at: http://techland.time.com/2012/05/07/six-reasons-why-apple-is-successful/ [Accessed: March 20, 2017].

148. *"Our story"*, Uber, [n.d.]. Available at: https://www.uber.com/our-story/ [Accessed: March 20, 2017]; *"What's fuelling Uber's growth story?"*, Growth Hackers, [n.d.]. Available at: https://growthhackers.com/growth-studies/uber [Accessed: March 20, 2017].

149. Comm, Joel. *"How American Airlines won Twitter"*, Inc., February 27, 2016. Available at: http://www.inc.com/joel-comm/how-american-airlines-won-twitter.html [Accessed: March 20, 2017]; Hutchings, Bob. *"How American Airlines gener-*

ates 33 billion social impressions", Business 2 Community, June 16, 2016. Available at: http://www.business2community.com/social-media/american-airlines-generates-33-billion-social-impressions-01573982#X25Cy4X4RgB7ssZI.97 [Accessed: March 20, 2017].

150. *"Our story: culture"*, Nucor Steel, [n.d.]. Available at: http://www.nucor.com/story/chapter4/ [Accessed: March 20, 2017]; Judd, Ron. *"Efficient, agile, smart, Seattle's steel mill keeps the fires burning"*, The Seattle Times, updated May 28, 2014. Available at: http://www.seattletimes.com/pacific-nw-magazine/efficient-agile-smart-seattlersquos-steel-mill-keeps-the-fires-burning/ [Accessed: March 20, 2017].

Chapter 9: Aligned Momentum Pivots

---

151. Regalado, Antonio. *"Technology is wiping out companies faster than ever"*, MIT Technology Review, September 10, 2013. Available at: https://www.technologyreview.com/s/519226/technology-is-wiping-out-companies-faster-than-ever/ [Accessed: March 21, 2017].

152. Lencioni, Patrick. *The Advantage: Why Organizational Health Trumps Everything Else in Business* (San Francisco, Calif.: Jossey-Bass, 2012).

153. Marquet, L. David. Turn the Ship Around!: A True Story of Building Leaders by Breaking the Rules (London: Portfolio Penguin, 2013).

154. For further discussion of how you could do this, see: Ferguson, Roger. *Finally! Performance Assessment that Works* (North Charleston, SC: CreateSpace, 2013).

155. Dweck, Carol S. *Mindset: The New Psychology of Success* (New York: Ballantine books, 2016 [2006]).

156. Greene, Robert. *Mastery* (New York: Penguin Books, 2013).

157. Kolhatkar, Sheelah. *"Elizabeth Warren and the Wells Fargo scandal"*, The New Yorker, September 21, 2016. Available at: http://www.newyorker.com/business/currency/elizabeth-warren-and-the-wells-fargo-scam [Accessed: February 28, 2017].

158. Egan, Matt. *"5,300 Wells Fargo employees fired over 2 million phony accounts"*, CNN, September 9, 2016. Available at: http://money.cnn.com/2016/09/08/investing/wells-fargo-created-phony-accounts-bank-fees/ [Accessed: February 28, 2017].

159. Dweck, Carol S. *"Mindset for Achievement"*, Mindset Online, [n.d.]. Available at: http://mindsetonline.com/howmindsetaffects/mindsetforachievement/index.html [Accessed: February 28, 2017].

160. *"Pike Place Fish Market"*, Wikipedia, Updated December 17, 2016. Available at: https://en.wikipedia.org/wiki/Pike_Place_Fish_Market [Accessed: February 28, 2017].

161. Yokoyama, John and Joseph Michelli. *When Fish Fly: Lessons for Creating a Vital and Energized Workplace from the World Famous Pike Place Fish Market* (New York: Hachette Books, 2015).

162. Peters, Thomas J. and Robert H. Waterman, Jr. *In Search of Excellence: Lessons from America's Best-run Companies* (New York: Collins Business Essentials, 2009, cop. 2004).

163. Nobel Prize Winner in Economics, Daniel Kahneman wrote the bestselling book, *Thinking, Fast and Slow* in 2011. Reviewer, Erik Johnson, summarizes the book's core concepts well. Our brains are comprised of two characters, one that thinks fast, System 1, and one that thinks slow, System 2. System 1 operates automatically, intuitively, involuntary, and effortlessly—like when we drive, read an angry facial expression, or recall our age. System 2 requires slowing down, deliberating, solving problems, reasoning, computing, focusing, concentrating, considering other data, and not jumping to quick conclusions— like when we calculate a math problem, choose where to invest money, or fill out a complicated form. These two systems often conflict with one another. System 1 operates on heuristics that may not be accurate. System 2 requires effort evaluating those heuristics and is prone to error. The plot of his book is how to, "recognize situations in which mistakes are likely and try harder to avoid significant mistakes when stakes are high". See: Kahneman, Daniel. *Thinking, Fast and Slow* (New York, NY: Farrar, Strauss and Giroux, 2011) and Johnson, Erik. "Book summary: Thinking fast and slow, by Daniel Kahneman (FSG: NY, 2001)" on Erik Reads (2014) Available at: https://erikreads.files.wordpress.com/2014/04/thinking-fast-and-slow-book-summary.pdf [Accessed: February 28, 2017].

164. *"The upside of daily line-up"*, Ritz Carlton Leadership Center Blog, December 3, 2014. Available at: http://ritzcarltonleadershipcenter.com/2014/12/upside-daily-line-up/ [Accessed: February 28, 2017].

165. *"Definition of strategic thinking"*, Business Dictionary, [n.d.]. Available at: http://www.businessdictionary.com/definition/strategic-thinking.html [Accessed: February 28, 2017].

166. Weinzweig, Ari. *Zingerman's Effective Organizational Change Process: Bottom-line Change* (Zingtrain, 2016) Available at: https://gazelles.com/static/resources/conf-materials/scaleup-2016/ari-weinzweig-opp.pdf [Accessed: February 27, 2017]. PDF.

167. Weinzweig, Ari. *"Changing the way we change: Zingerman's approach to organizational change"*, The Great Game of Business, July 17, 2015. Available at: http://greatgame.com/annual-gathering-of-games/changing-way-change-zingermans-approach-organizational-change/ [Accessed: February 27, 2017].

168. Hsieh, Tony. *"Holacracy and self-organization"*, Zappos Insights (2016). Available at: https://www.zapposinsights.com/about/holacracy [Accessed: February 27, 2017].

169. See Chapter 8 under *"Grow people and watch greater profitability follow"*, and also: Paul Nunes and Tim Breene, *"Jumping the S-Curve"* Accenture, [n.d.]. Available at: https://www.accenture.com/us-en/insight-jumping-s-curve [Accessed: February 28, 2017].

Chapter 10: Your Best Next Step

170. Spicer, André. *"Stupefied"*, Aeon, September 27, 2016. Available at: https://aeon.co/essays/you-don-t-have-to-be-stupid-to-work-here-but-it-helps [Accessed: February 28, 2017].

171. Ruiz, Don Miguel. *The Four Agreements: A Practical Guide to Personal Freedom* (San Rafael, CA.: Amber-Allen Publishing, 1997).

ACKNOWLEDGMENTS

Writing a book came neither naturally nor easily to me. It was a calling that I chose to say "yes" to. Purpose pulls. I have many people to thank for both encouraging me and challenging me, so that this book is the best it can be. Many are named in the testimonials that will travel with this book where ever it lands. I am grateful.

There are two people who were instrumental in bringing this book to life: Emily C. Evans and Simone Hutchinson. Emily, you helped me let go of what wasn't working and get on with it! You challenged me when I was writing in the same way I find with leaders (and challenge them on this); as if those I'm communicating with had been with me during its creation. This book is better because of you. Simone, to me you are the personification of a four leaf clover. You showed such a high level of discipline to professionally edit this book, and see it through to publication. No shortcuts. You also kept me optimistic and focused. Emily and Simone, this book would not exist without you.

Also instrumental, but in a less direct way, are those individuals who were so generous to share their thought leadership with one or more of my leadership peer groups. In alphabetical order: Frumi Rachel Barr, Jim Bergquist, Bob Burg, Frank Cook, Dennis Cummins, Peter DiGiammarino, Nancy Eberhardt, Roger Ferguson, Brian Formato, Maria Gamb, Bob Gibson, Hart Hodges, Randy Hall, Stijn Hendrikse, Brad Kuik, Jim Kouzes, George Labovitz, Michael McIntosh, Karina Miller, Brian Mohr, John Mullins, Greg Olson, Roy Osing, Chuck Pettinger, Kim Shepherd, Stan Silverman, Koen Smets, Robert Spector, Jeff Spencer, Andrew Thorn, and Ari Weinzweig. *I've learned from you and from working with leaders as they learn from what you've shared, in talks, books, and more. Thank you for aligning with me and my purpose of improving business vibrancy while catalyzing momentum for leaders and teams. This is what Aligned Momentum is all about!*

ABOUT THE AUTHOR

Lori Michele Leavitt, also known as *The Pivot Catalyst*, will guide you with this book to your best next steps toward extraordinary business momentum. Just as she coaches leaders around the world, with this book she will coach you. Learn more about Lori and LML Services at www.lorimicheleleavitt.com.

Lori Michele Leavitt is founder and president of Abrige Corp. Her leadership services are delivered through business and performance coaching, leading peer groups, and consulting for M&A due diligence and turnarounds. Abrige software, branded as Aligned Momentum™, has catalyzed momentum for organizations with thousands of employees. An IoT company she founded was the first to enable cashless water vending in Africa.

Lori speaks globally to groups from 10 to 2000 on performance momentum and culture change.

Lori has an MBA and certifications in speaking, coaching, facilitation, and financial management. Her favorite role is as Emily's Mom.

www.ingramcontent.com/pod-product-compliance
Lightning Source LLC
Chambersburg PA
CBHW020830210326
41598CB00019B/1856